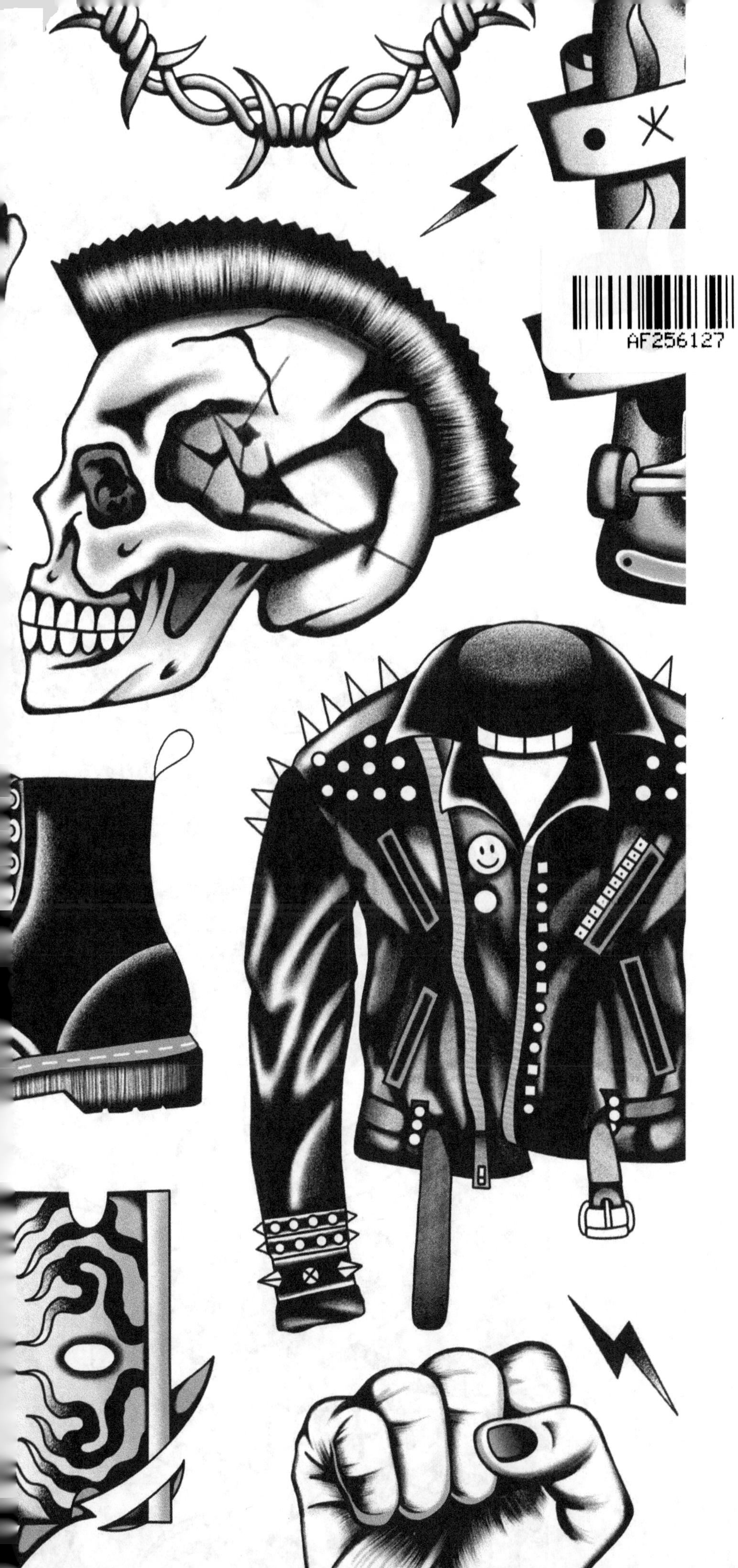

THE VAULT EDITIONS GUIDE TO
MASTERING
THE ART OF
DRAWING

HOW TO DRAW
PUNK THINGS

A HELPFUL MANUAL FOR
ARTISTS AND DESIGNERS

STEP BY STEP

HAND DRAWN
UNIQUE 40 DESIGNS
BEST QUALITY

EDITIONS
Vault

AF256127

INTRODUCTION

Welcome to *How to Draw Punk Things*—a celebration of raw creativity, rebellious energy, and the unapologetic spirit of punk. This book isn't just about learning to draw; it's about embracing the DIY ethos, breaking the rules, and creating bold and radical artwork that makes a statement.

Whether you're a beginner picking up a pencil for the first time or an artist looking to infuse your work with a punk attitude, this guide inspires and empowers you. The designs in these pages—ranging from leather jackets and barbed wire to skulls, snakes, and combat boots—aren't just images; they're symbols of individuality and defiance.

We've broken each design into simple, step-by-step instructions to ensure anyone can follow along. You'll start with basic shapes and gradually build each piece into a striking finished artwork. But don't stop there—punk is all about personalisation, so make these designs your own. Add your flair, distort the lines, and push the boundaries.

Punk culture has always been about more than just music or fashion; it's a movement, a mindset, and a creative force that challenges the status quo and thrives on individuality. The same applies to this book. Use it to create art for zines, posters, album covers, t-shirts, or whatever project inspires you. Let your imagination run wild, experiment, and most importantly, don't be afraid to break the mould, push your own boundaries, and redefine what art means to you.

Grab your pencil and get ready to unleash punk's raw, untamed power on the page. This is your chance to create art that's not just cool—it's revolutionary. Let's go!

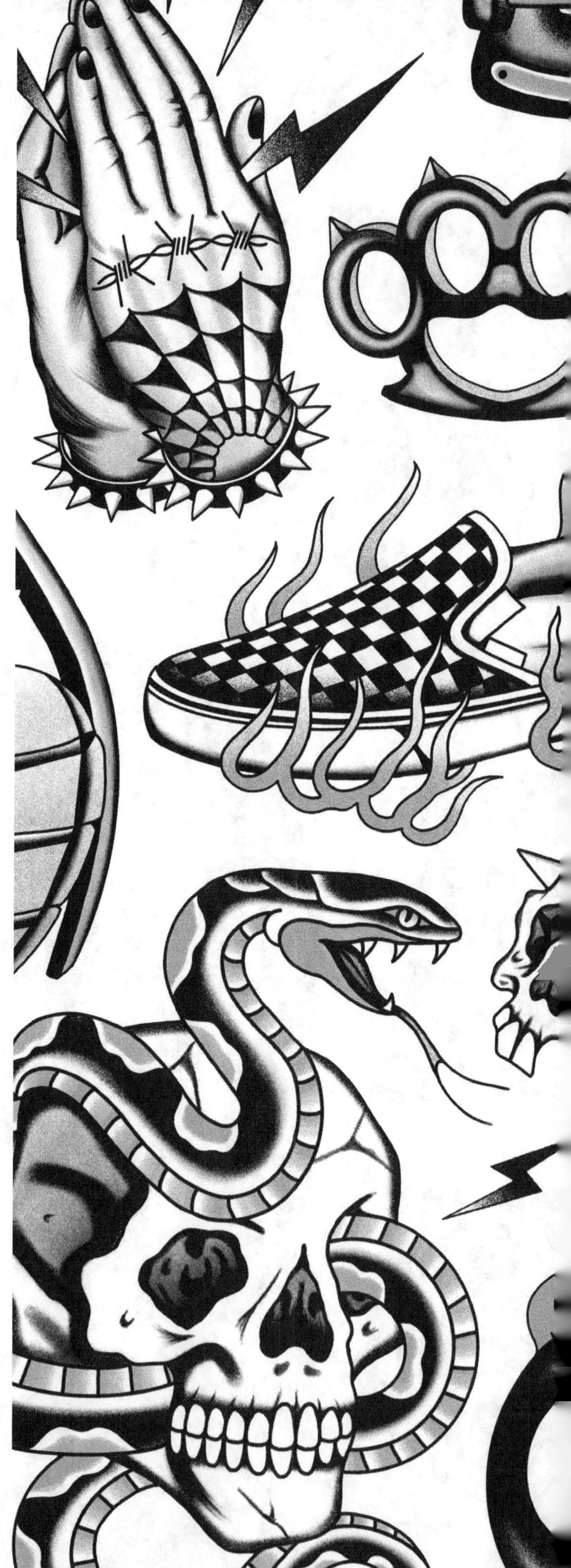

TABLE ◆ OF ◆ CONTENTS

DOWNLOAD YOUR FILES

Downloading your files is simple. To access your digital files, please go to the last page of this book and follow the instructions provided.

For technical assistance, please email: info@vaulteditions.com

Copyright
Copyright © Vault Editions Ltd 2024.

Bibliographical Note
This book is a new work created by Vault Editions Ltd.

ISBN: 978-1-922966-54-4

VAULT EDITIONS

MACE & CHAIN

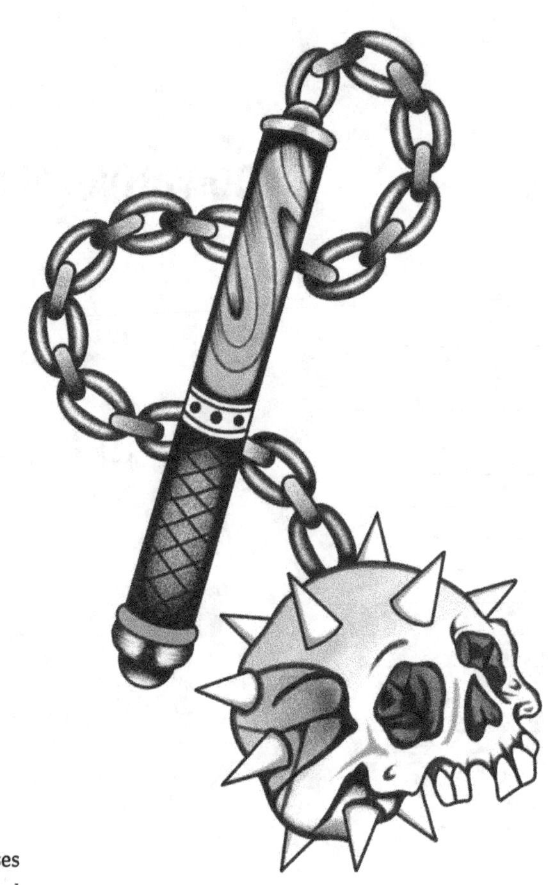

A weapon of rebellion, the mace symbolises punk's readiness to confront oppression and stand firm against conformity.

01   02   03

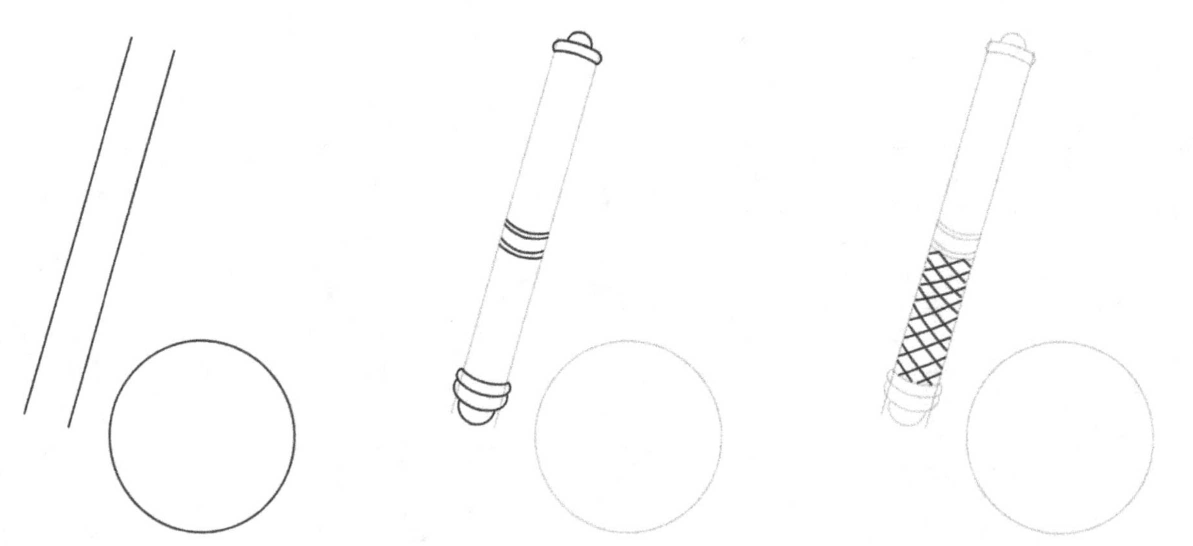

04

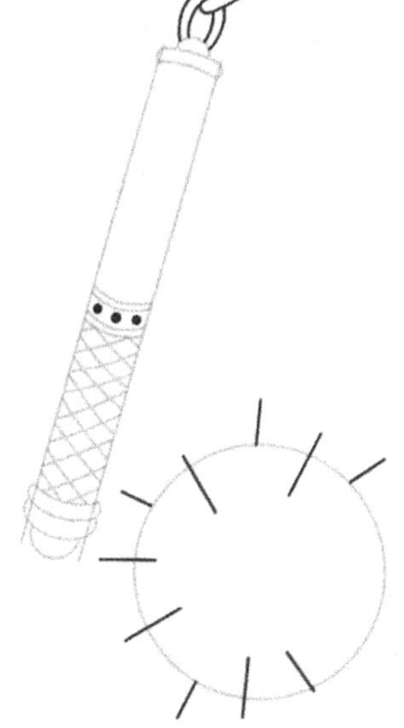

05

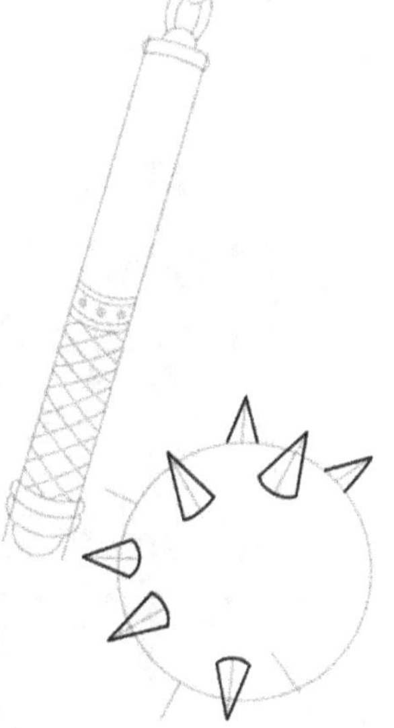

06

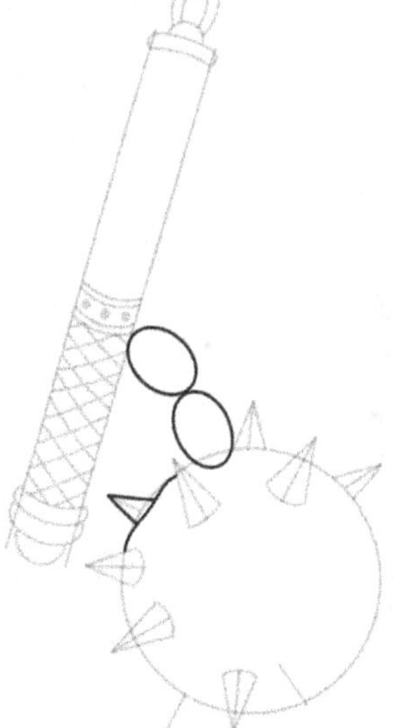

07

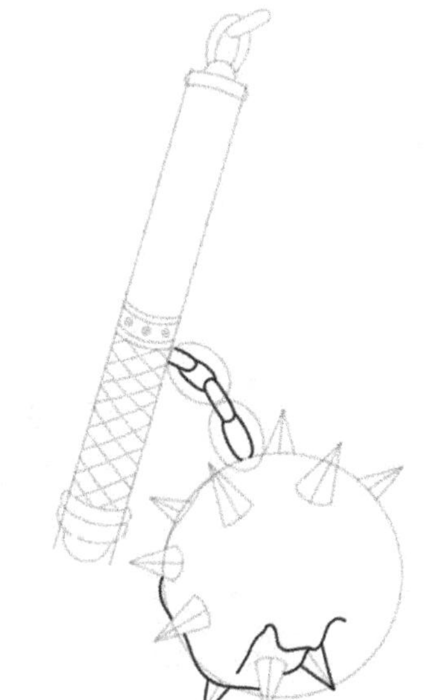

08

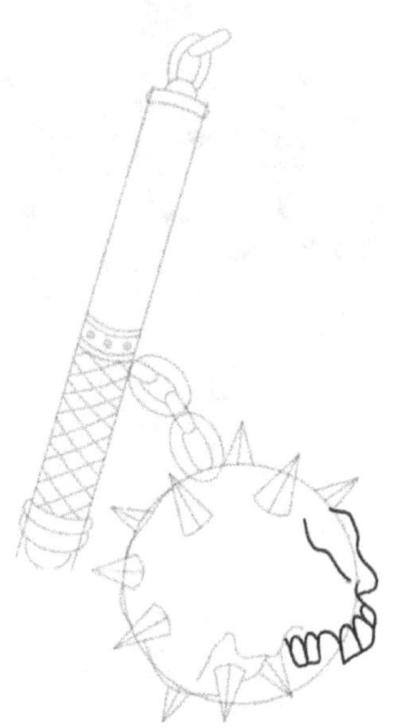

09

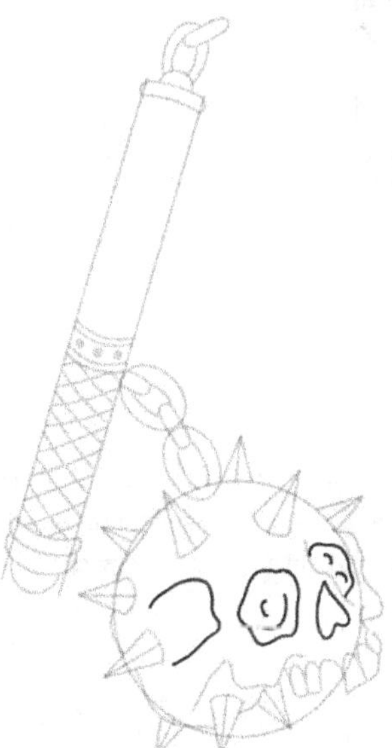

10

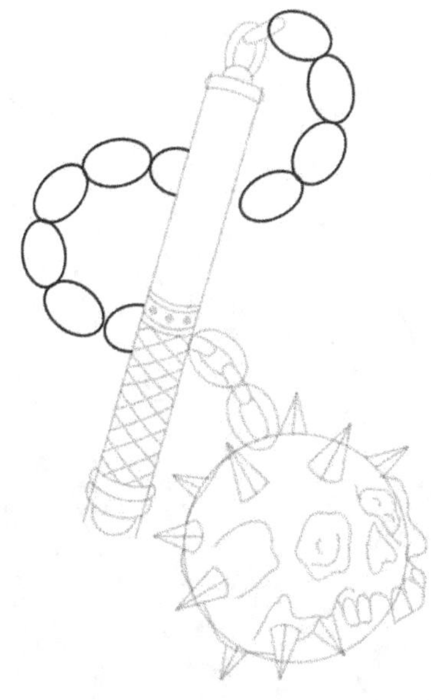

11

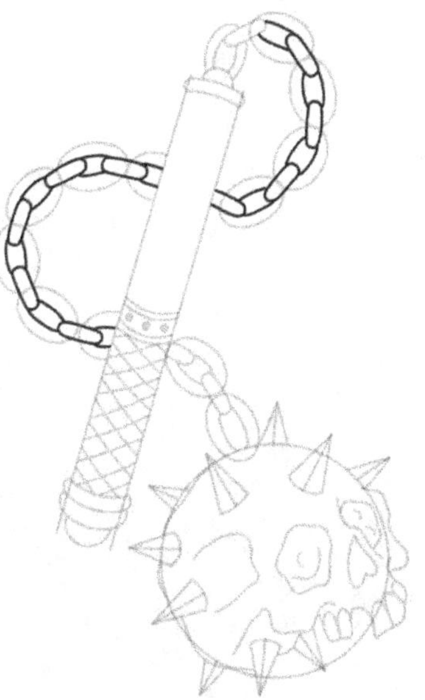

12

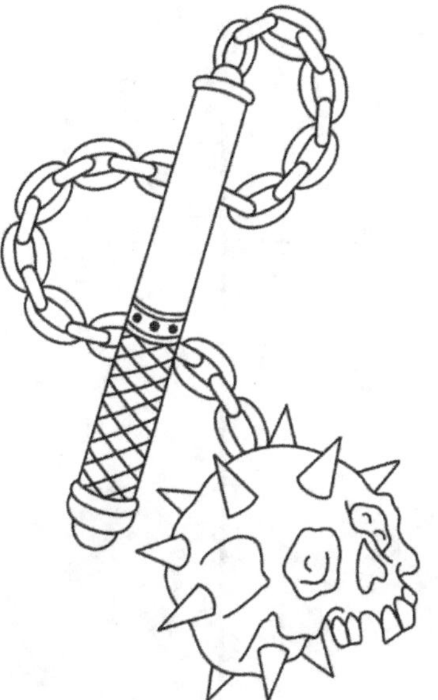

HEART GRENADE

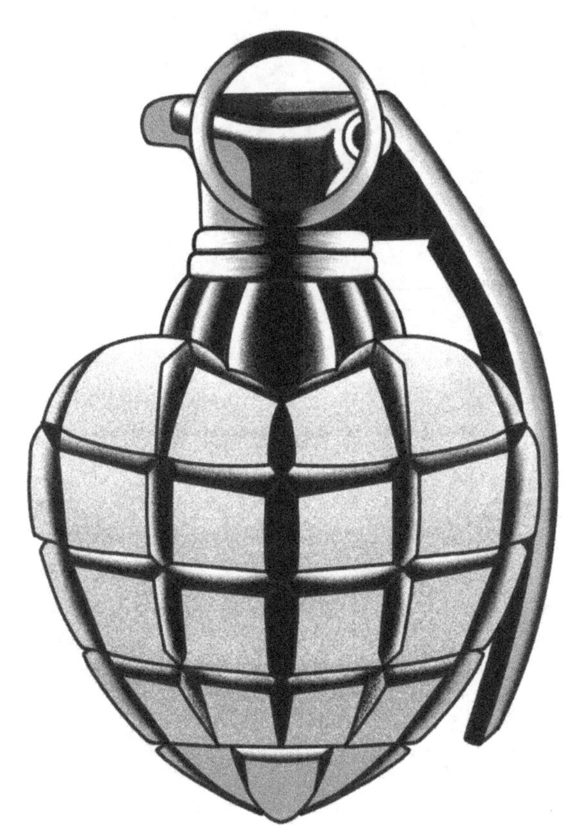

A visceral symbol of love as a destructive force, the heart grenade represents punk's raw emotion and explosive passion.

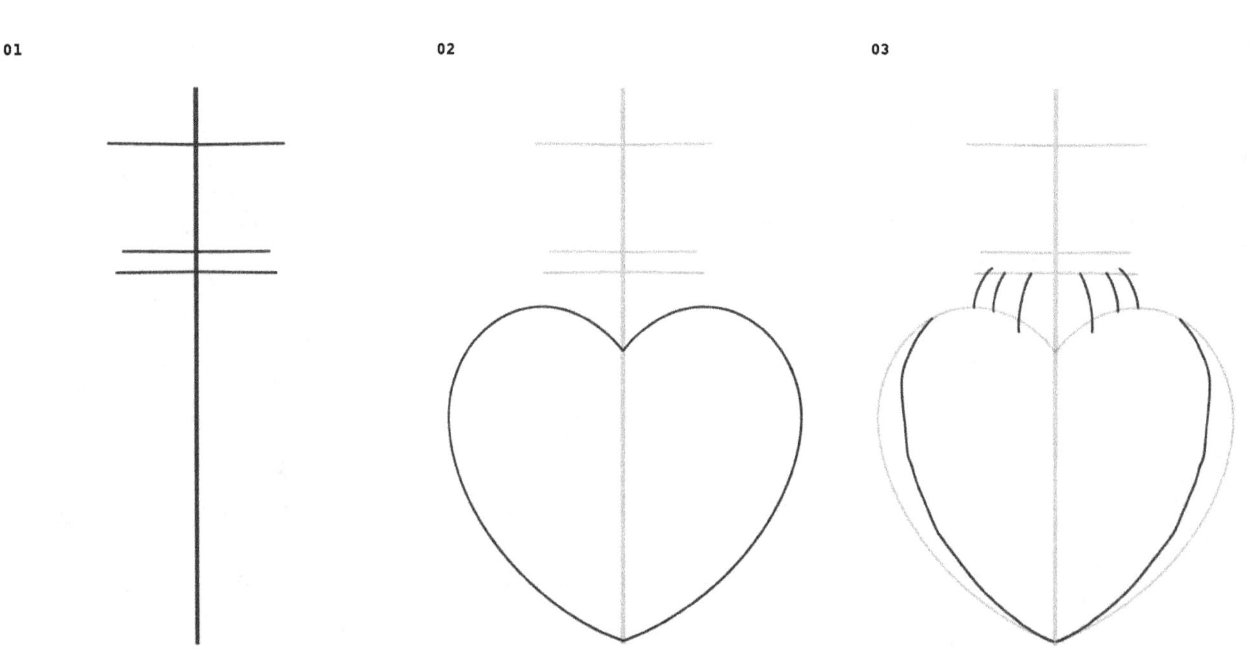

01

02

03

04

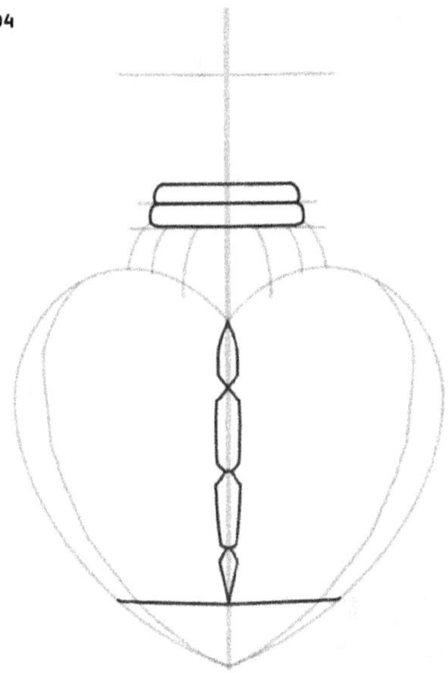

05

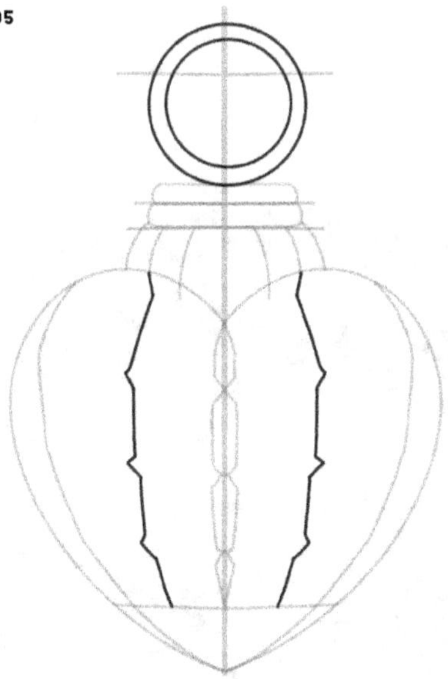

06

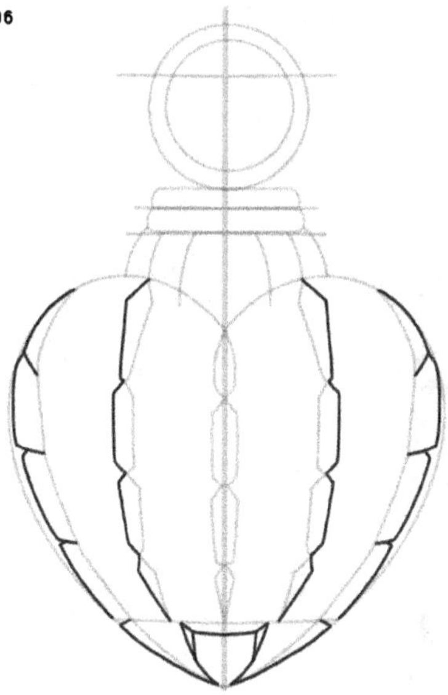

07

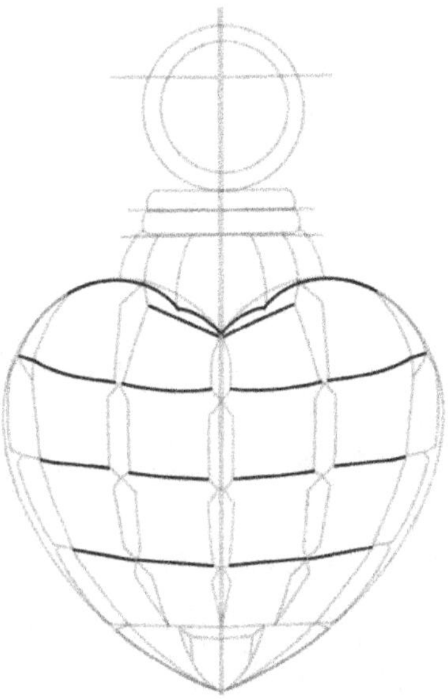

08

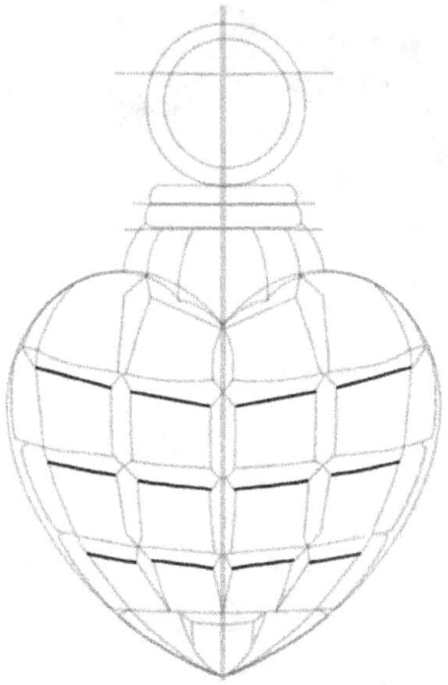

09

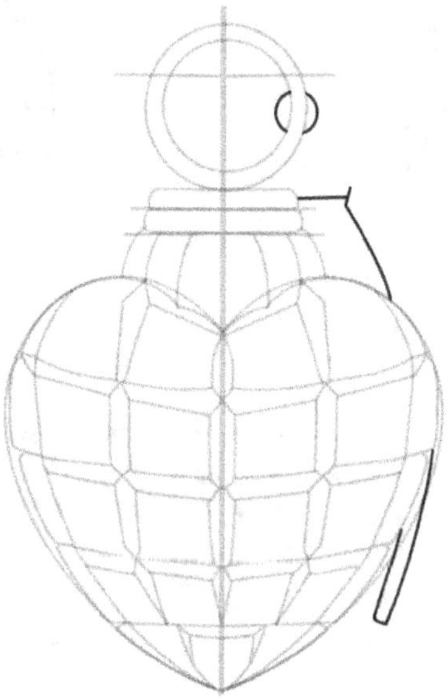

10

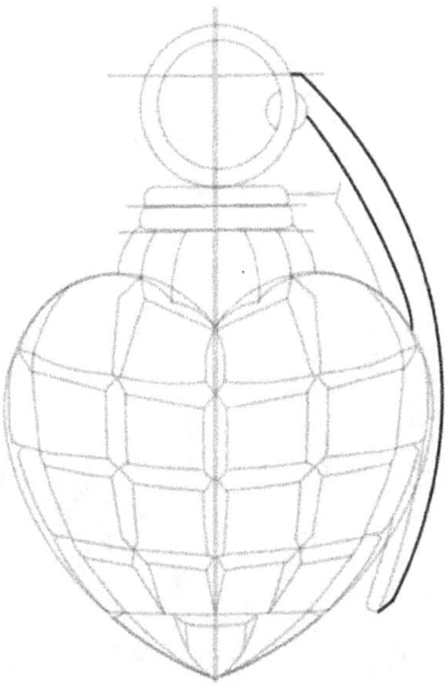

11

12

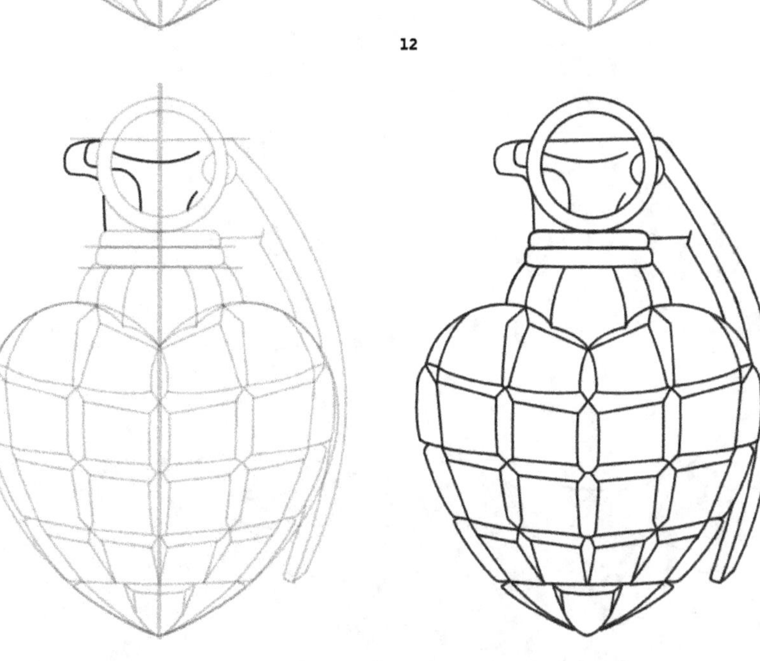

MOHAWK SKULL

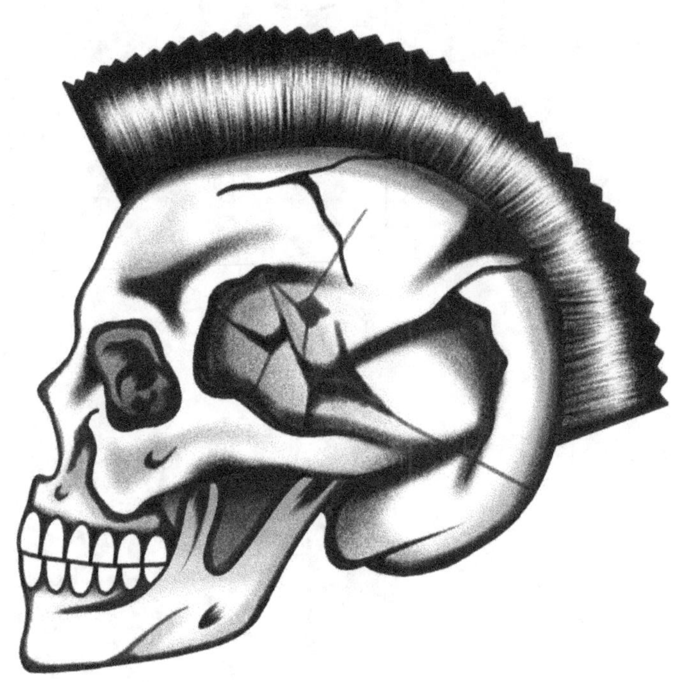

A punk icon of ultimate rebellion, the mohawk skull embodies fearless individuality and defiance of societal norms.

01

02

03

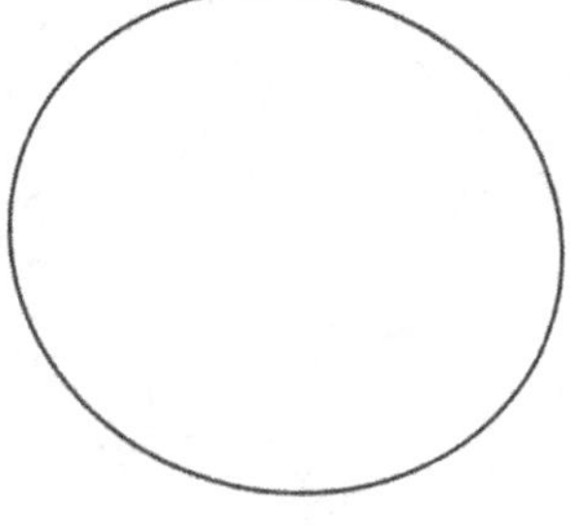

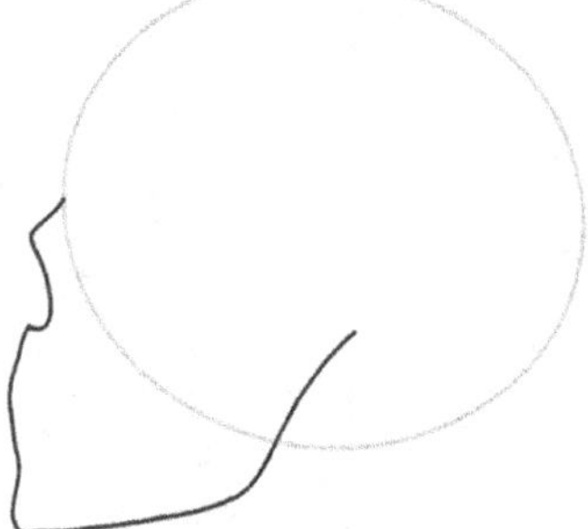

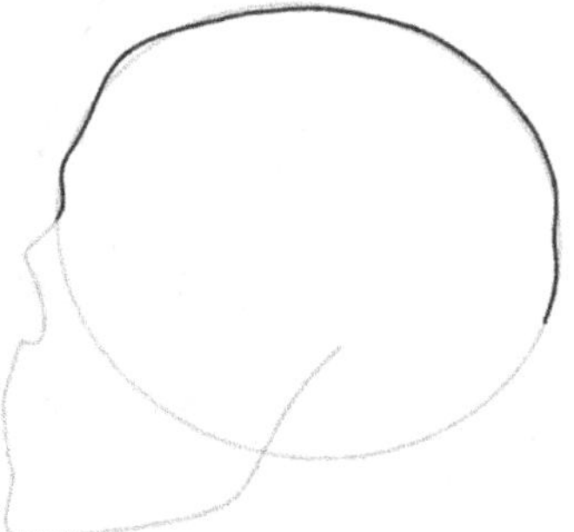

04

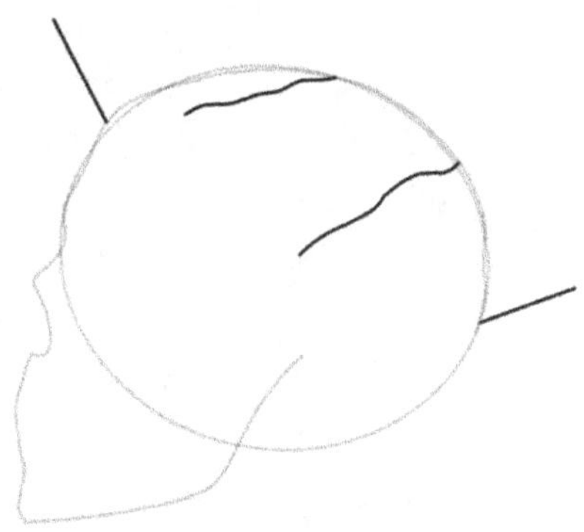

05

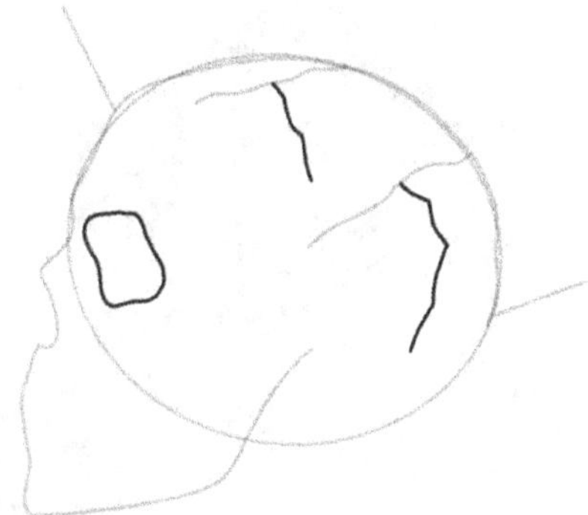

06

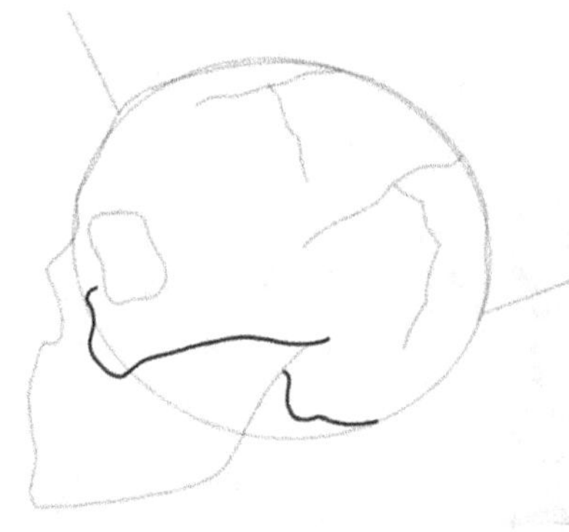

07

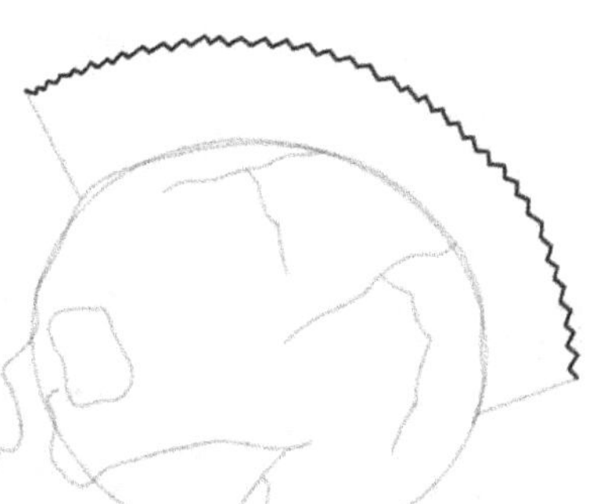

08

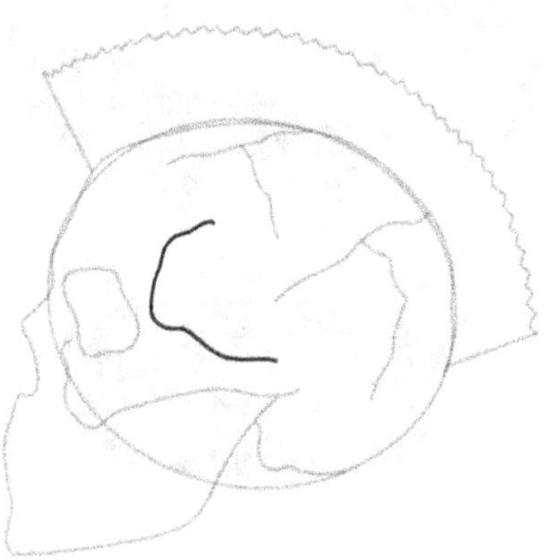

09

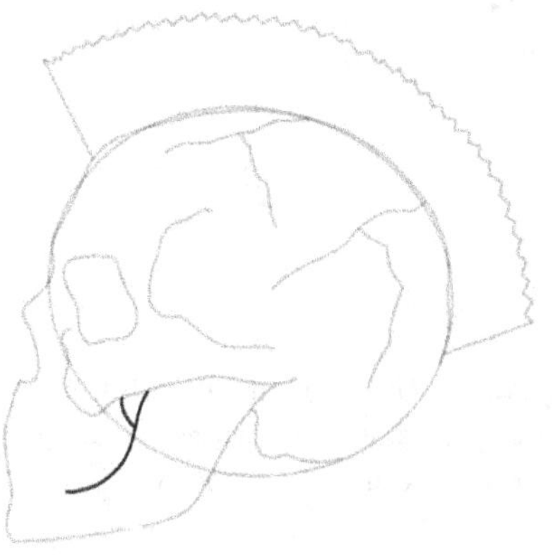

10

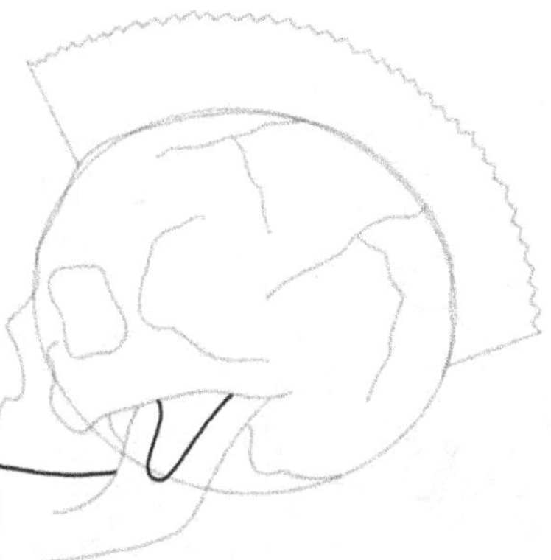

11

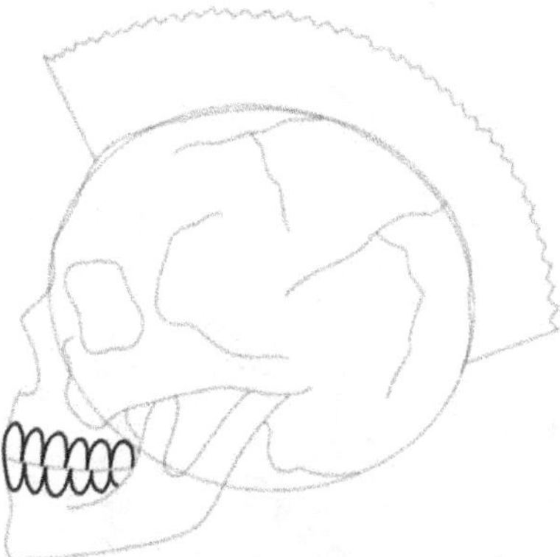

12

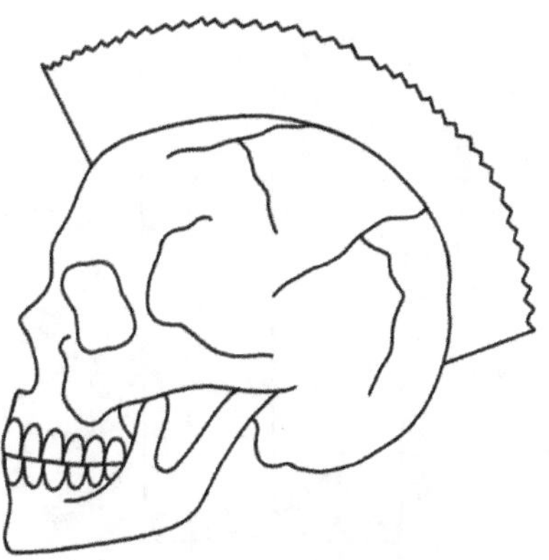

HOW TO DRAW PUNK THINGS

SKATEBOARD

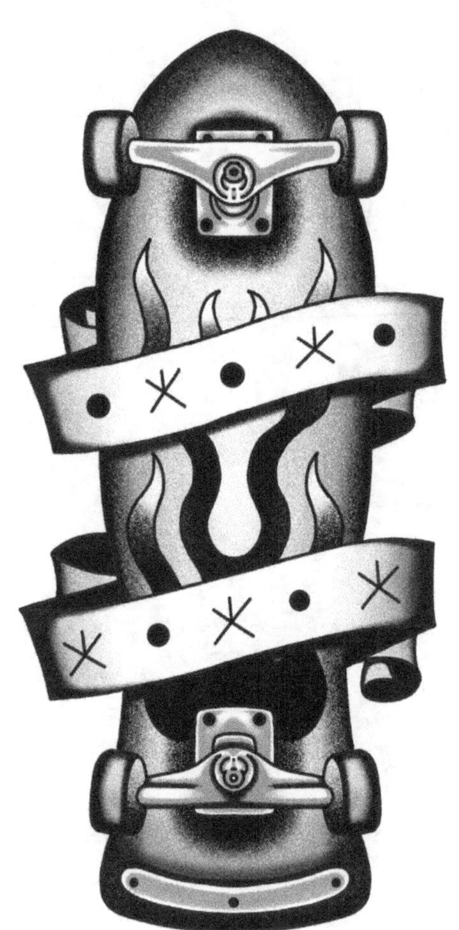

A symbol of freedom and anti-establishment energy, the skateboard embodies punk's spirit of rebellion and youthful defiance.

01

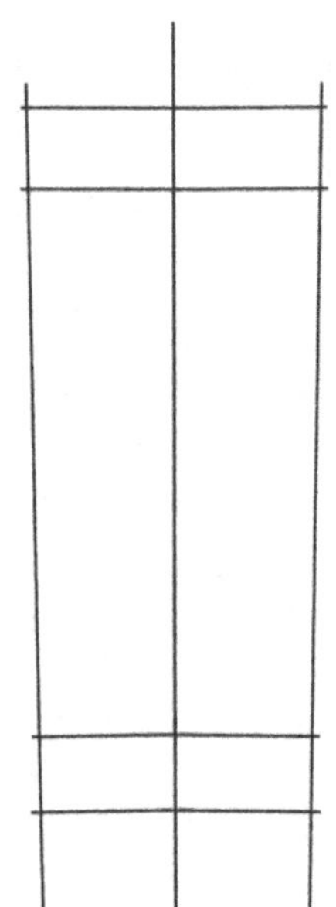

02

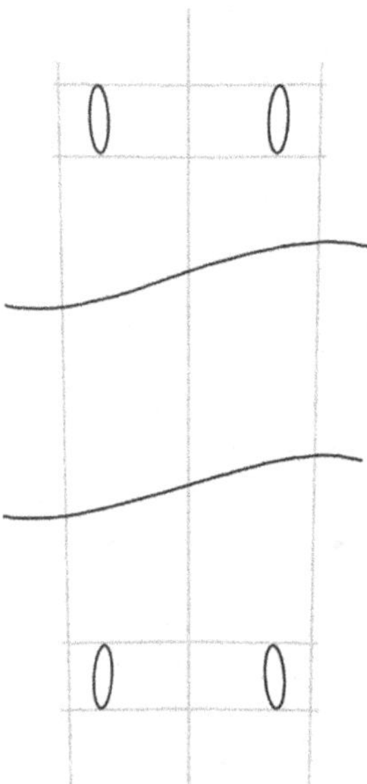

03

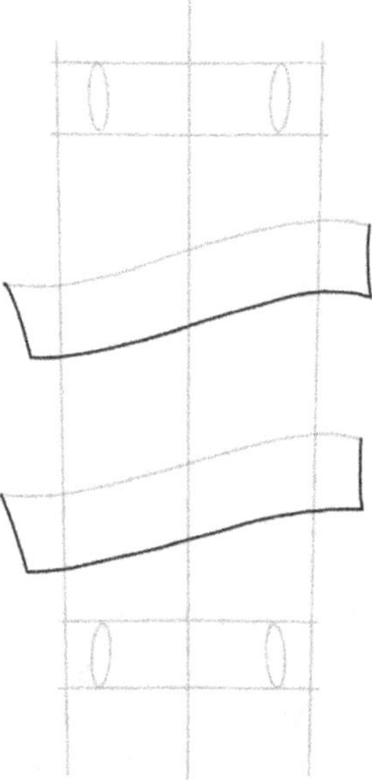

04

05 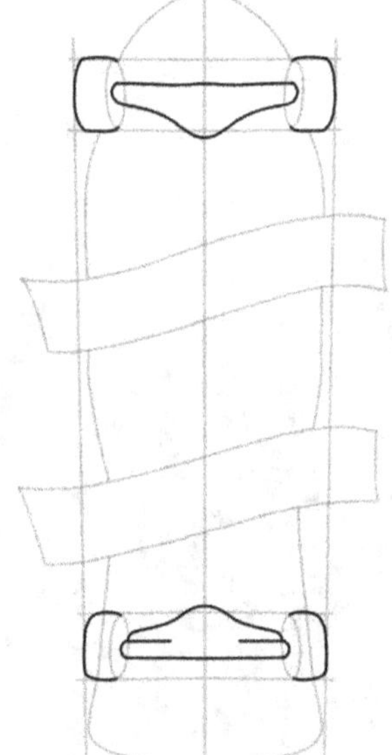

06 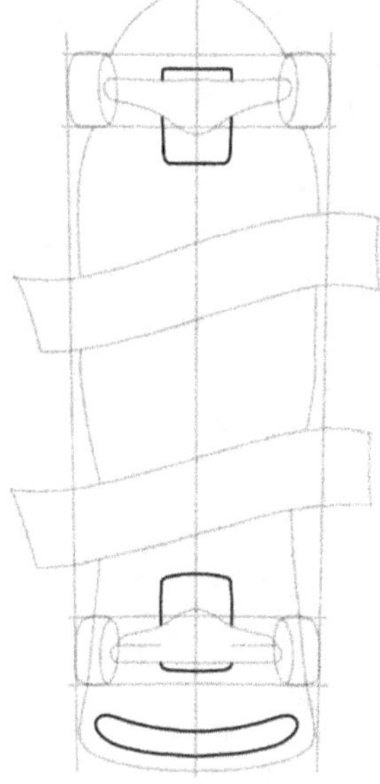

07 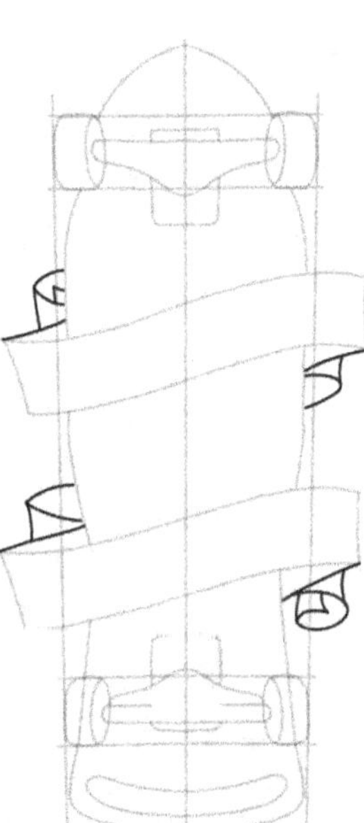

08 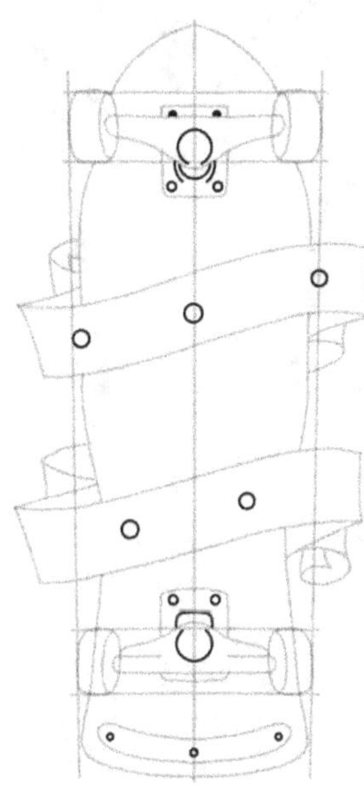

09 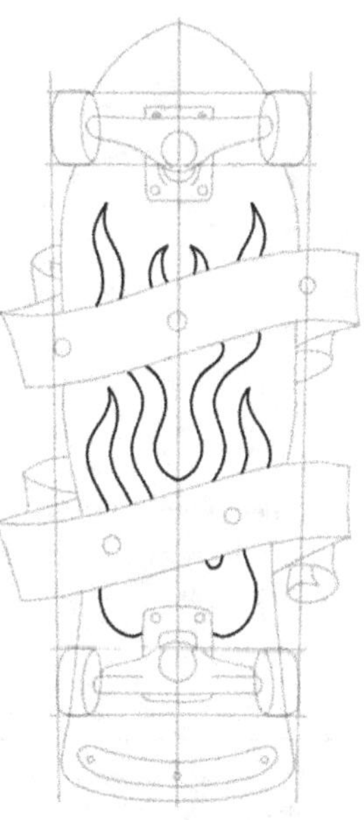

10 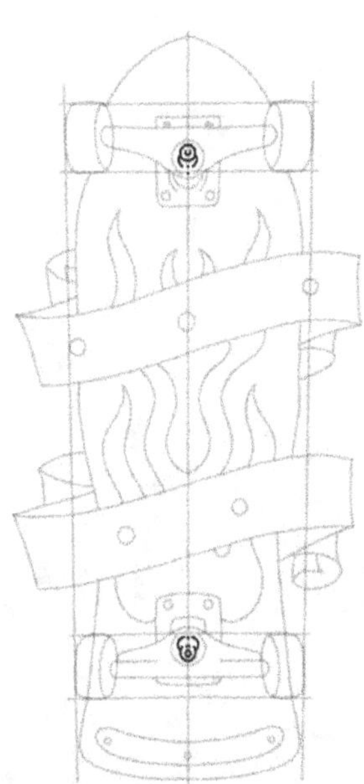

11 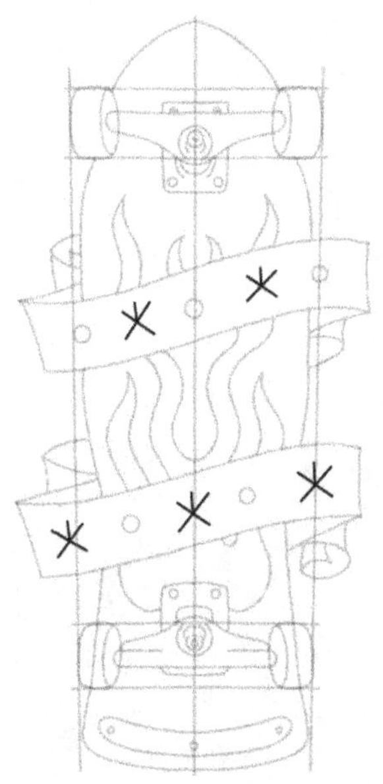

12 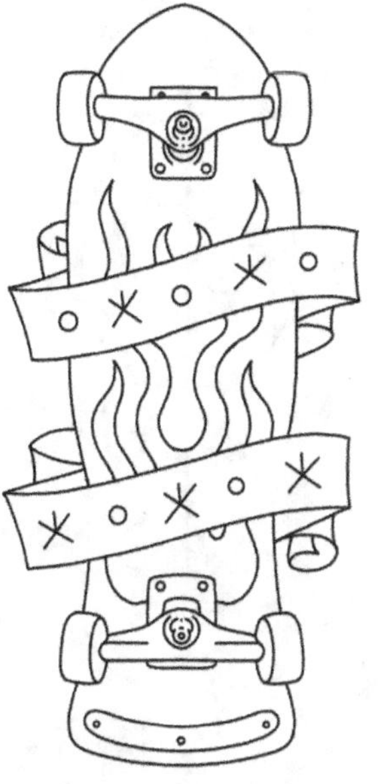

SPIDER

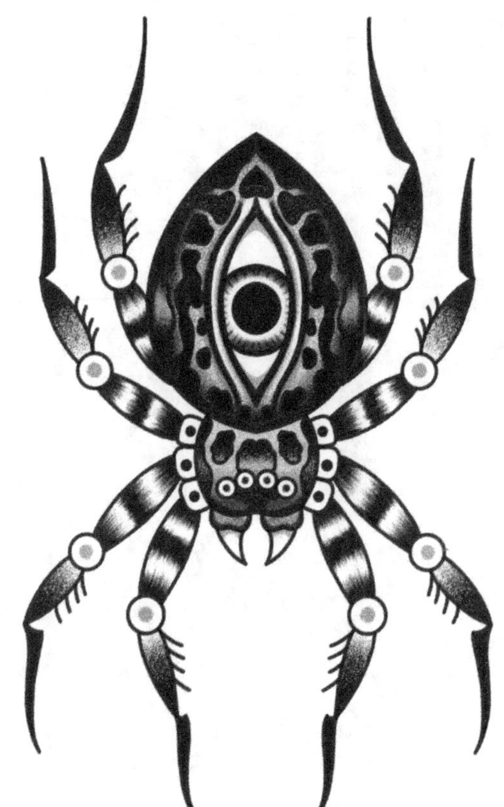

A symbol of patience and resilience, the spider reflects punk's embrace of the outsider.

01

02

03

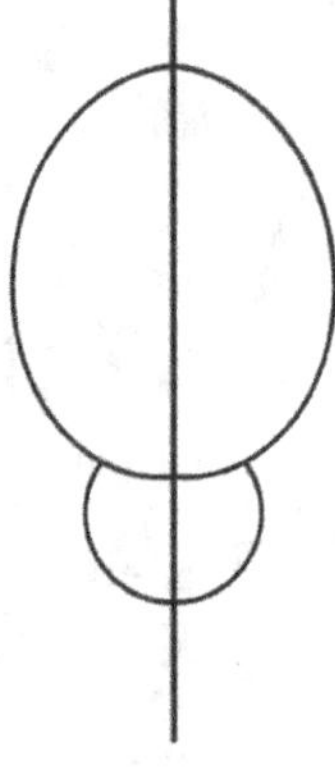

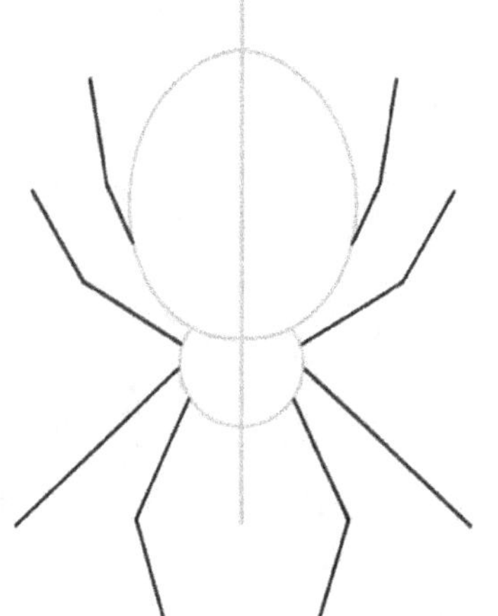

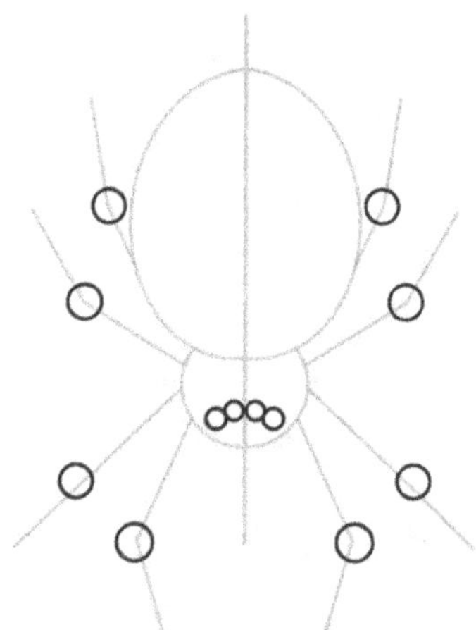

04

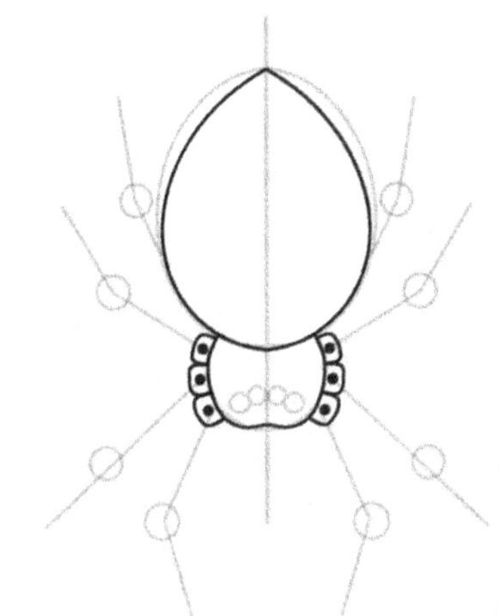

05

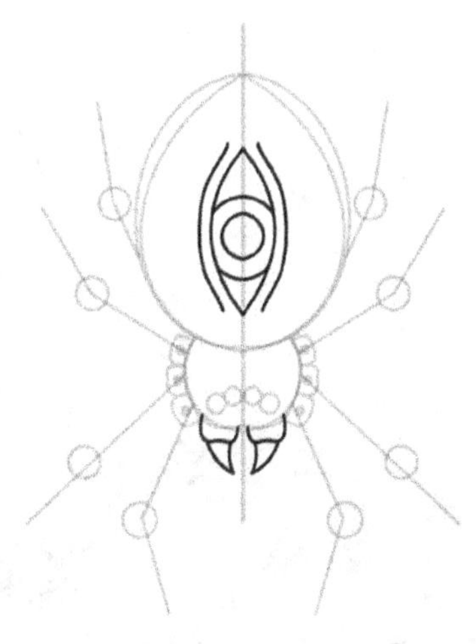

06

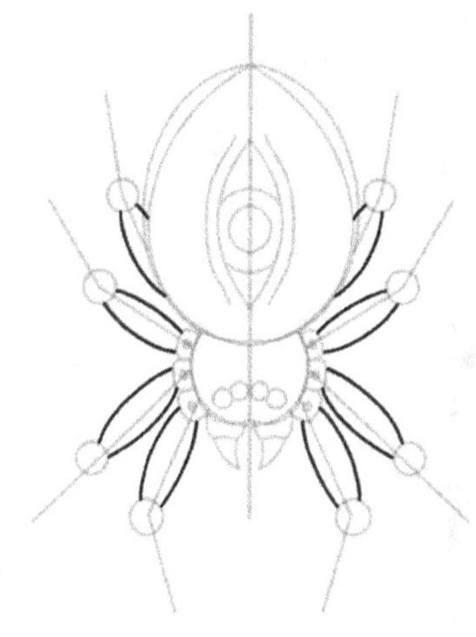

07

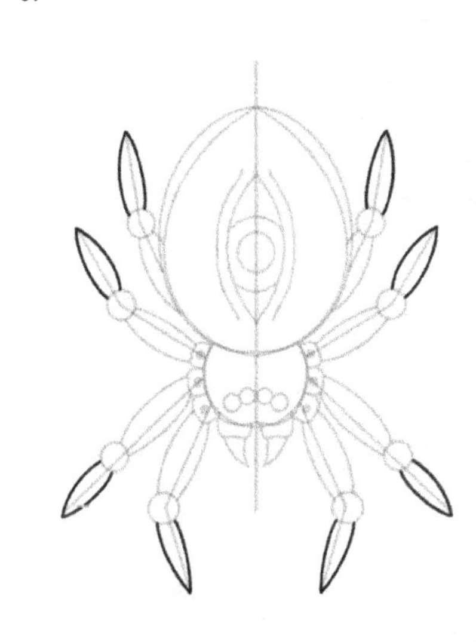

08

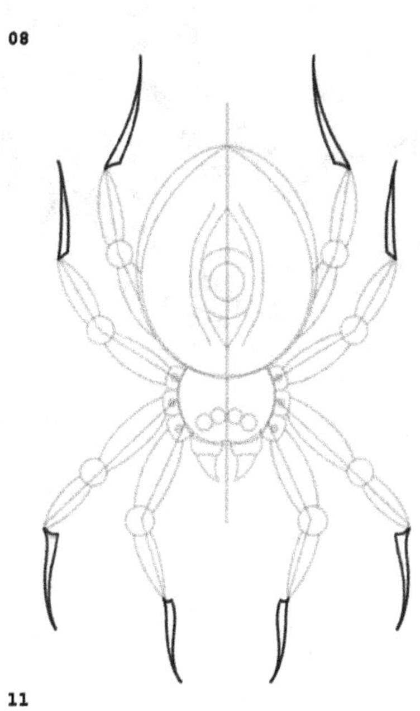

09

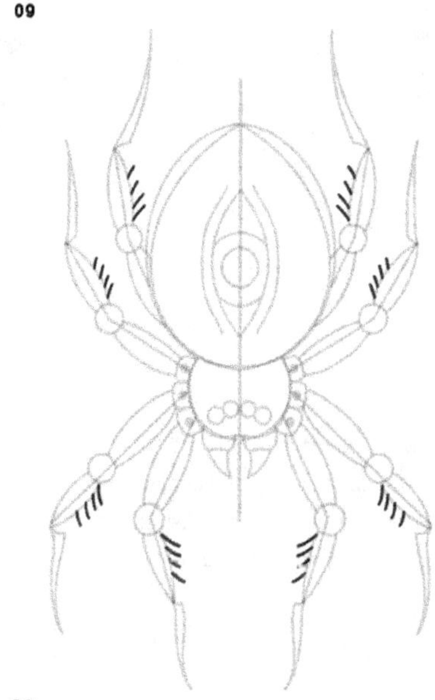

10

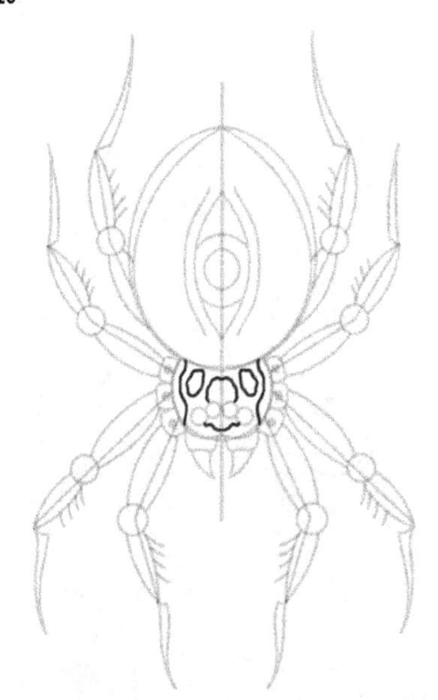

11

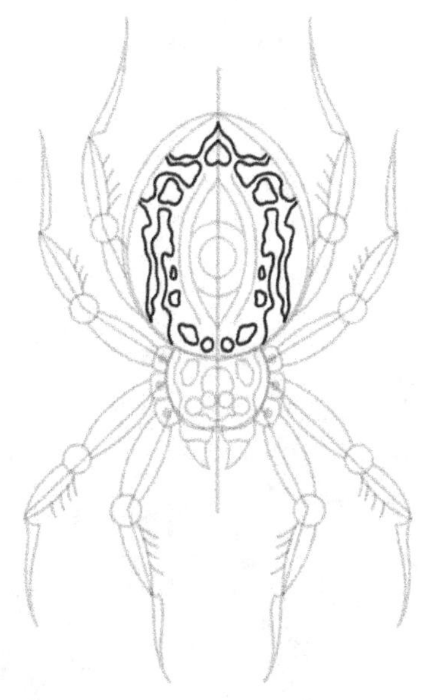

12

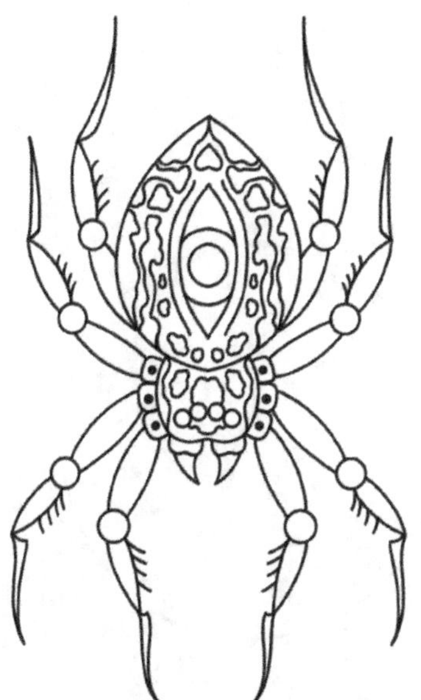

EIGHT BALL

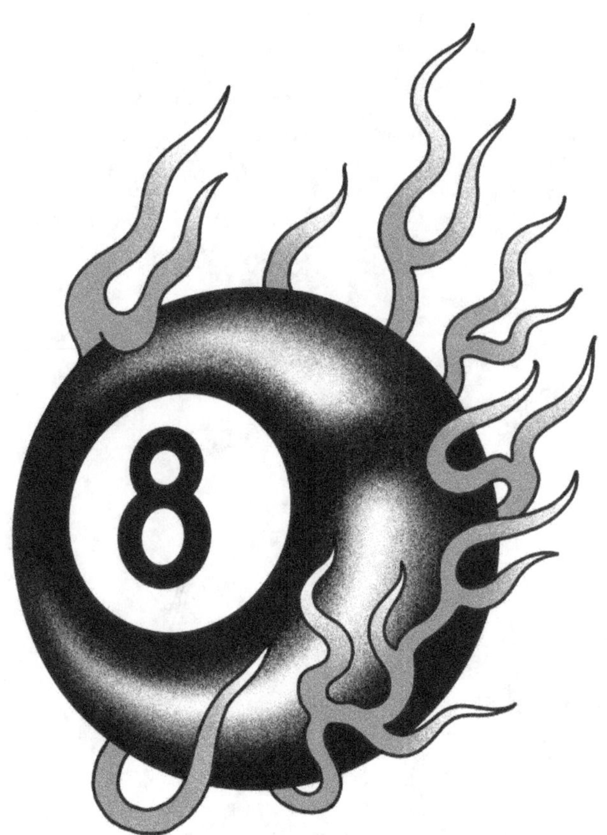

The 8 Ball reflects the punk ethos of embracing uncertainty and challenging conventional rules by symbolising risk, rebellion, and unpredictability.

01   **02**   **03**

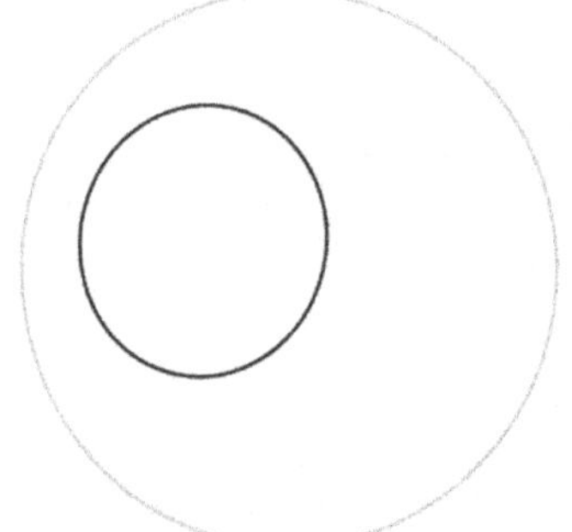

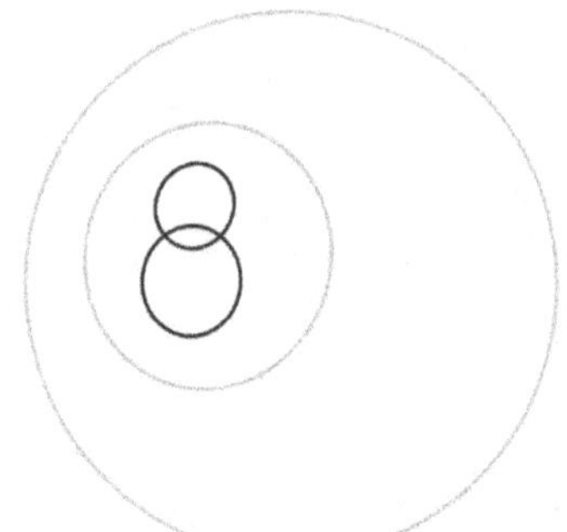

04

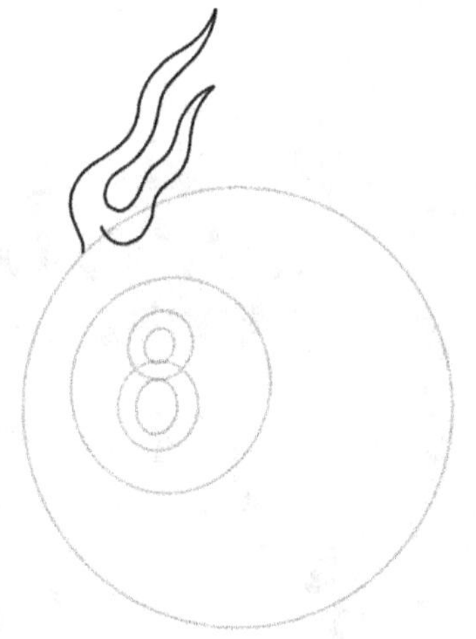

05

06

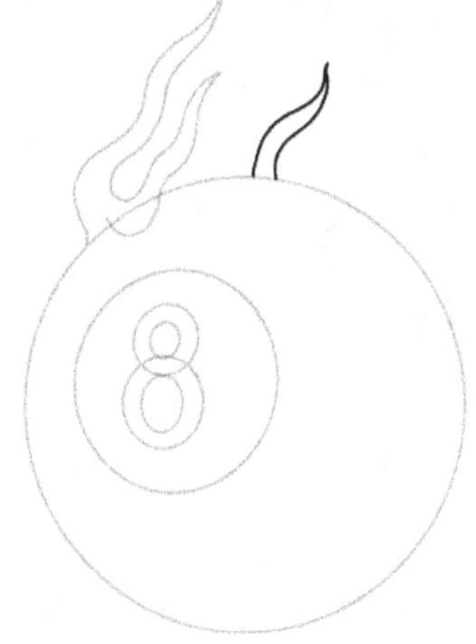

07

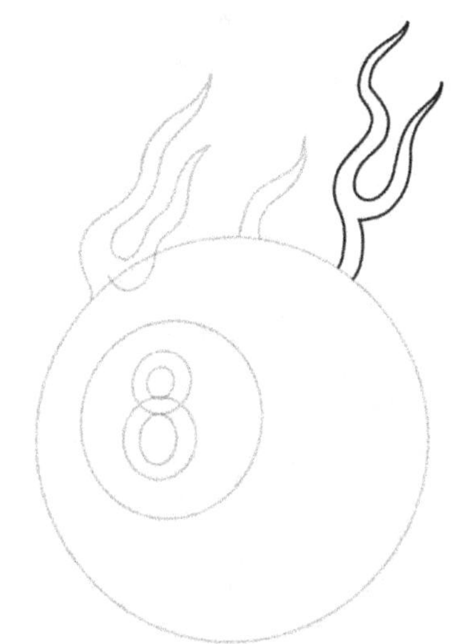

08

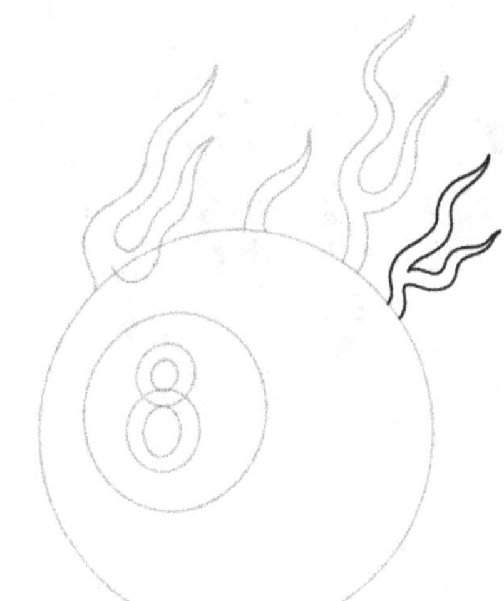

09

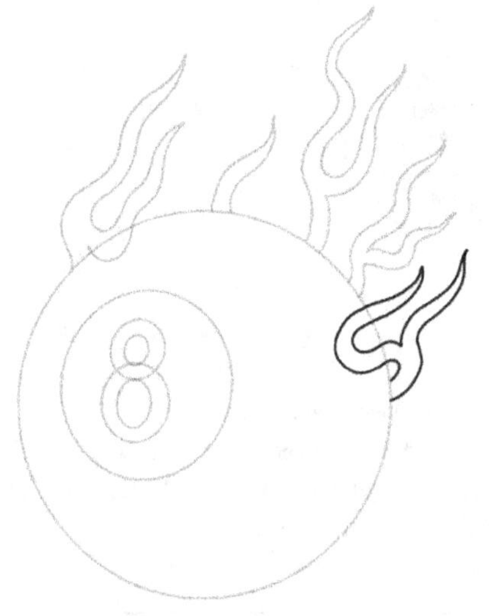

10

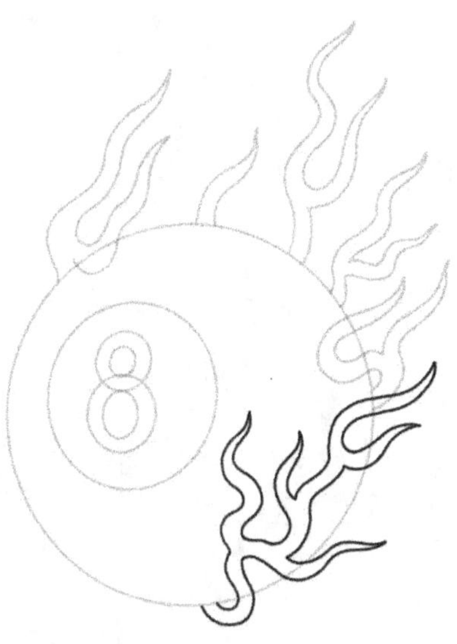

11

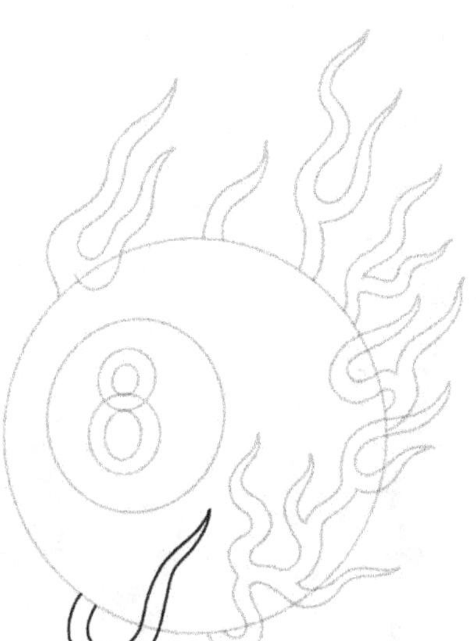

12

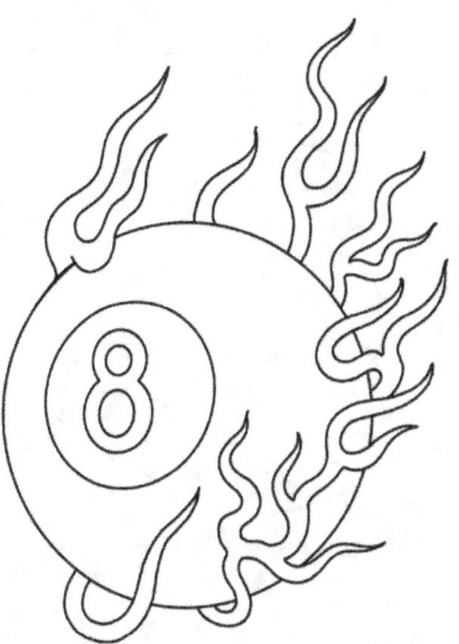

ANATOMICAL HEART

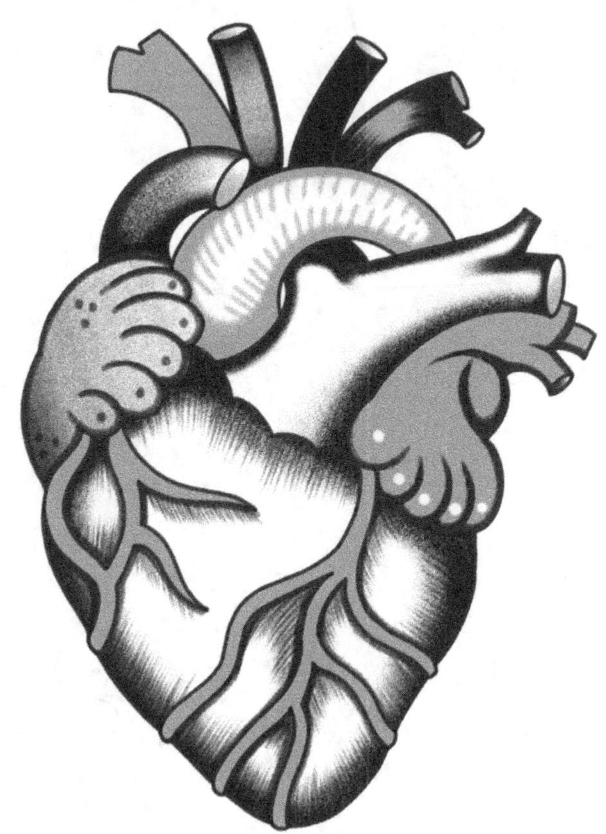

It is a raw emblem of authenticity, vulnerability, and emotional intensity, reflecting punk's unapologetic honesty and passion for individuality.

01

02

03

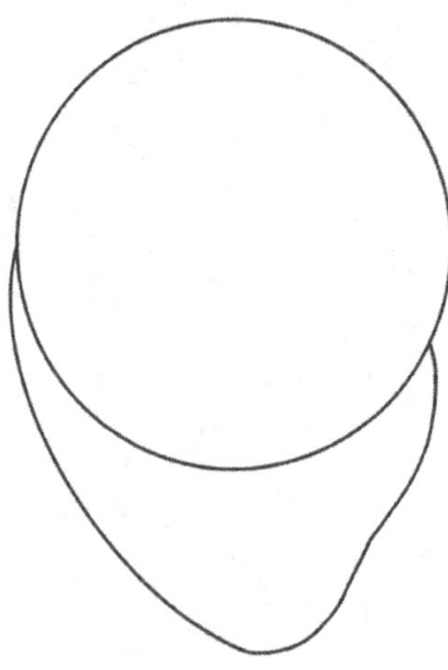

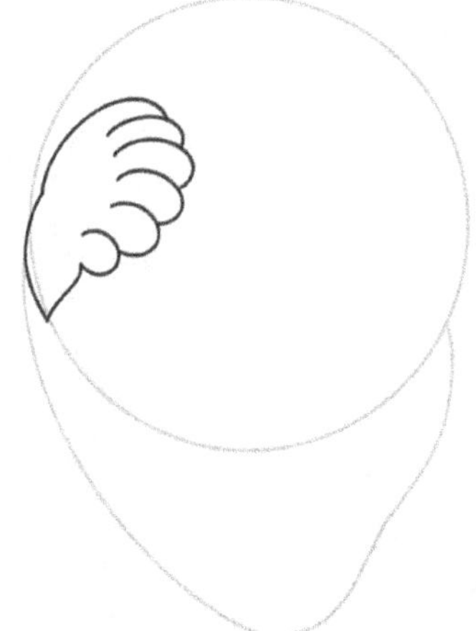

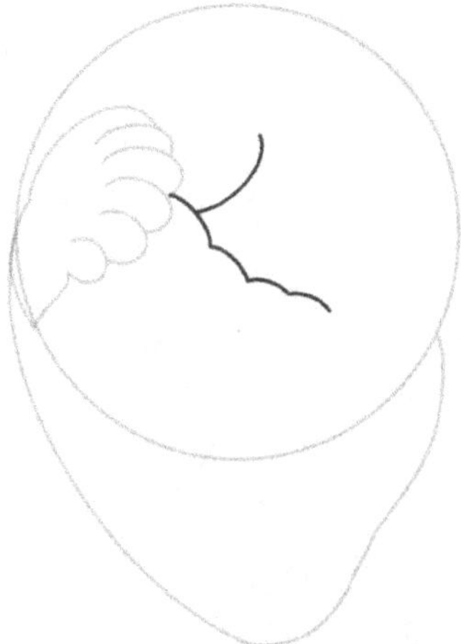

04

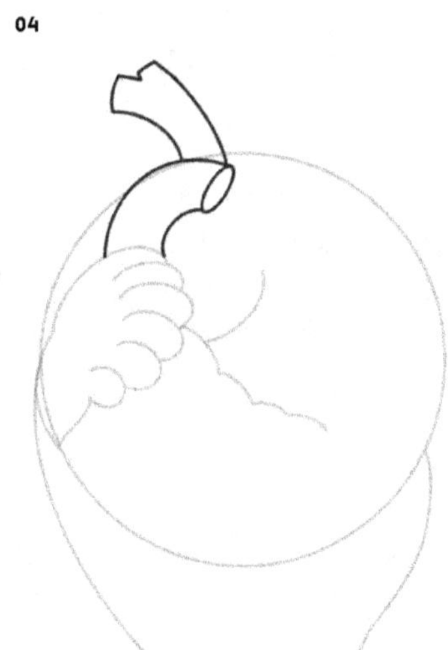

05

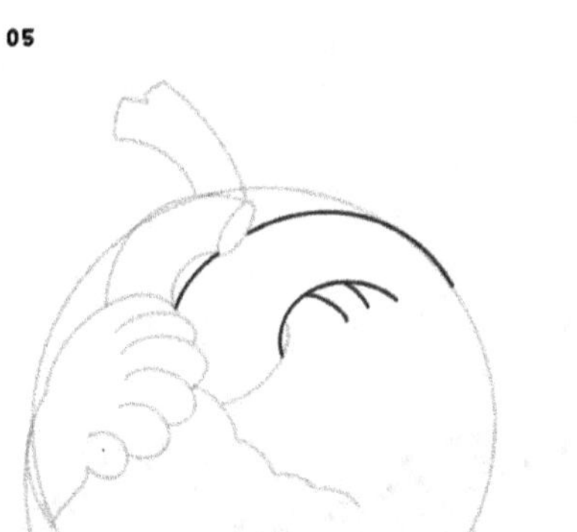

06

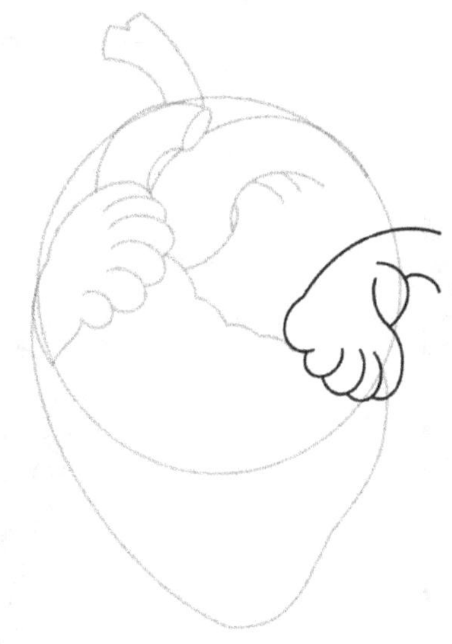

07

08

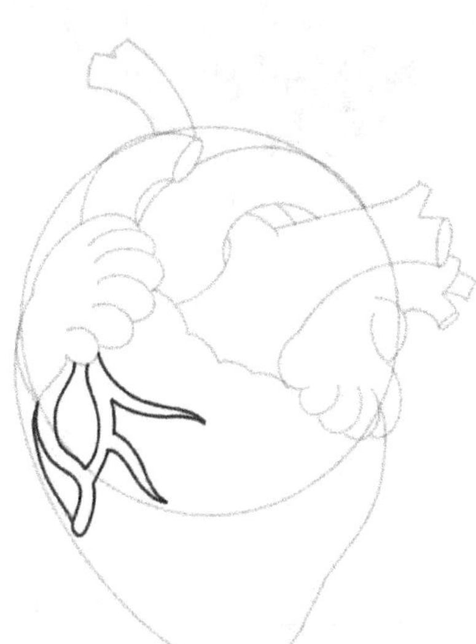

09

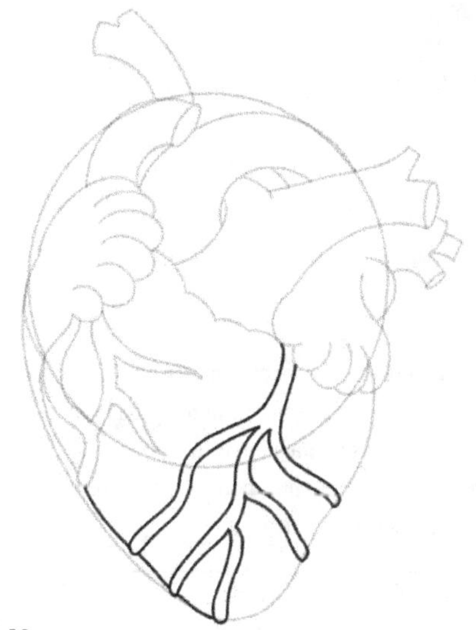

10

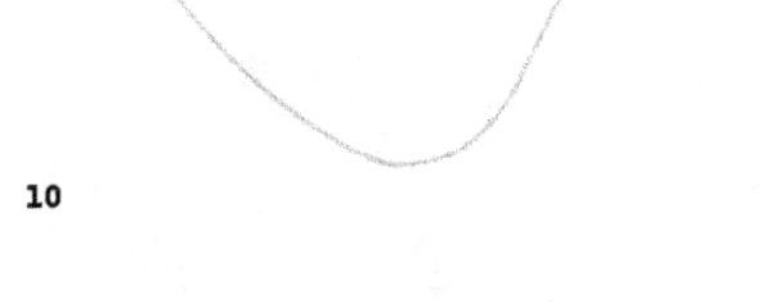

11

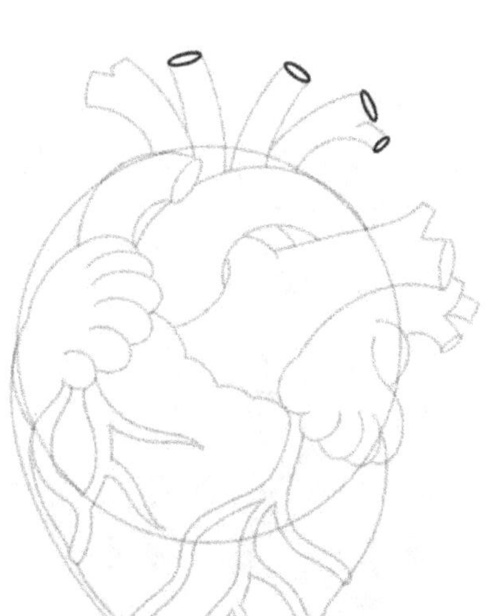

12

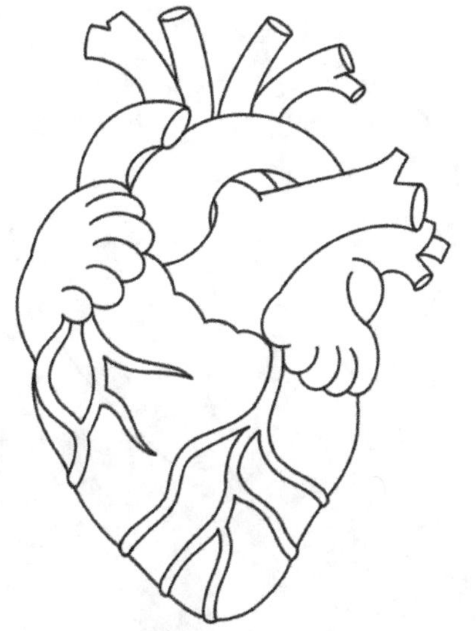

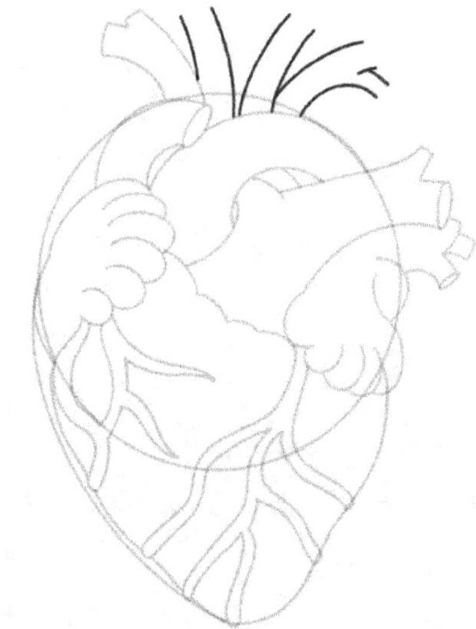

BROKEN HEART

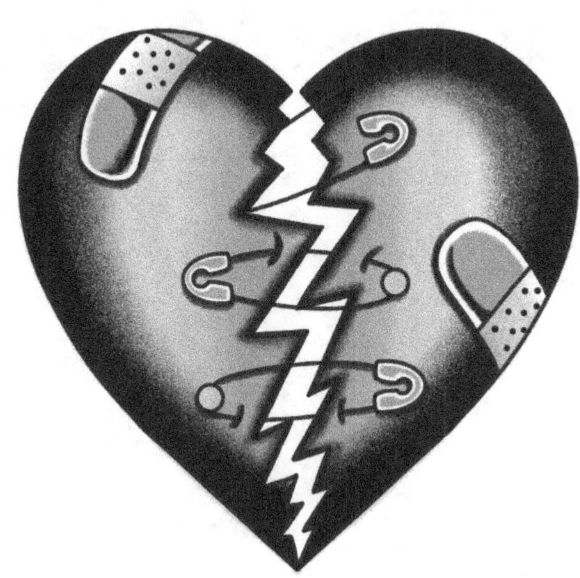

A symbol of emotional defiance and resilience, the broken heart reflects punk's ability to transform personal pain into a powerful anthem of self-expression and rebellion against societal norms.

01

02

03

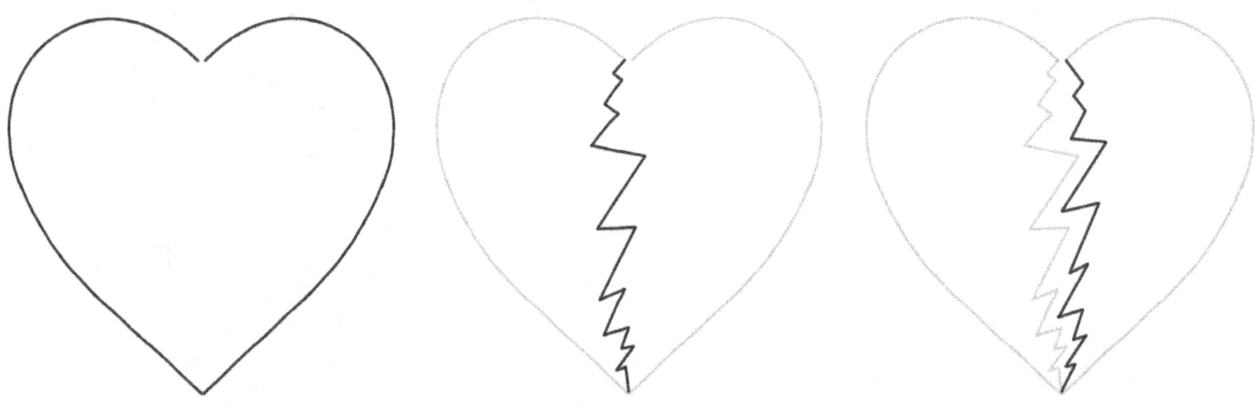

04

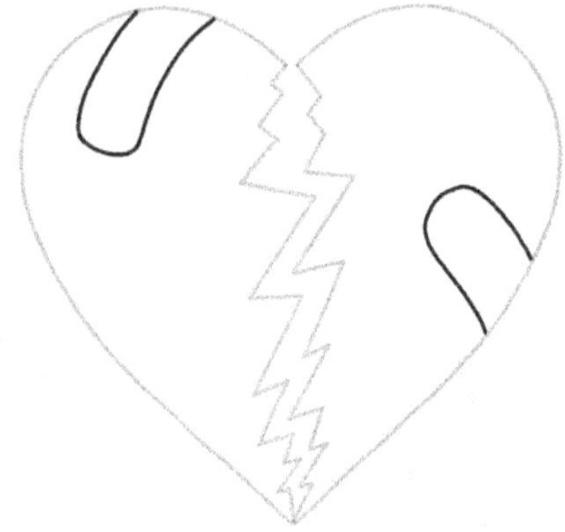

05

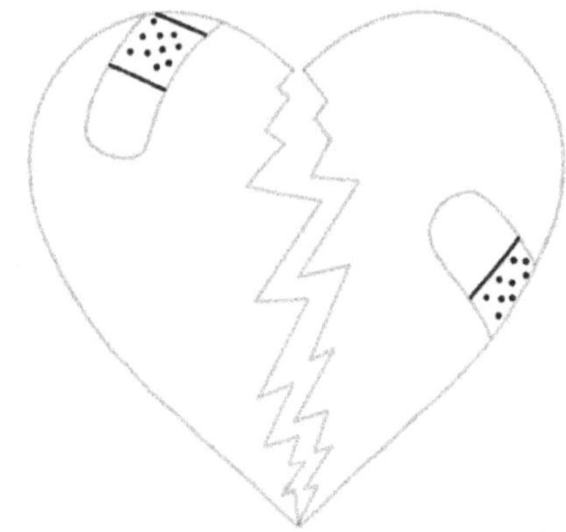

06

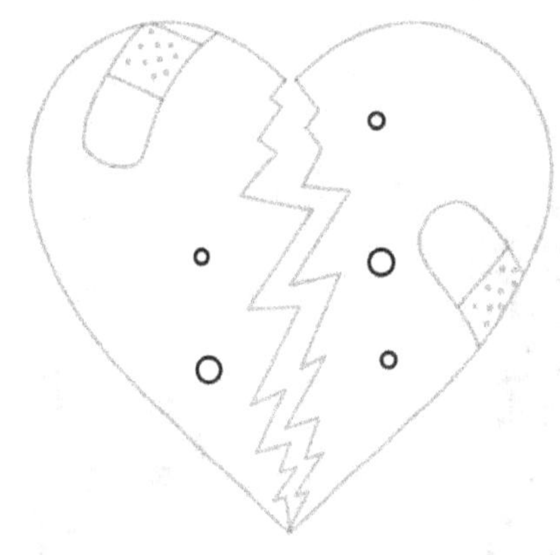

07

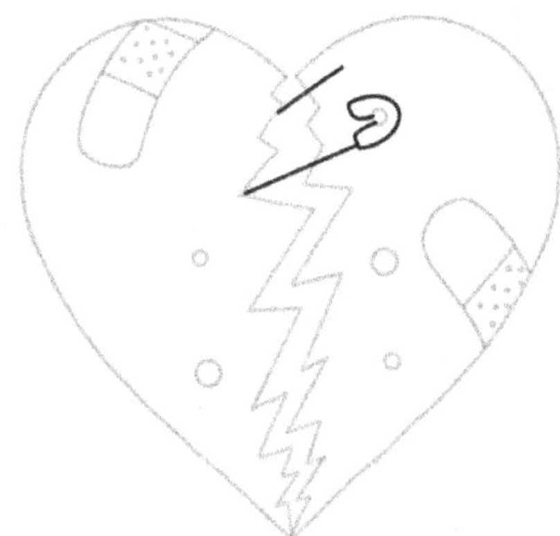

08

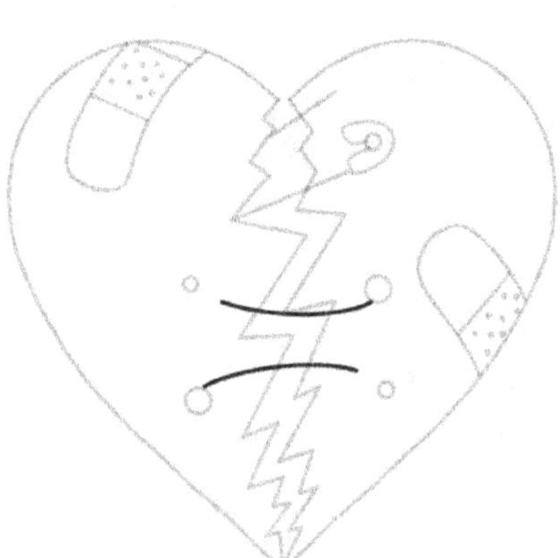

09

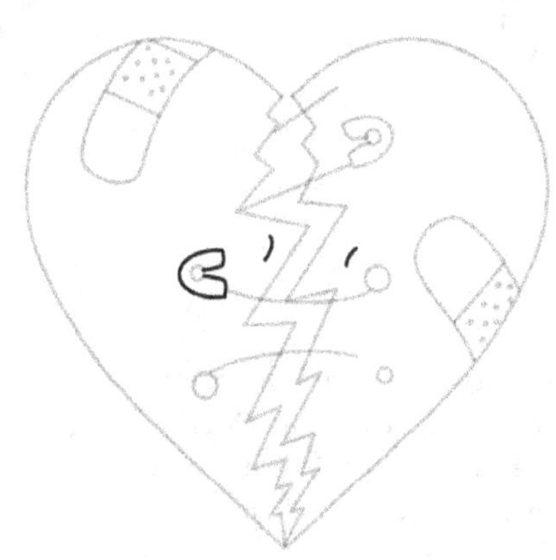

10

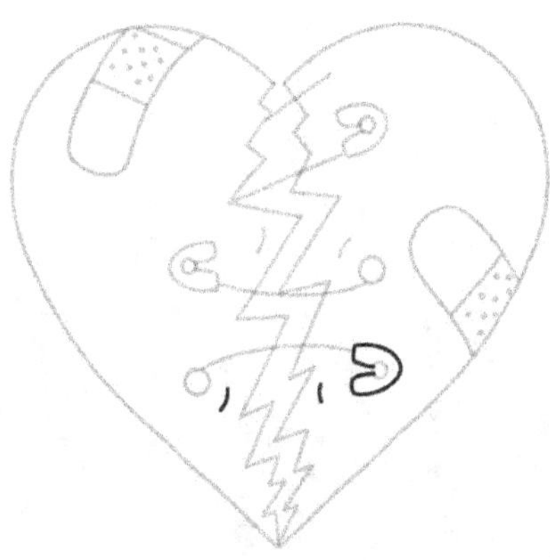

11

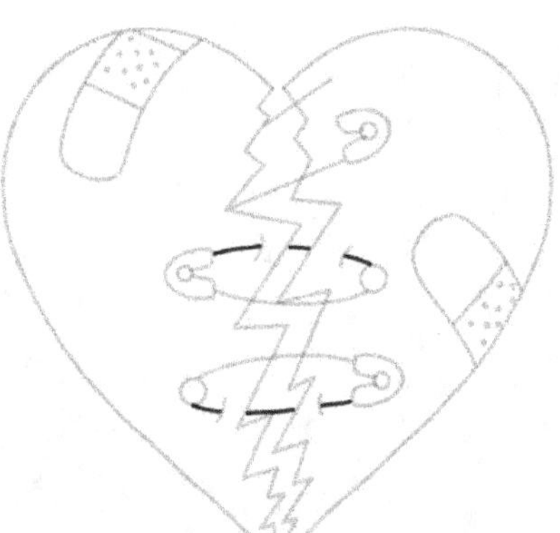

12

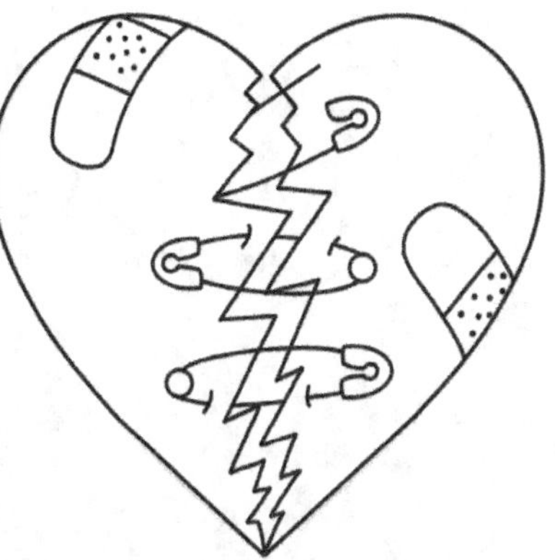

BARBED WIRE

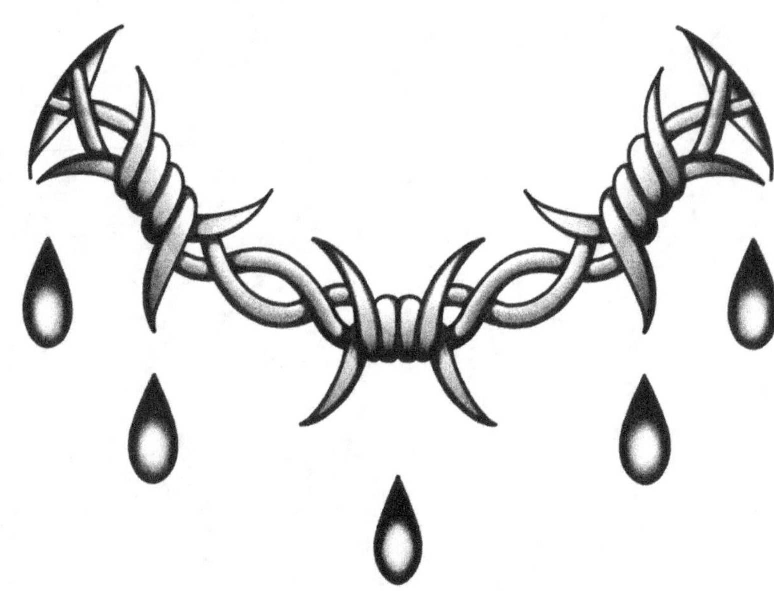

A symbol of resistance, defiance, and protection, barbed wire embodies the punk rejection of conformity and the barriers imposed by societal norms.

01

02

03

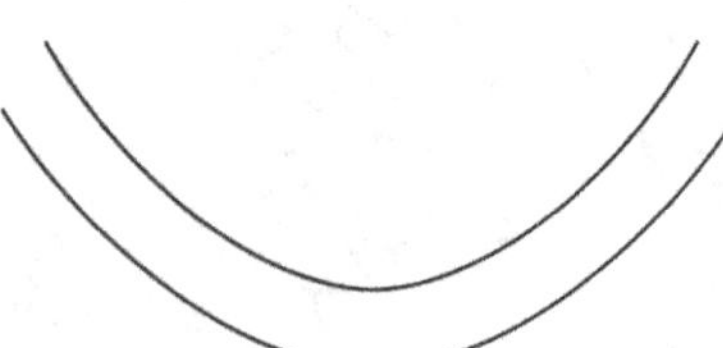

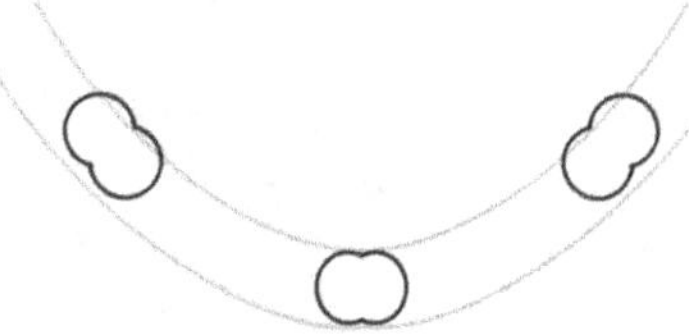

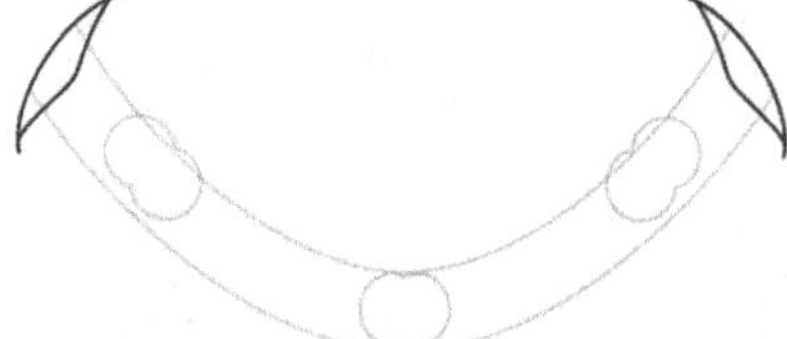

04

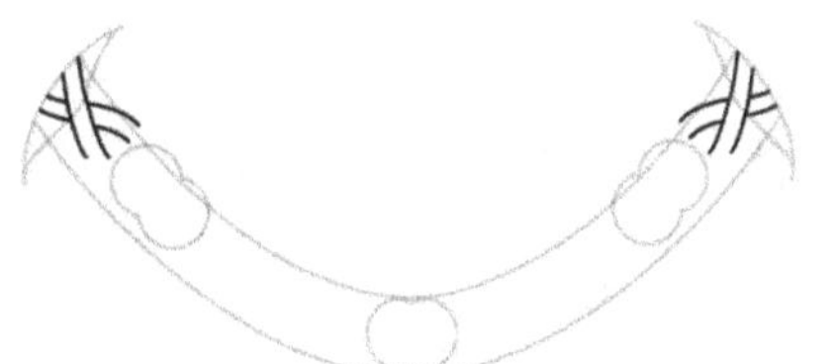

05

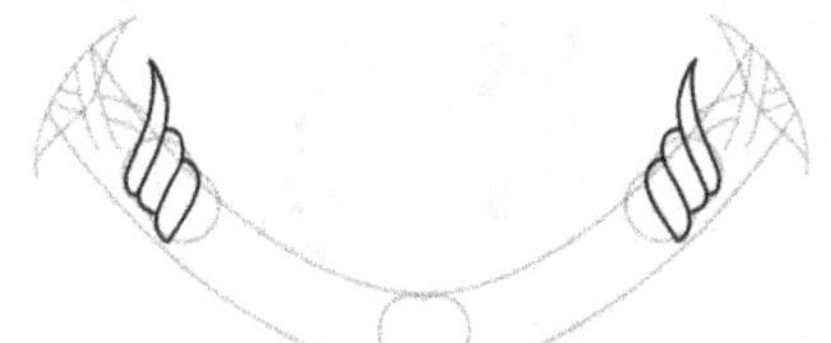

06

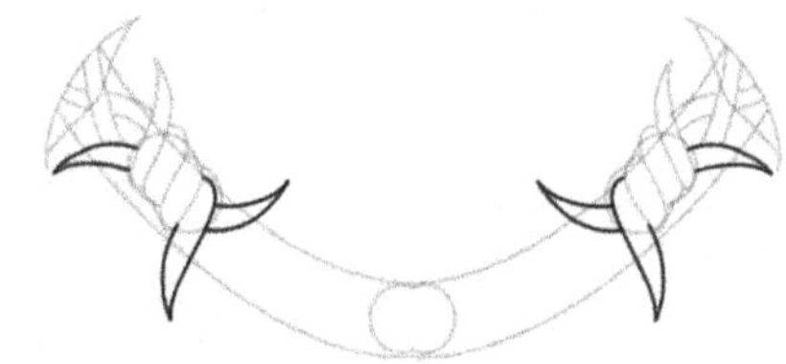

07

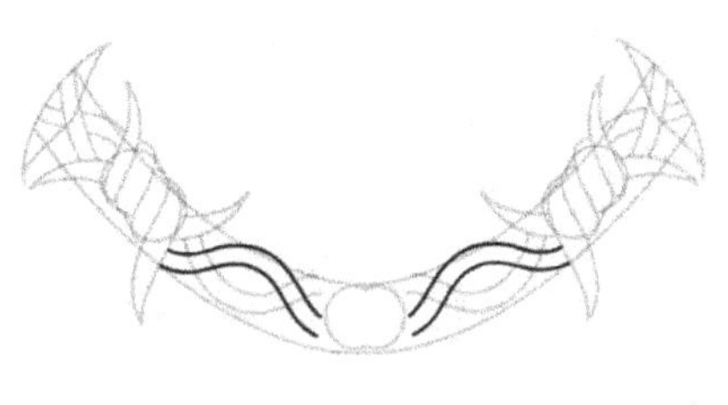

08

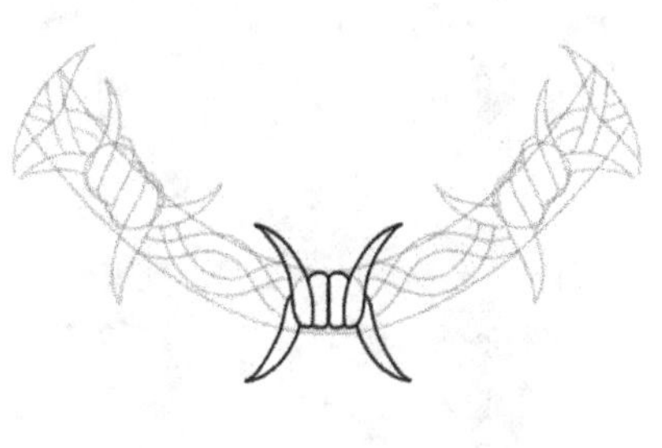

09

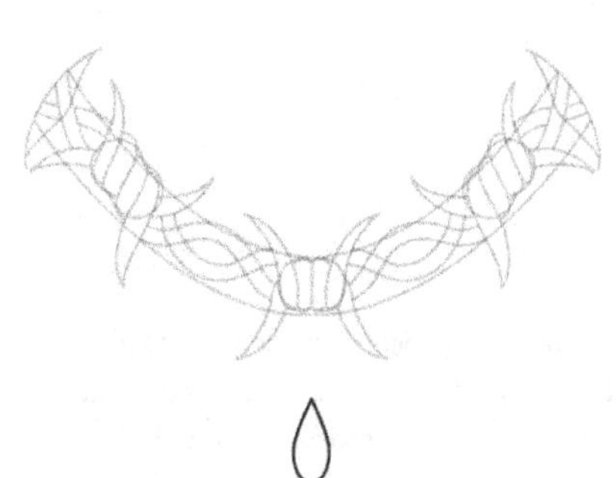

HOW TO DRAW PUNK THINGS

10

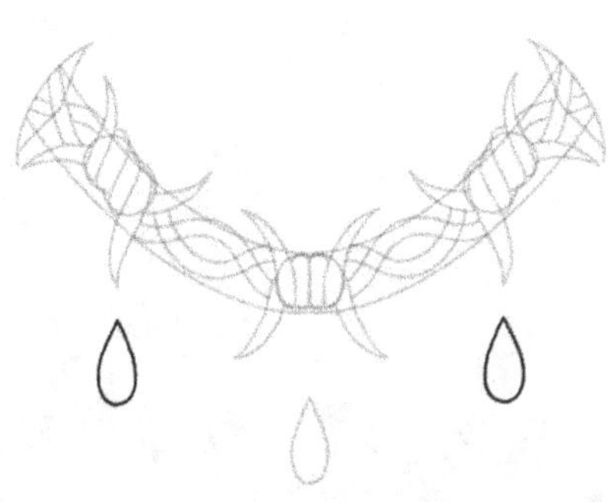

11

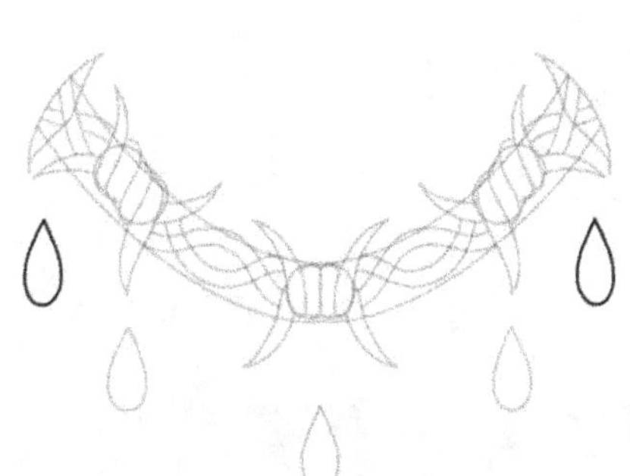

12

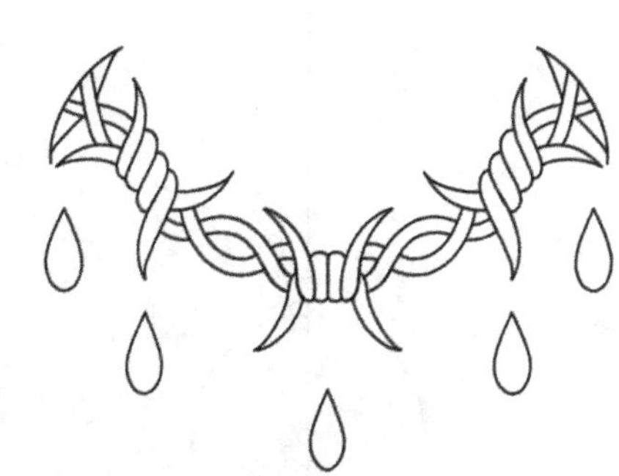

BAT

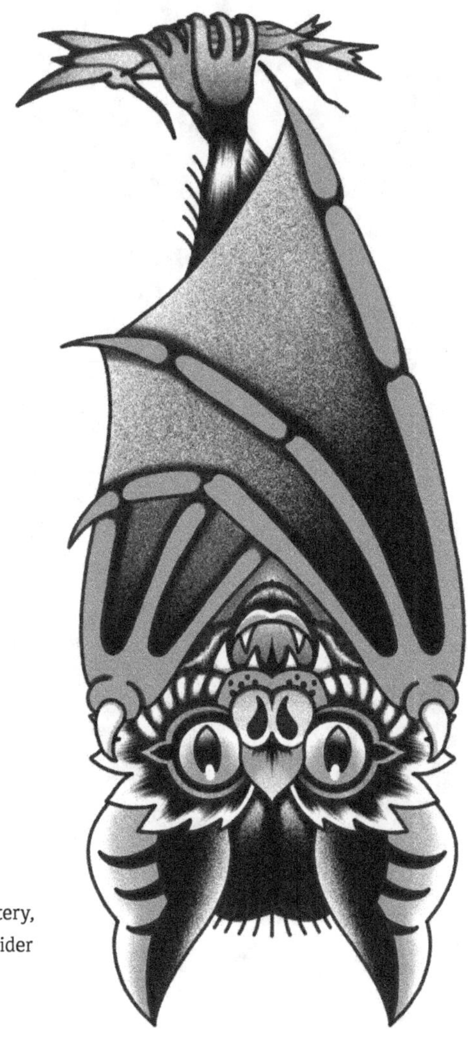

Representing nocturnal rebellion and mystery, bats symbolise punk's embrace of the outsider and the rejection of societal norms.

01

02

03

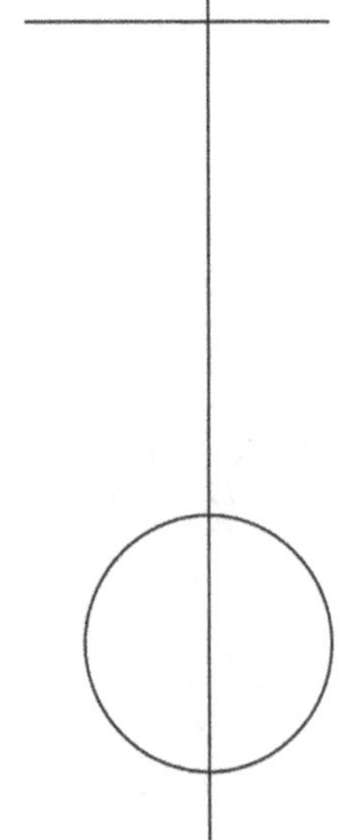

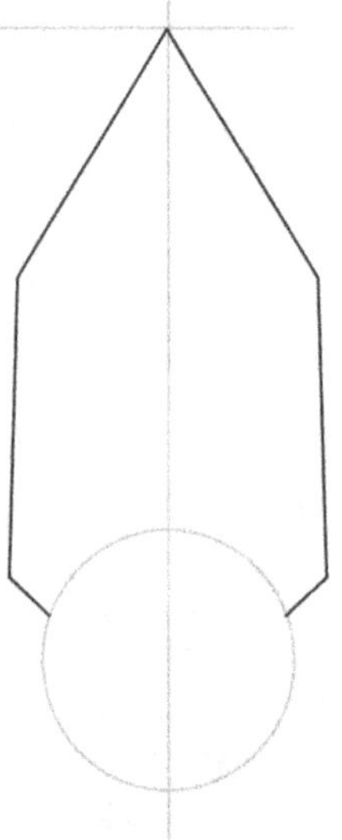

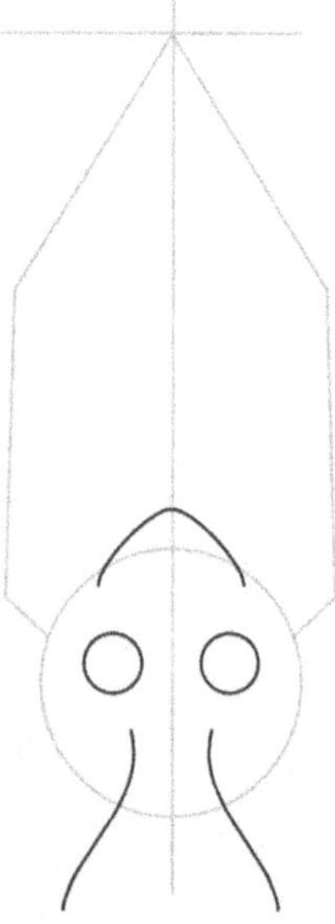

04

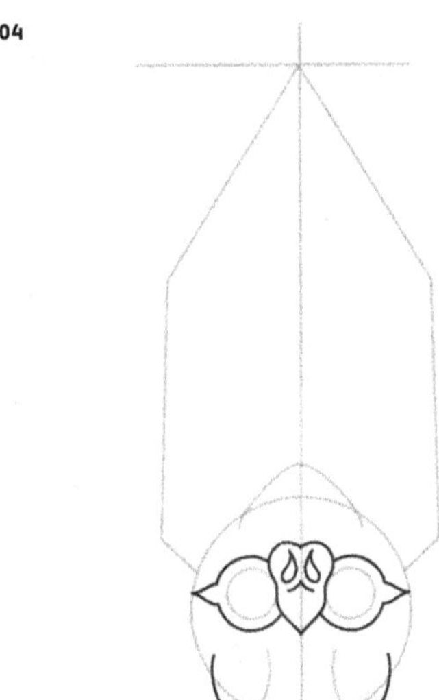

05

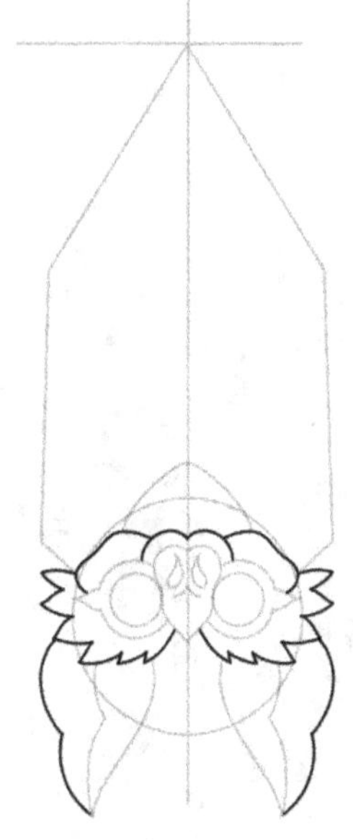

06

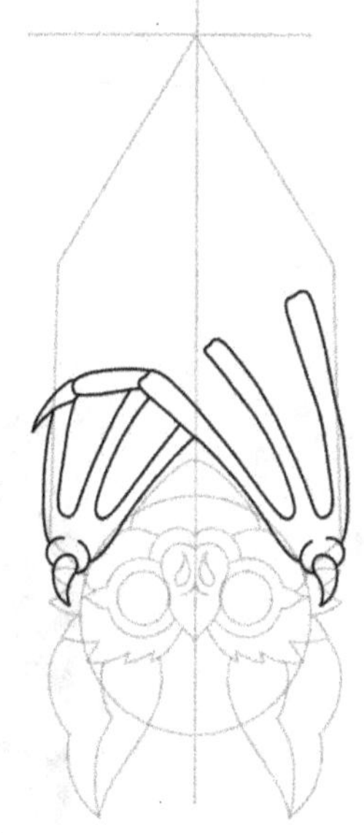

07

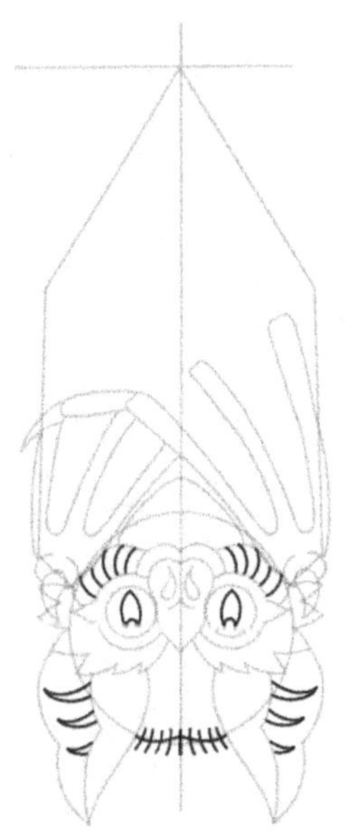

08

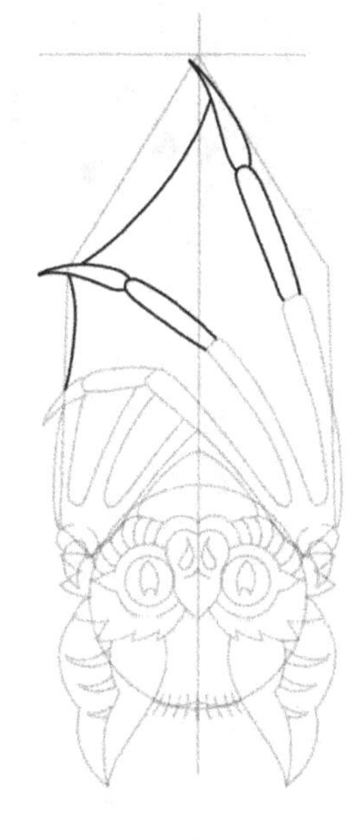

09

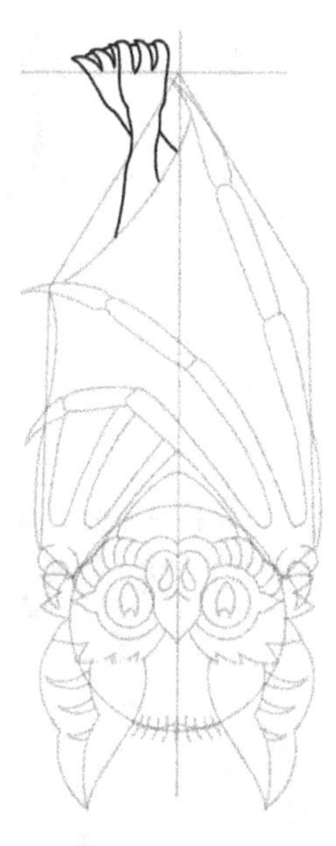

10

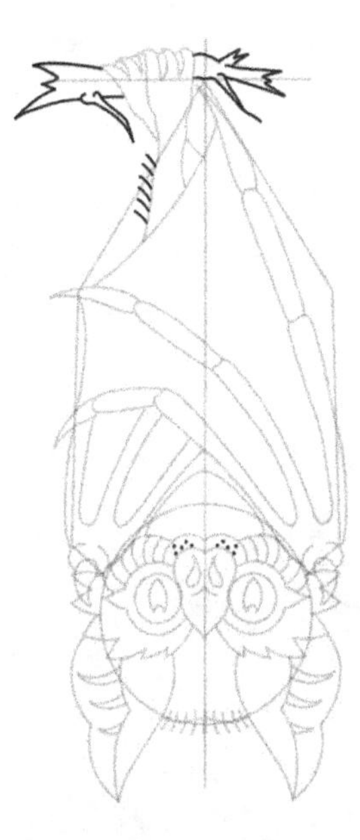

11

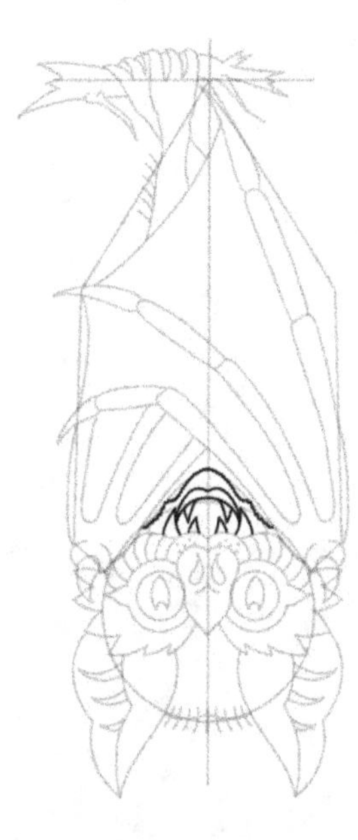

12

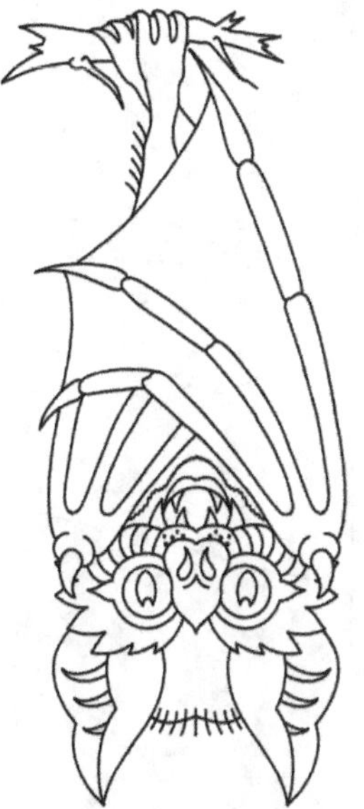

BOOM BOX

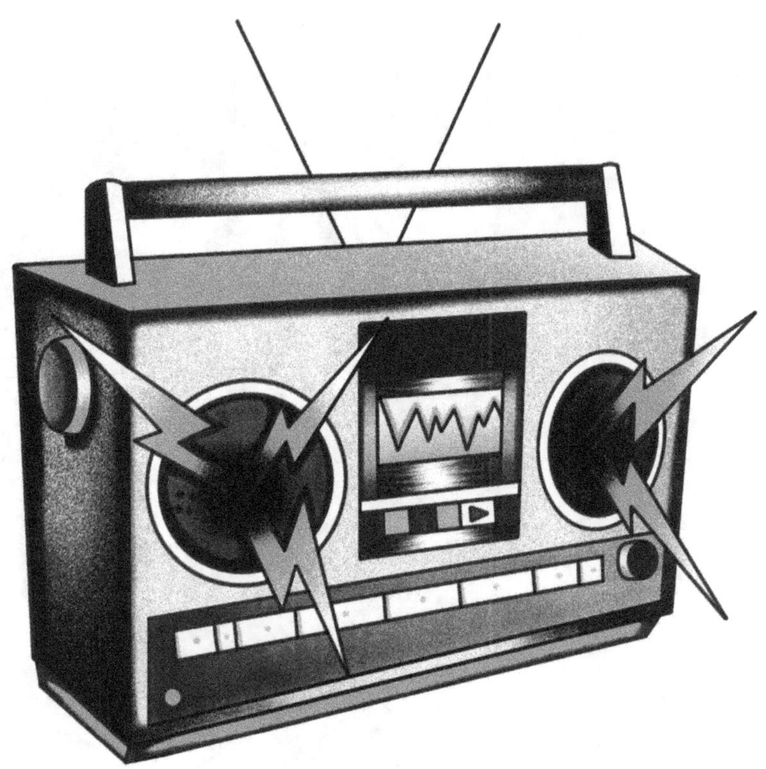

A portable voice of revolution, the boombox symbolises the DIY spirit of punk, spreading raw energy and countercultural messages.

01

02

03

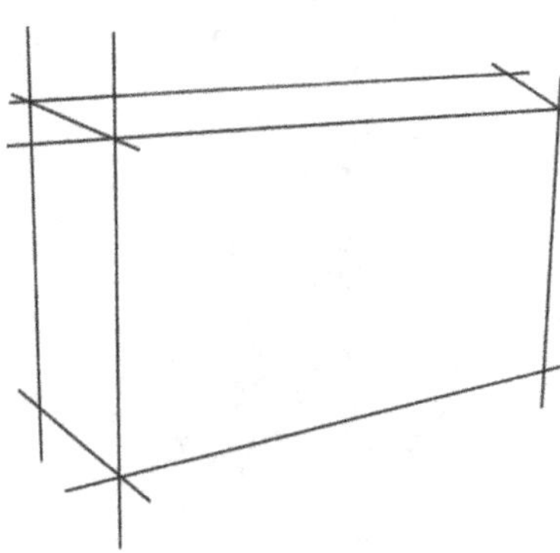

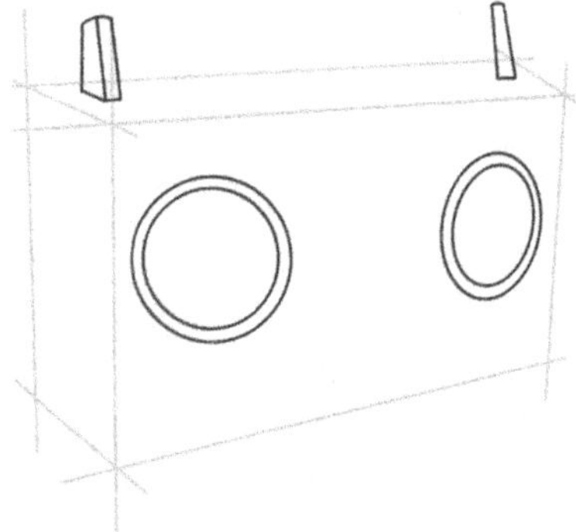

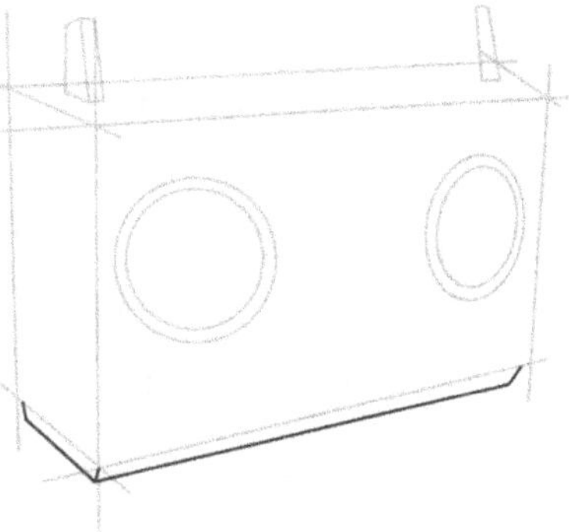

04

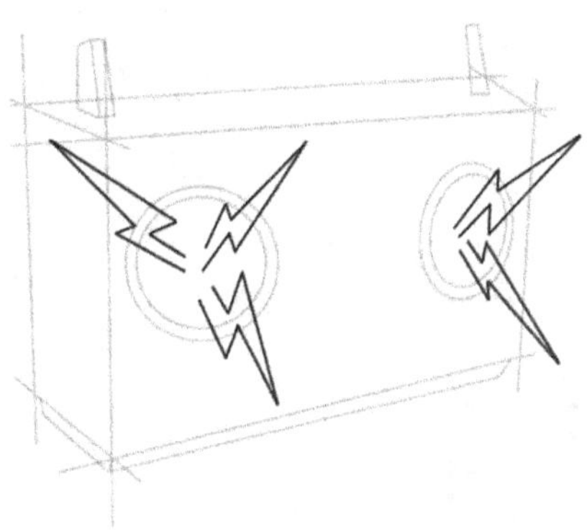

05

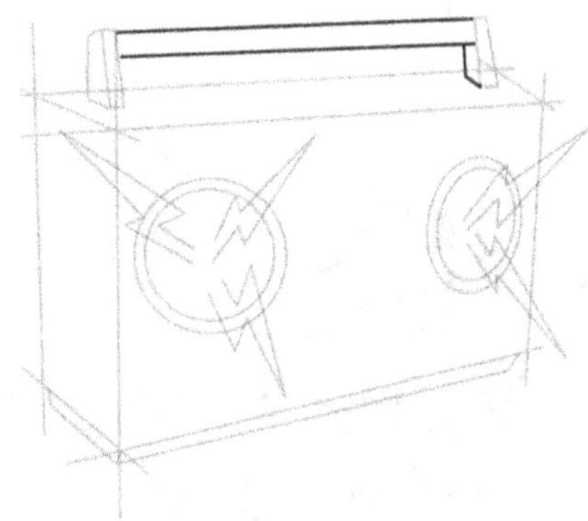

06

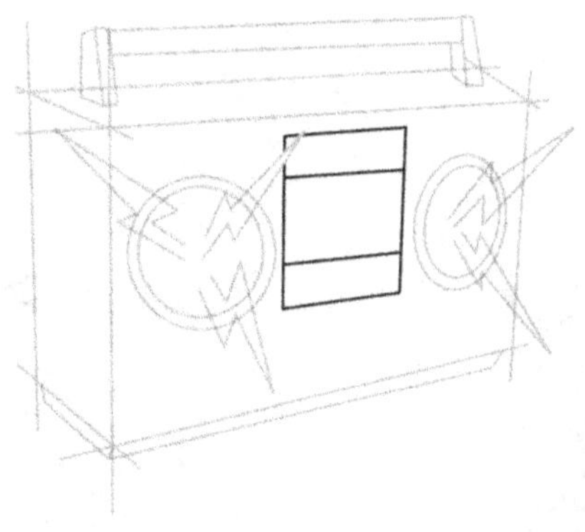

07

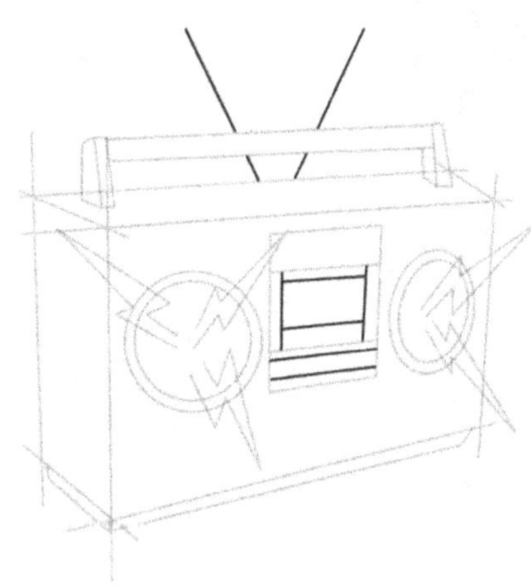

08

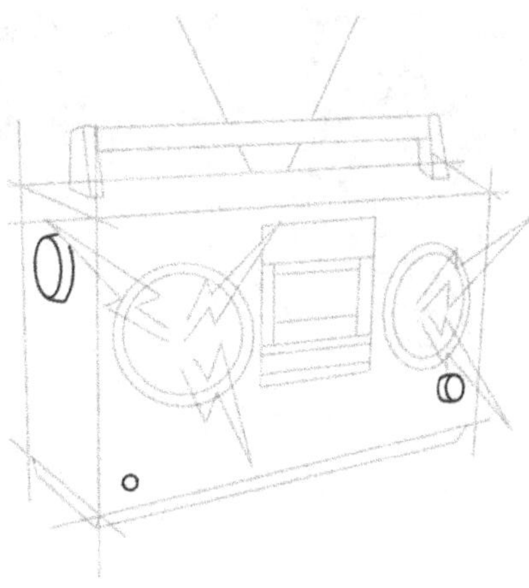

09

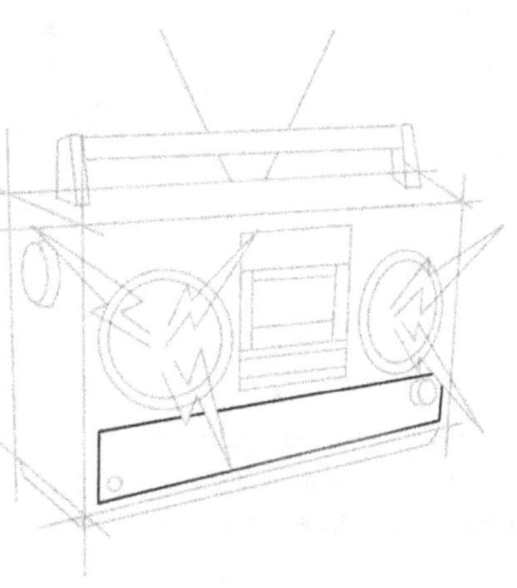

10

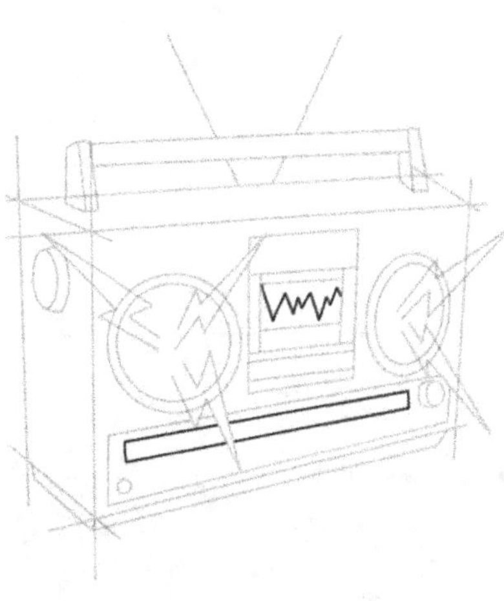

11

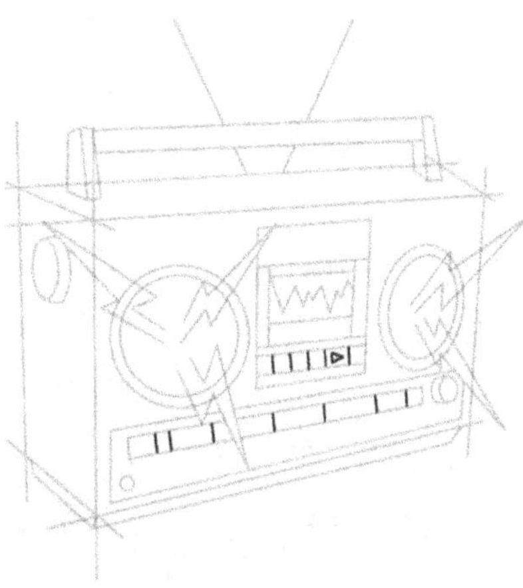

12

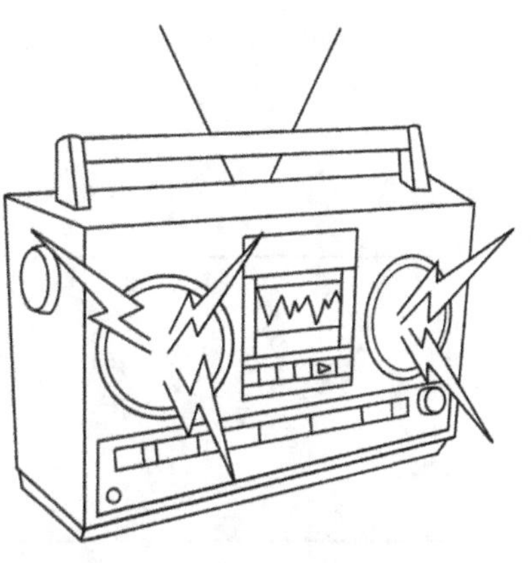

CASSETTE

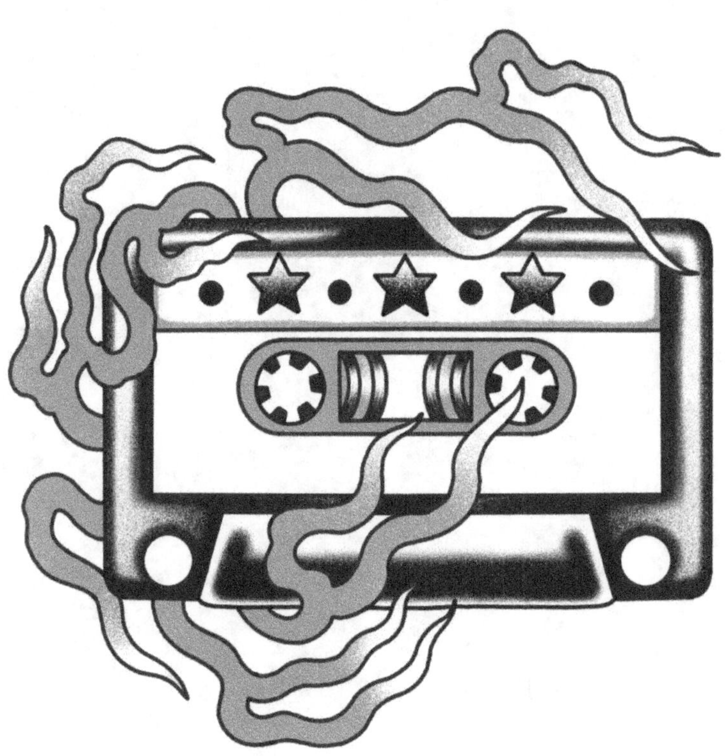

An icon of underground music culture, cassettes represent the raw, unfiltered creativity and DIY ethos that define punk.

01

02

03

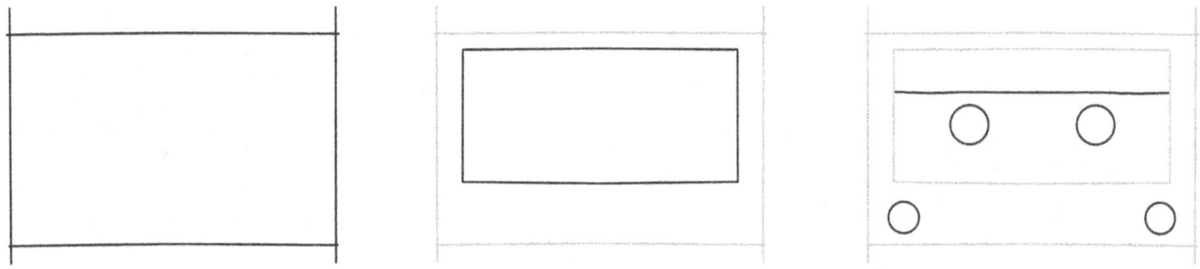

04

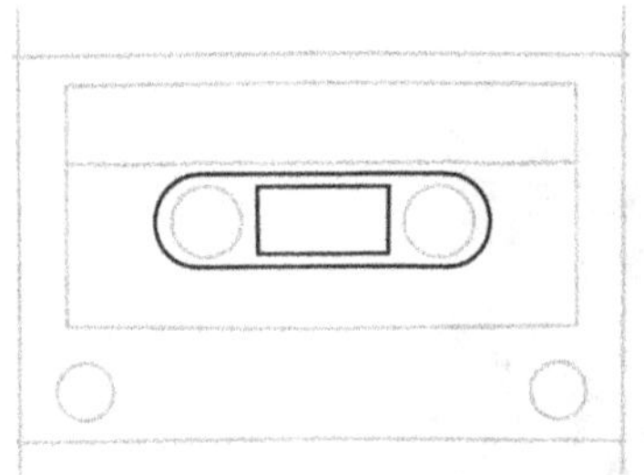

05

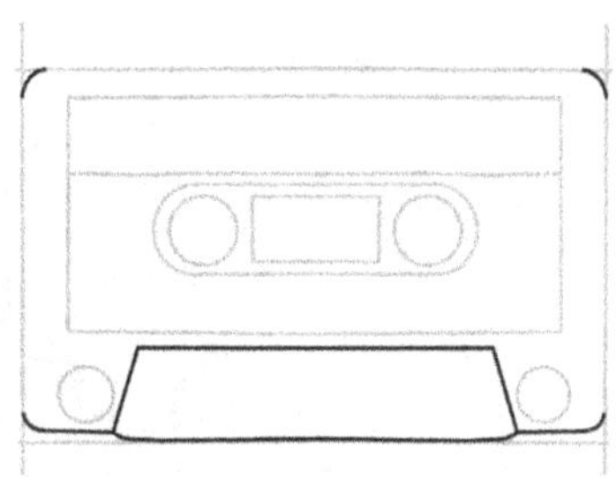

06

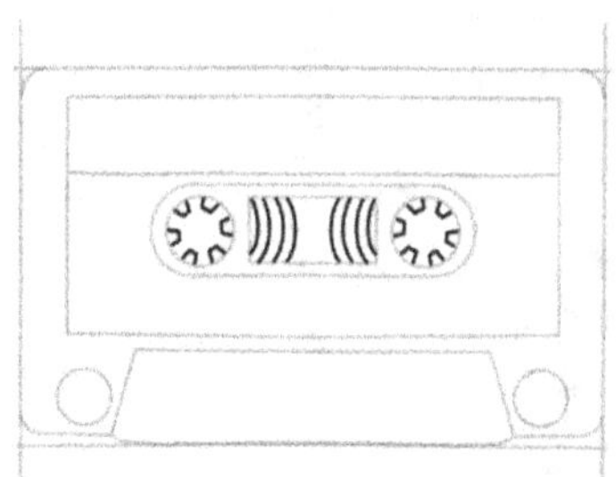

07

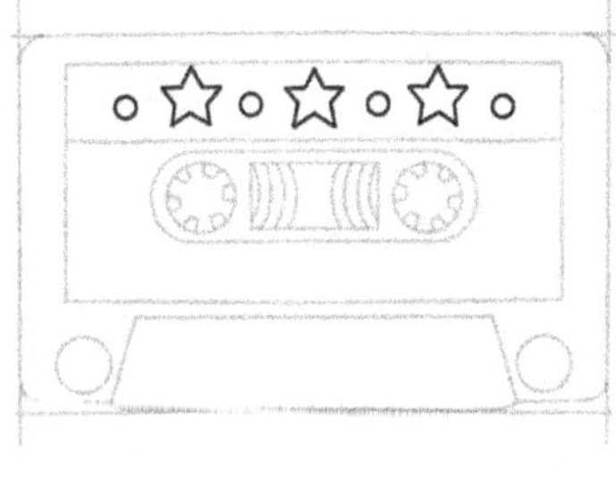

08

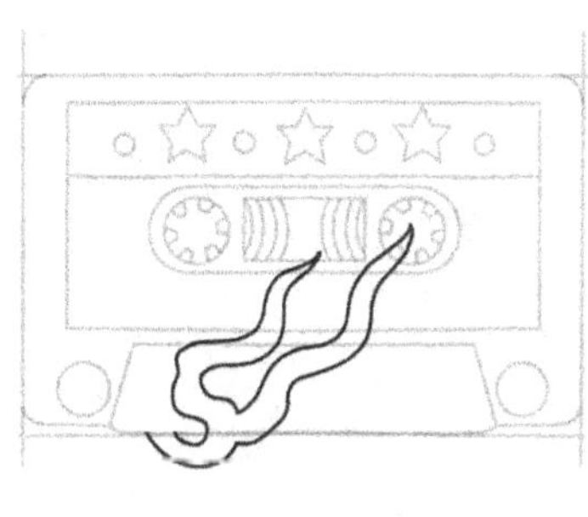

09

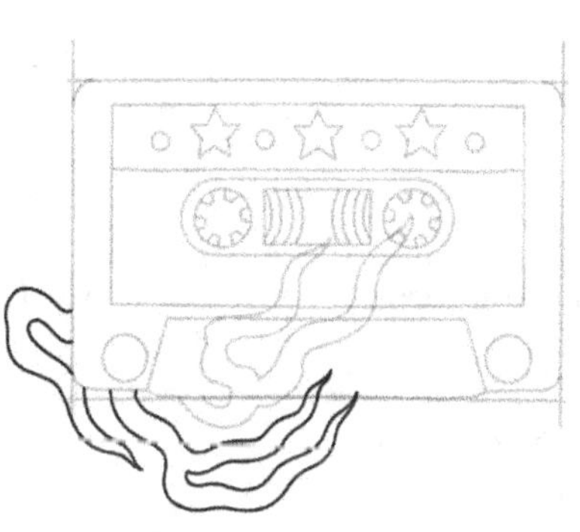

10

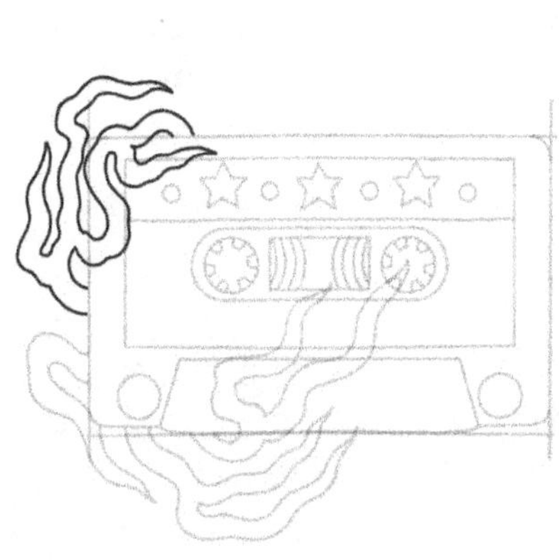

11

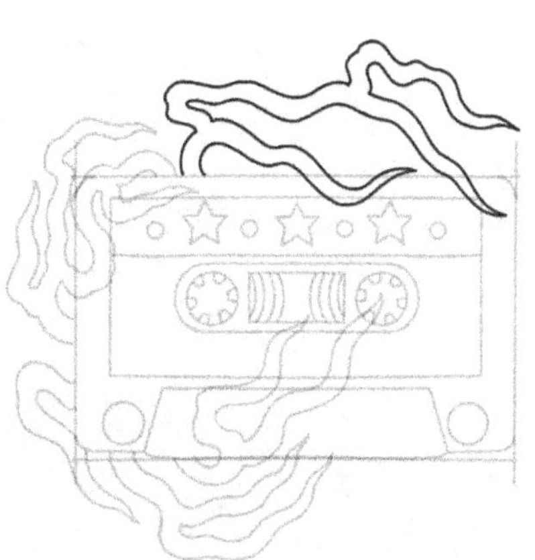

12

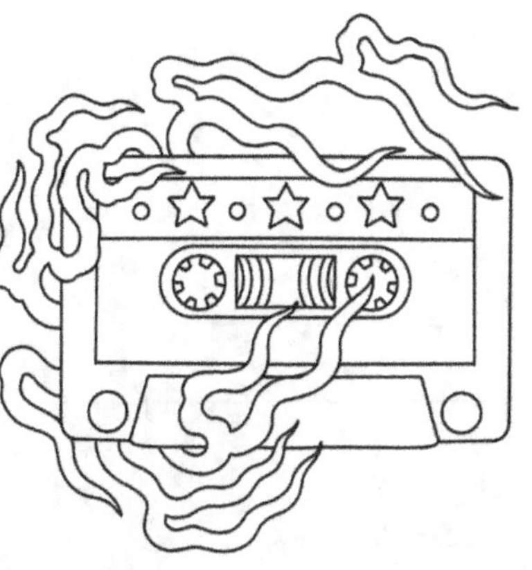

SNEAKER

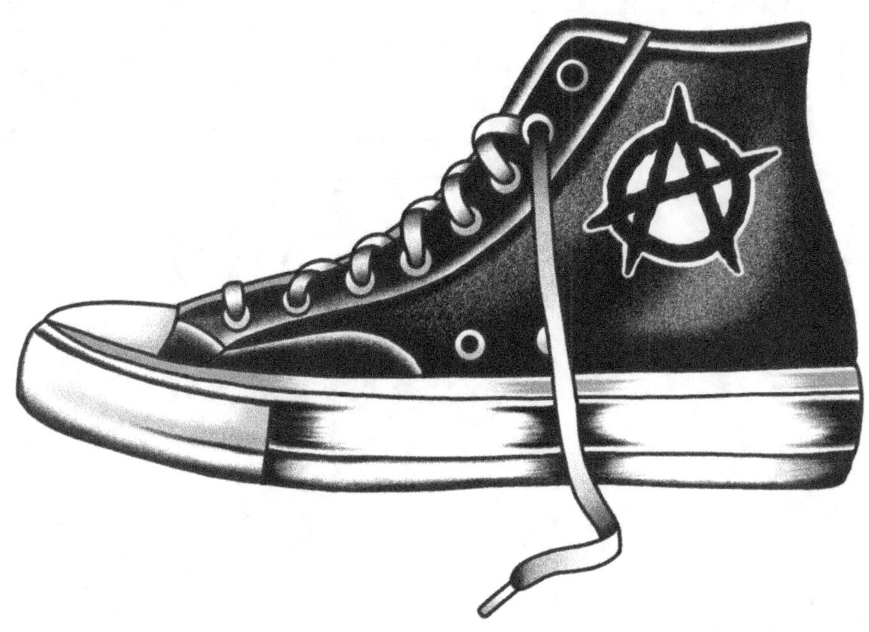

A nod to skate culture and youthful rebellion, this iconic sneaker design symbolises freedom, individuality, and the energetic defiance of punk.

01

02

03

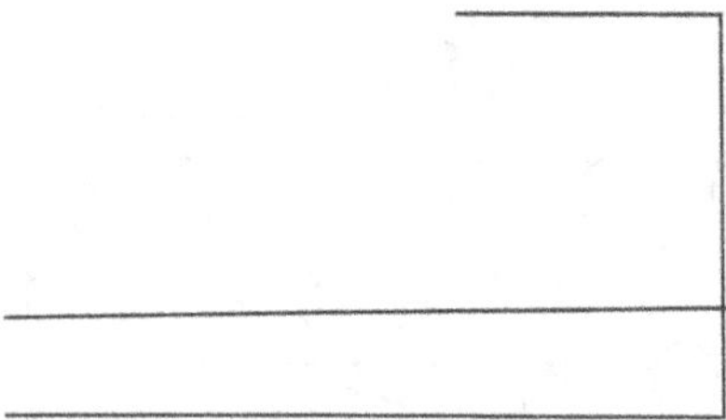

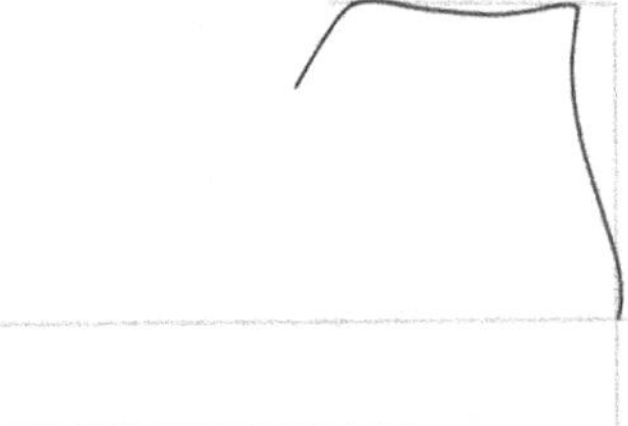

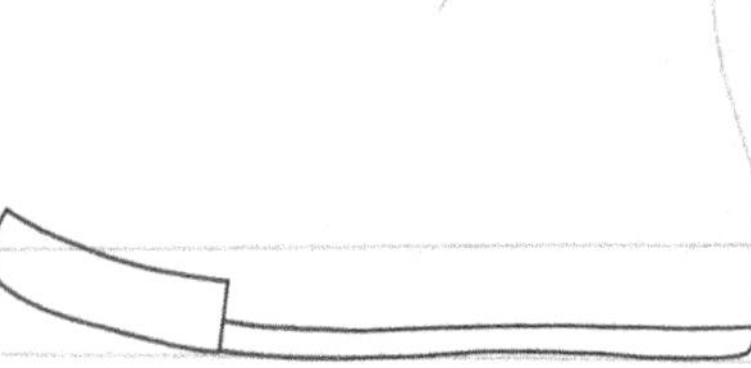

04

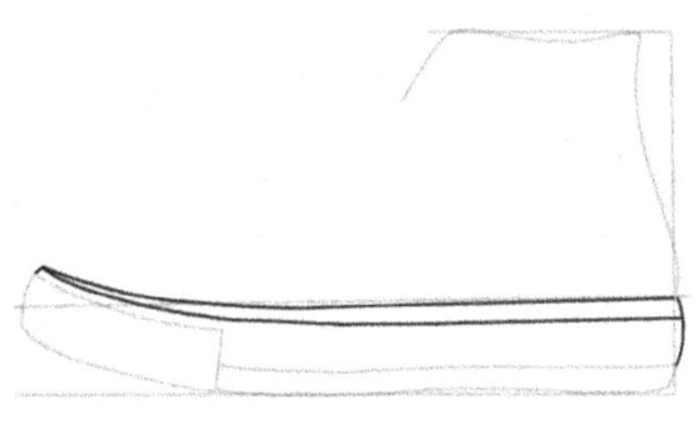

05

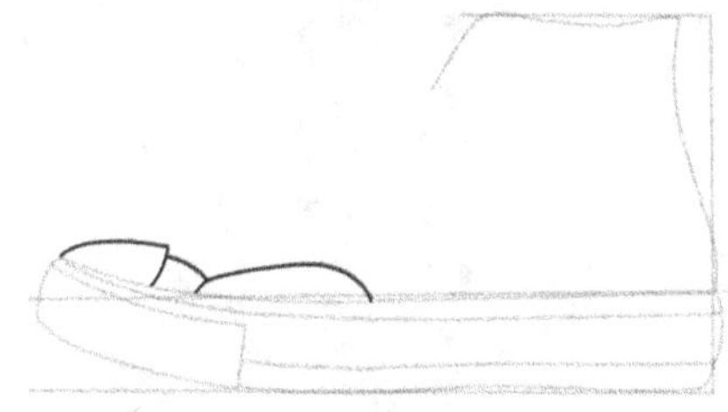

06

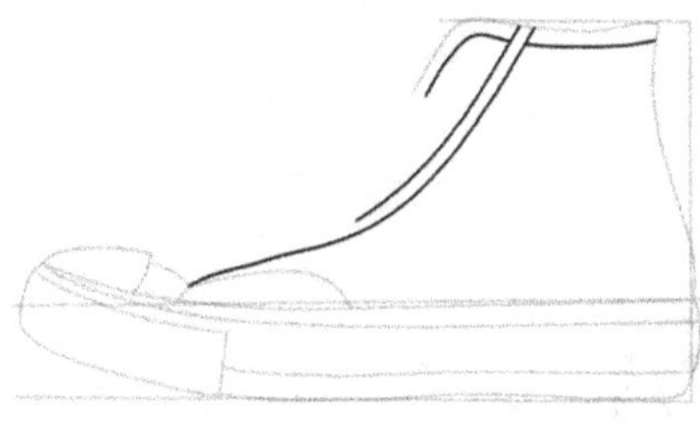

07

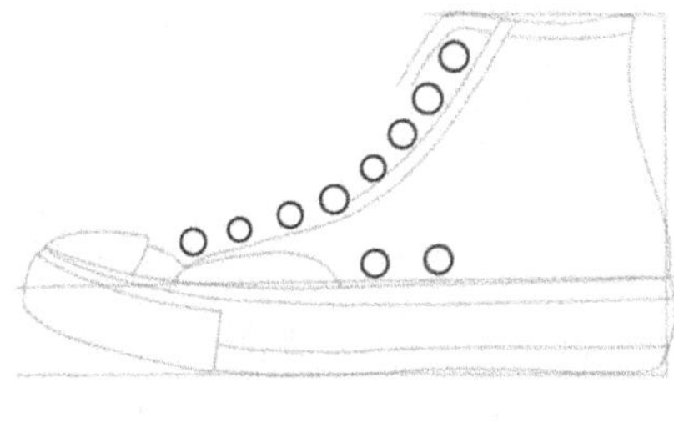

08

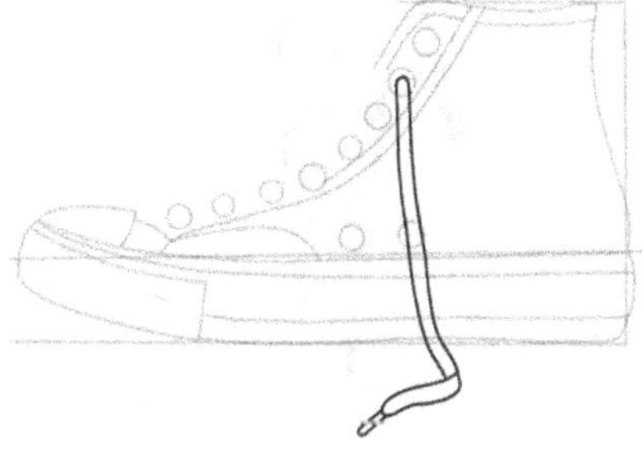

09

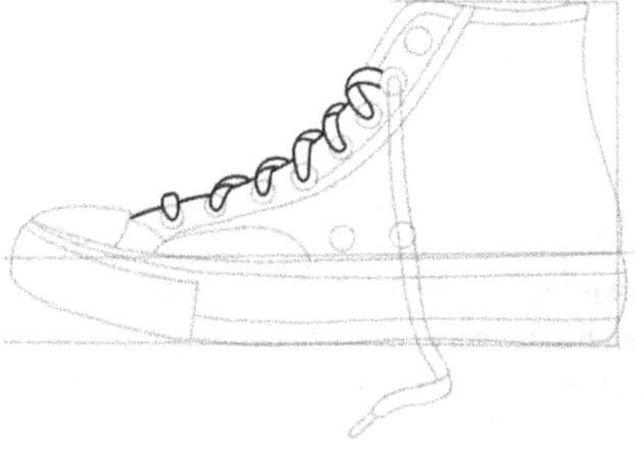

10

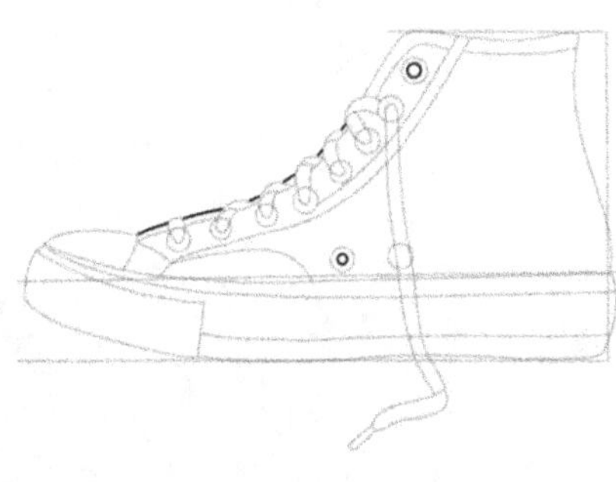

11

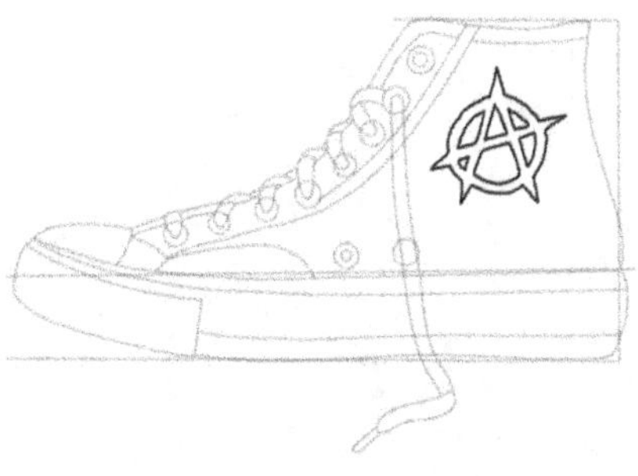

12

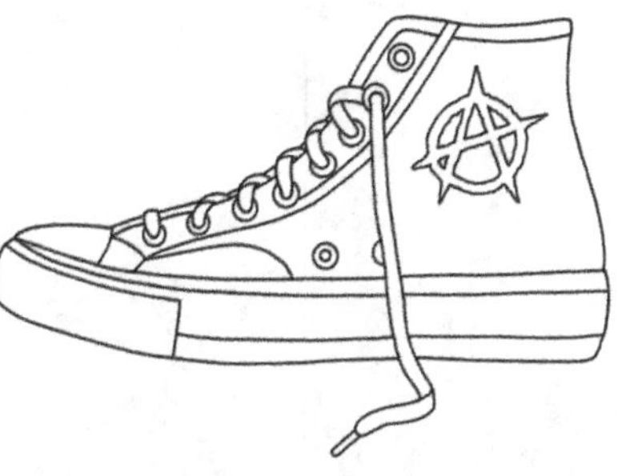

HOW TO DRAW PUNK THINGS

DAGGER

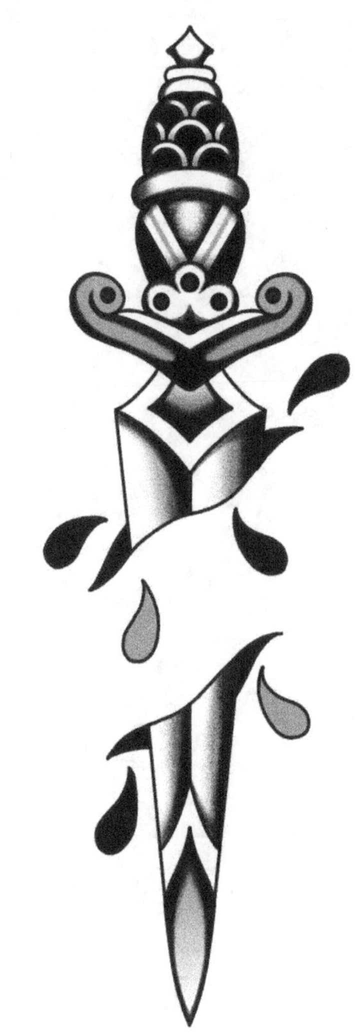

Representing rebellion and danger, the dagger embodies punk's cutting-edge defiance and refusal to be subdued.

01

02

03

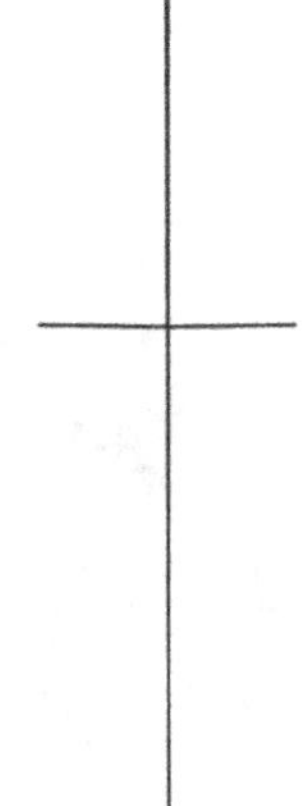

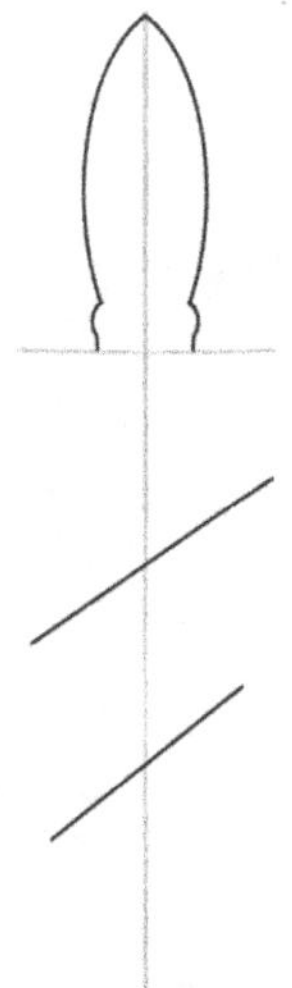

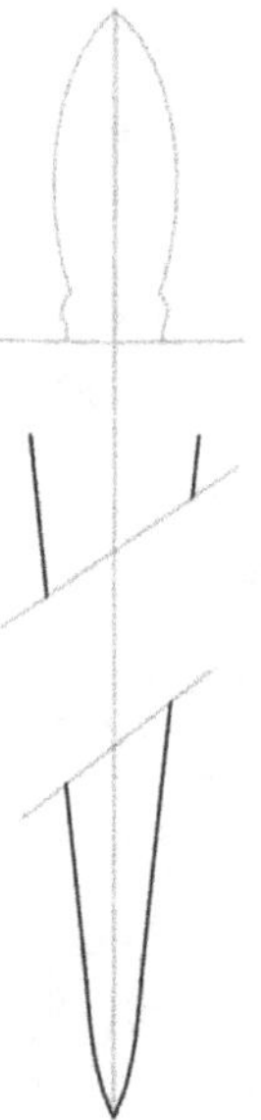

04

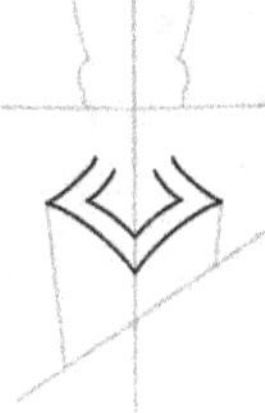

05

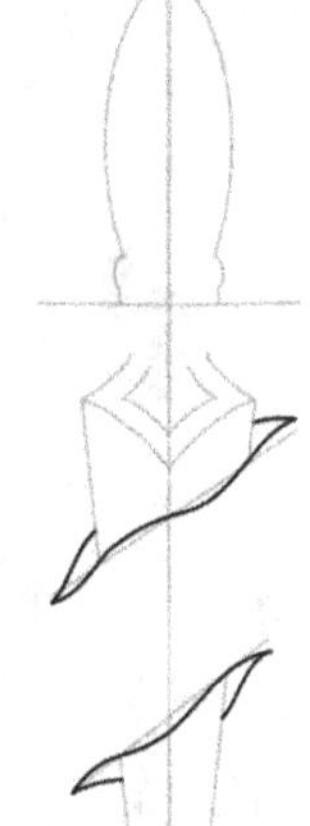

06

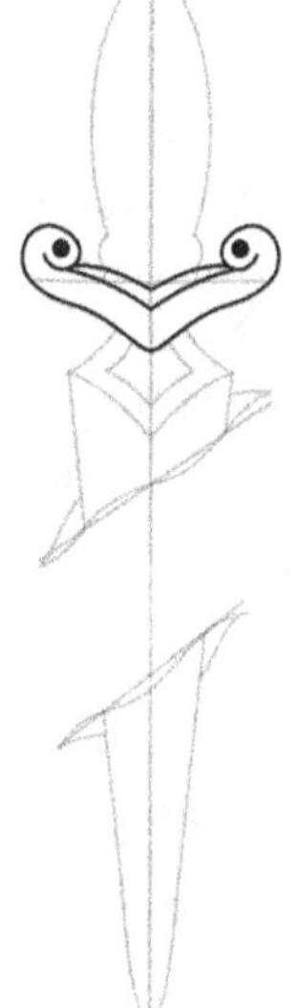

07

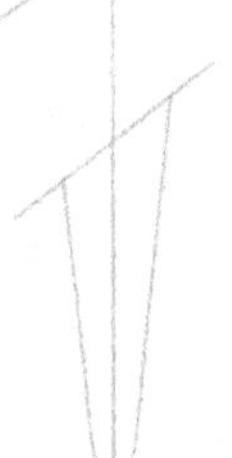

08

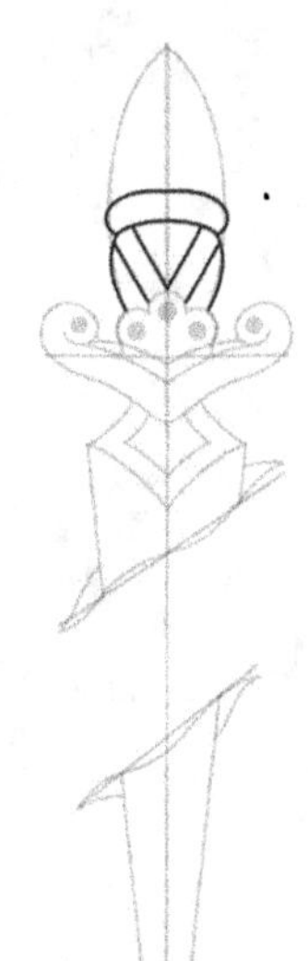

09

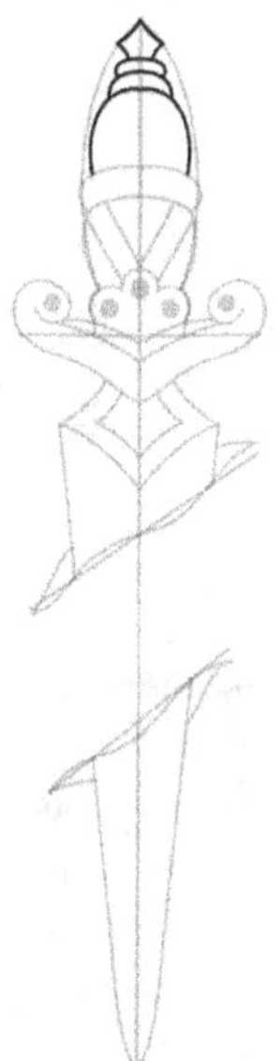

10

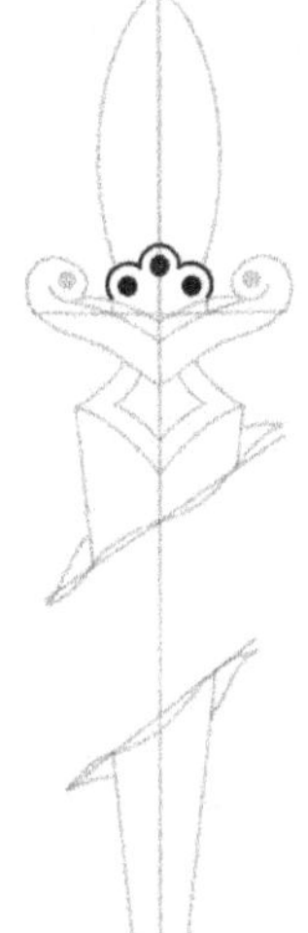

11

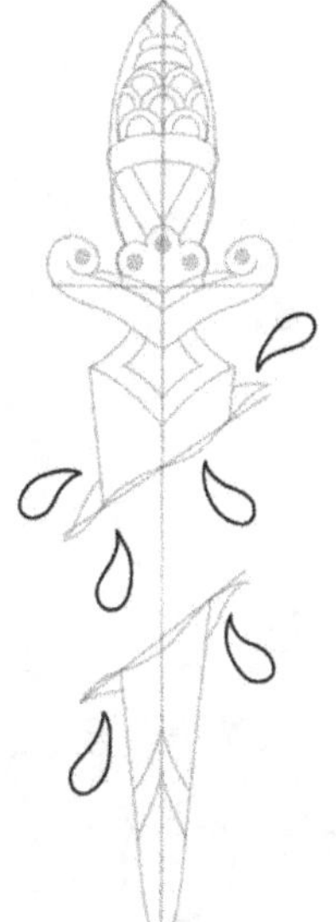

12

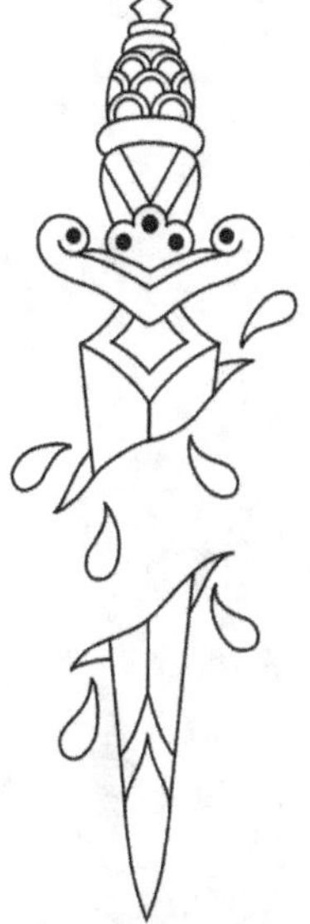

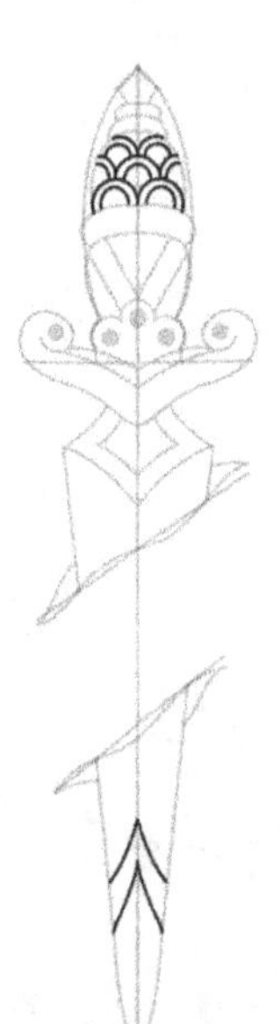

EYE BALL

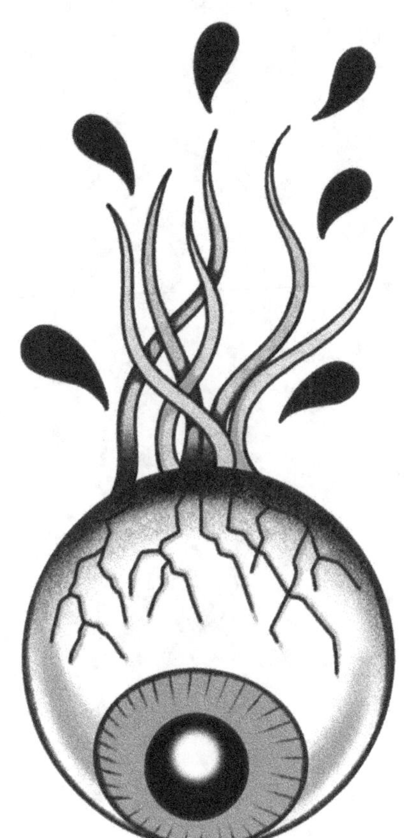

The eyeball symbolises heightened awareness and vigilance, reflecting the punk movement's critical scrutiny of societal norms and injustices. It serves as a visual reminder to remain observant and question authority.

01

02

03

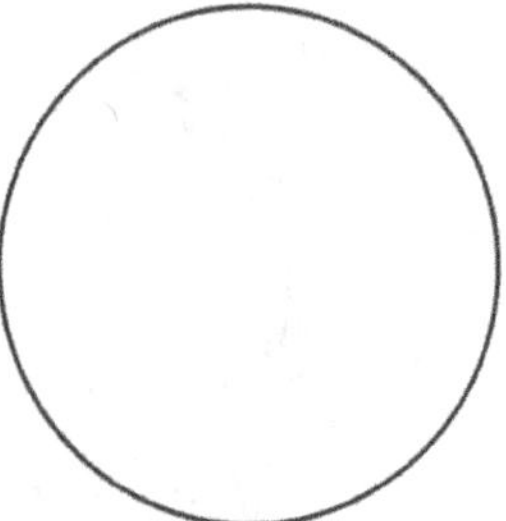

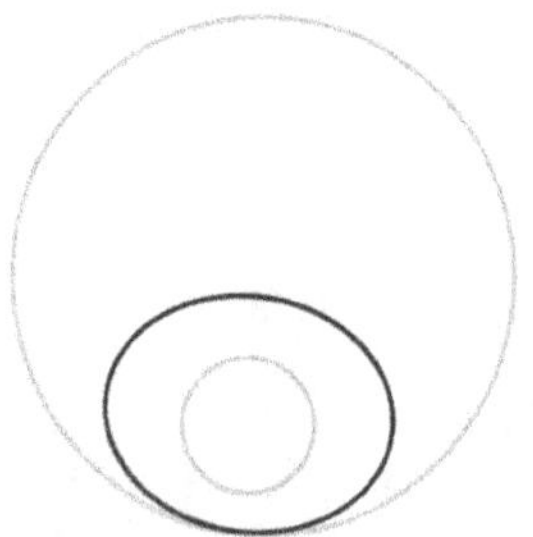

04

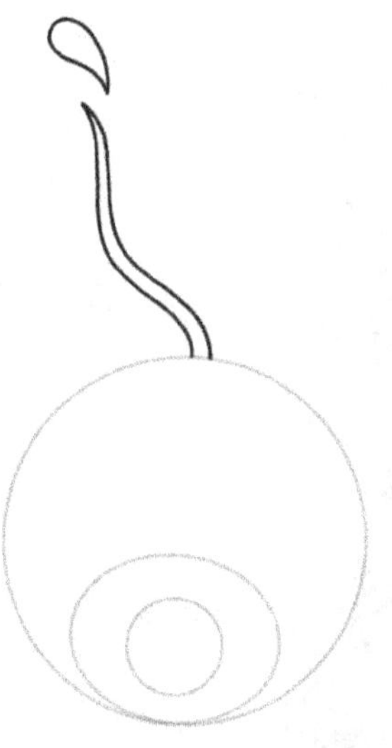

05

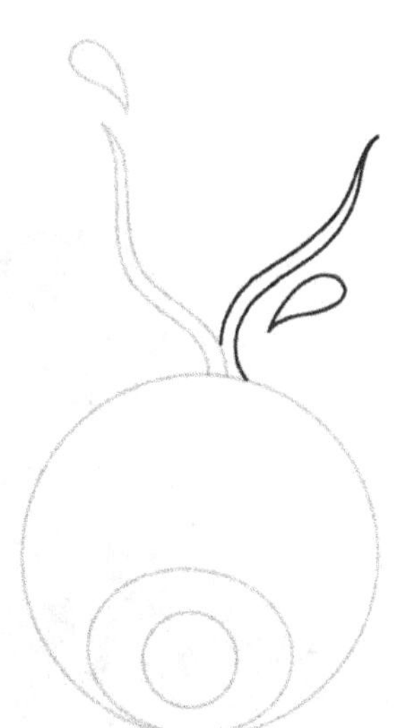

06

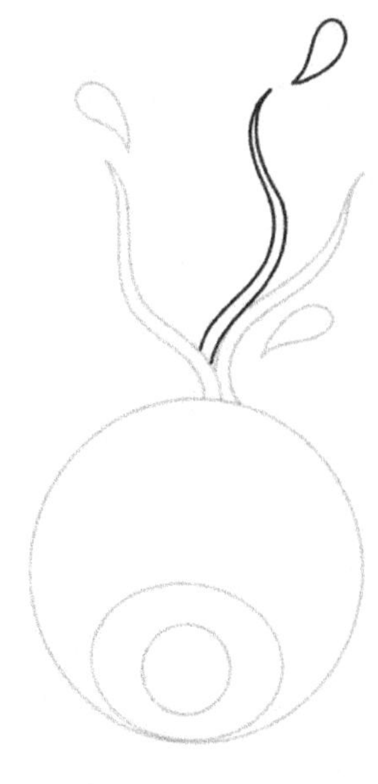

07

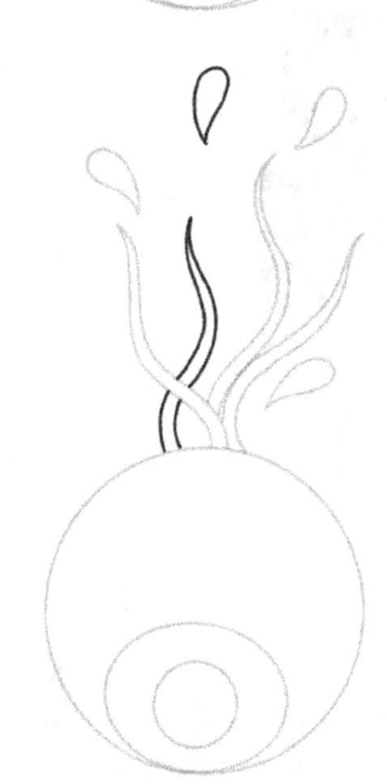

08

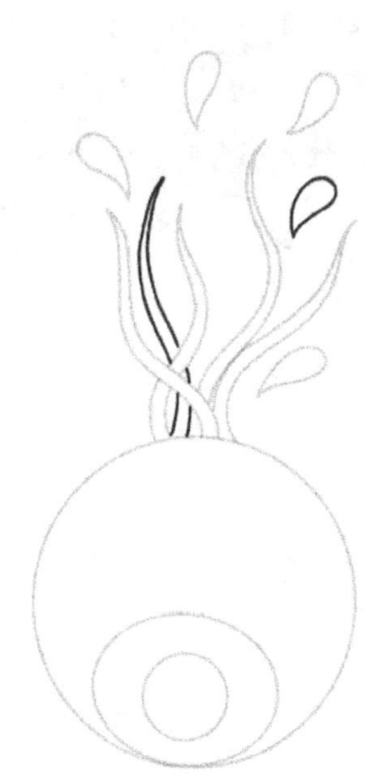

09

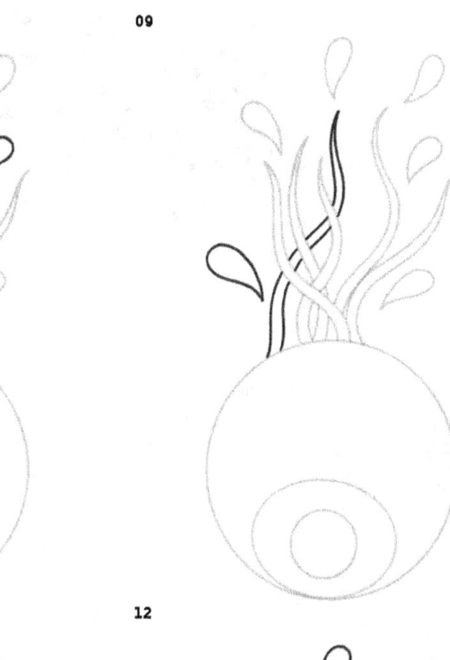

10

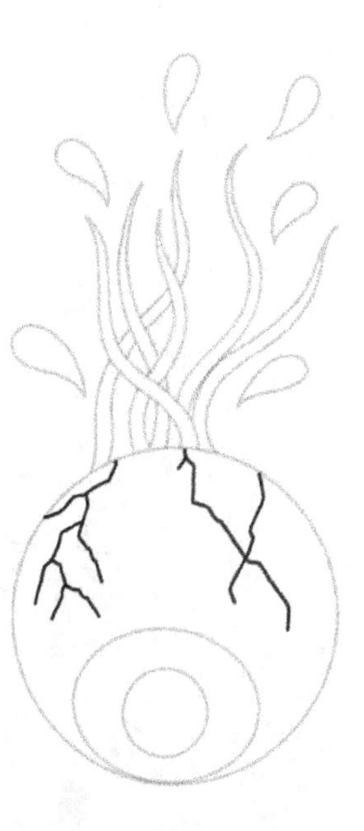

11

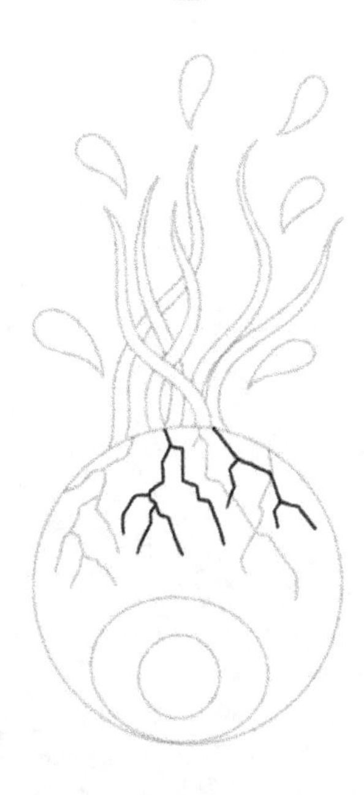

12

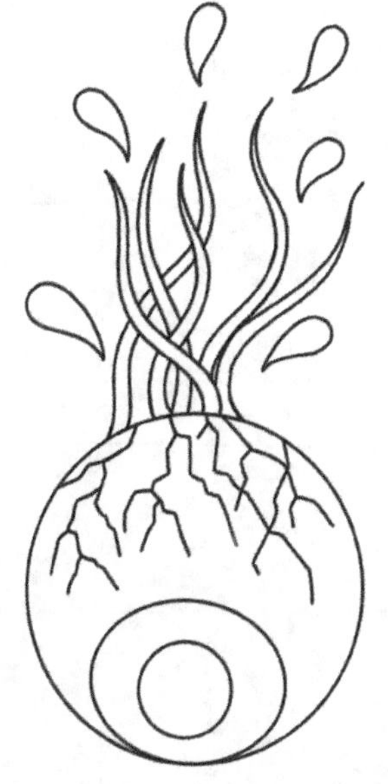

COMBAT BOOT

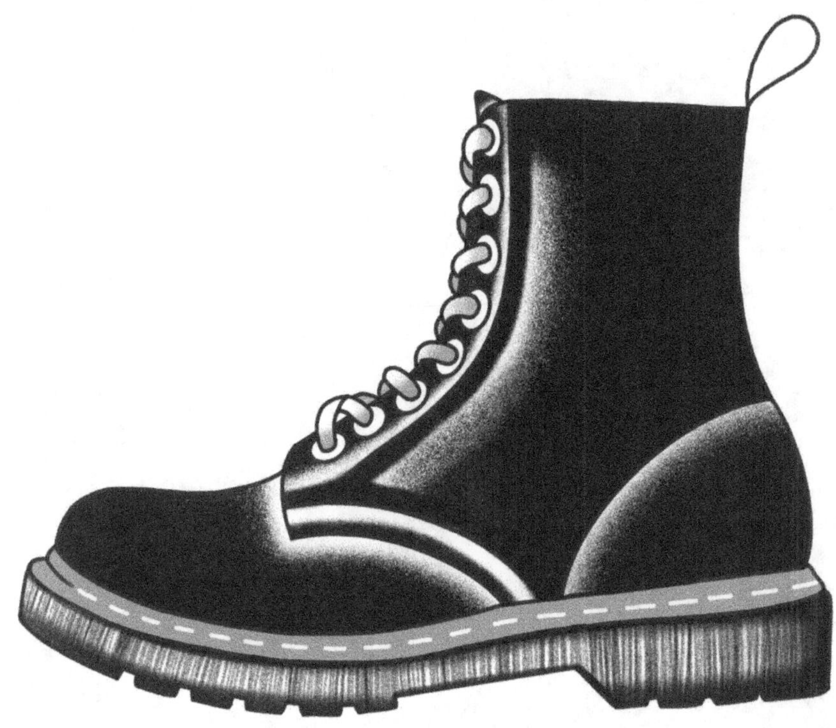

A symbol of rebellion and resistance, the
combat boot represent standing firm against
oppression and the rugged individuality of
punk culture.

01   02   03

04

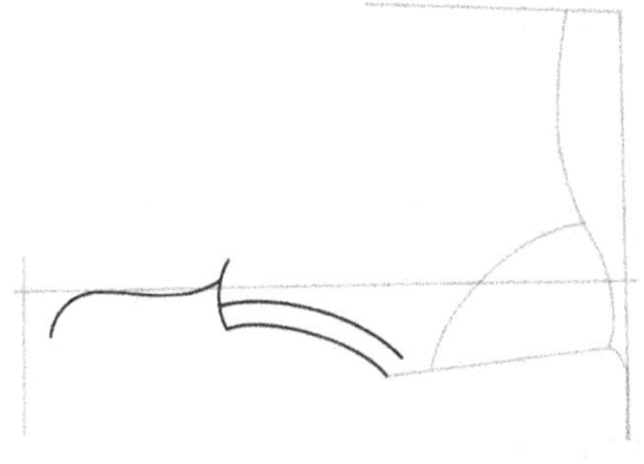

05

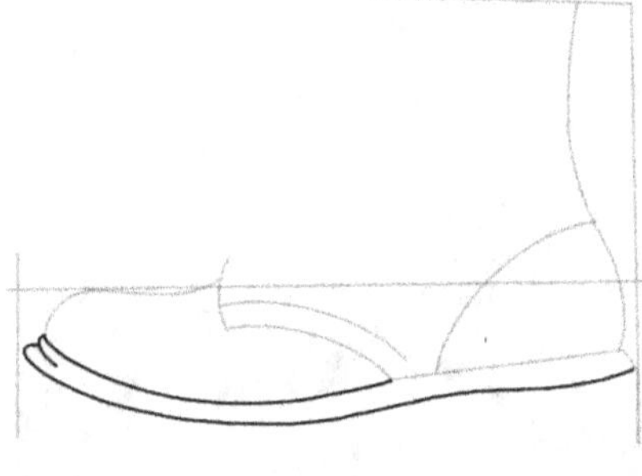

06

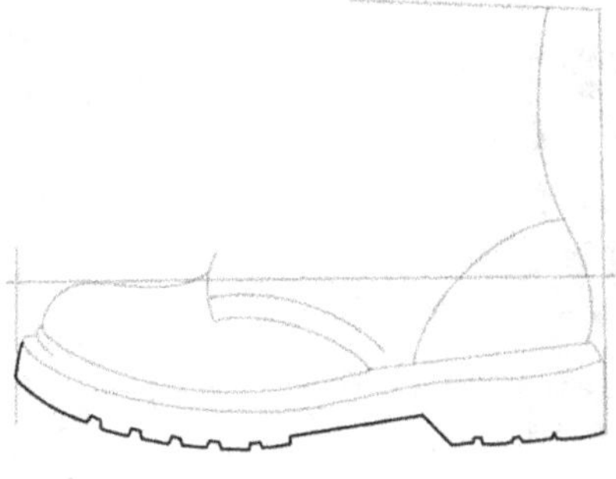

07

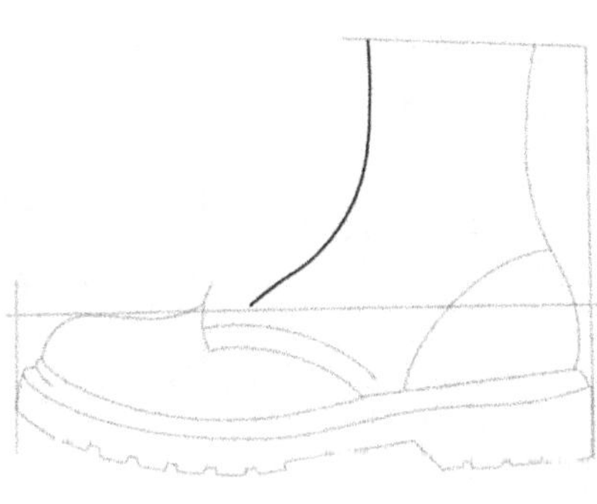

08

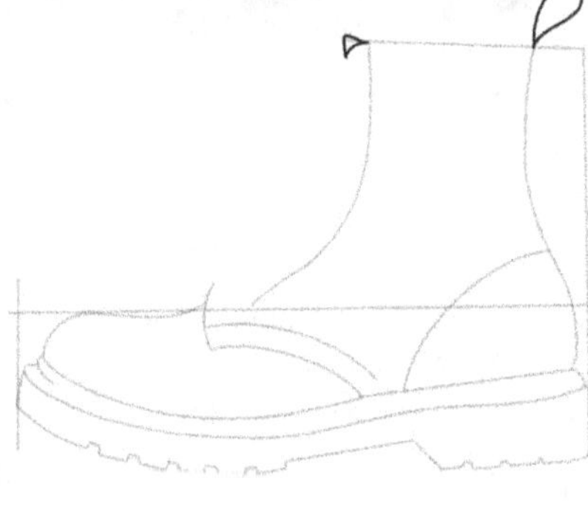

09

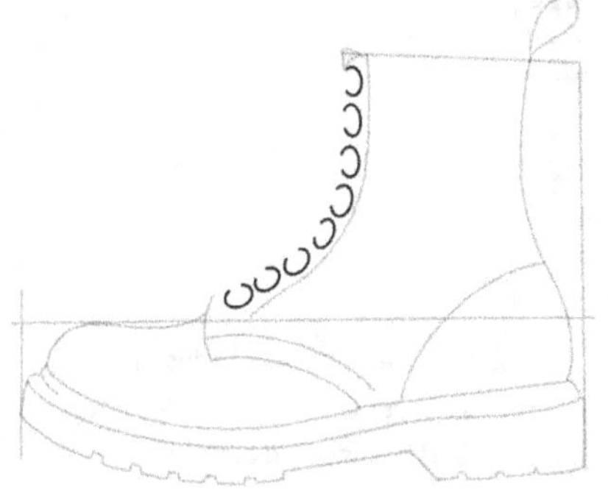

10

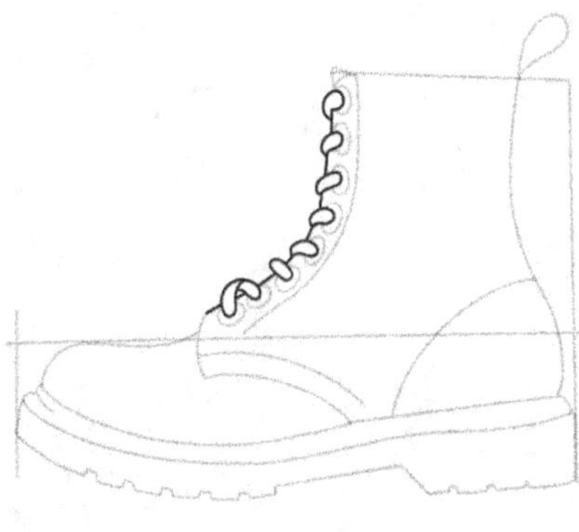

11

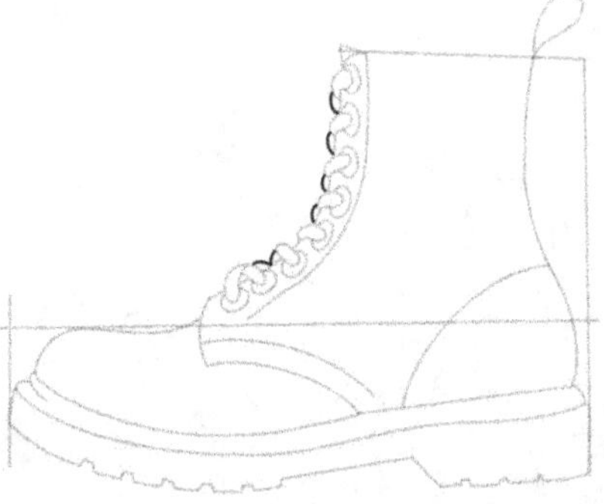

12

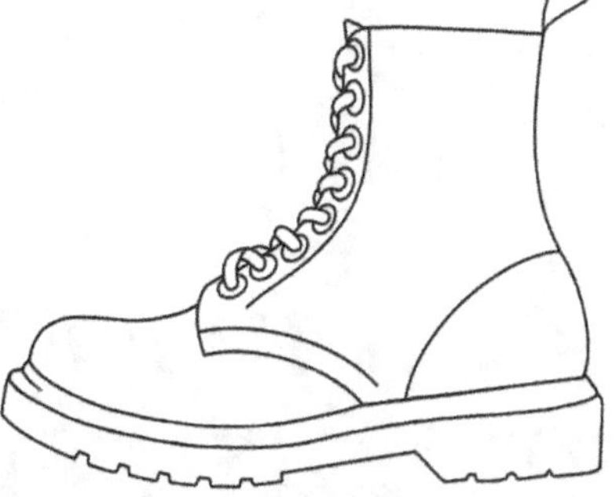

KNUCKLE DUSTER

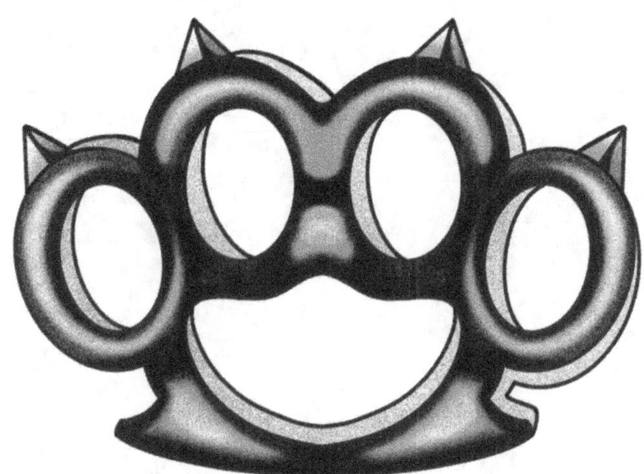

A tool of defiance, the knuckle duster represents the punk spirit of self-defence, rebellion, and readiness to fight for beliefs.

01   02   03

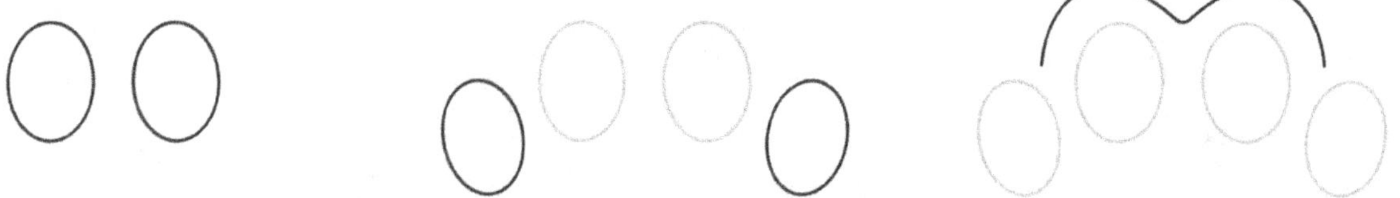

04

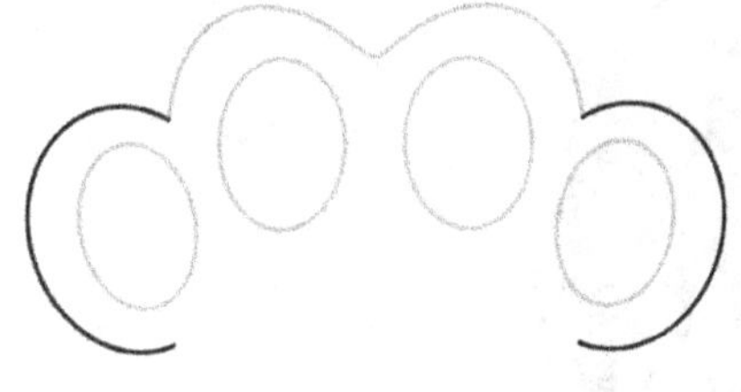

05

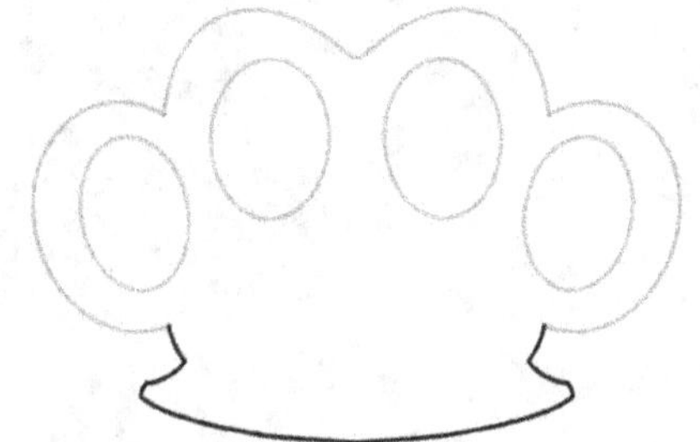

06

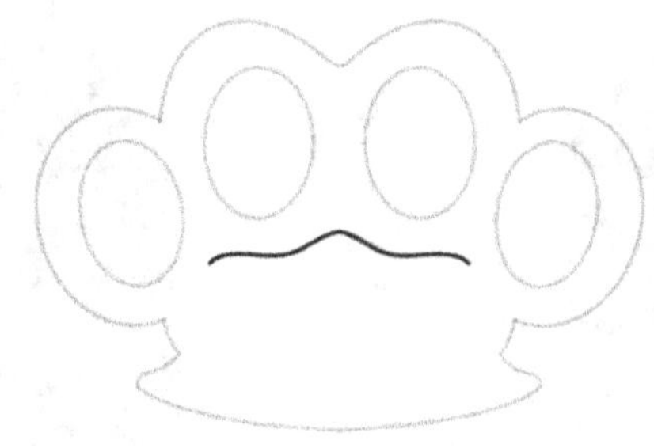

07

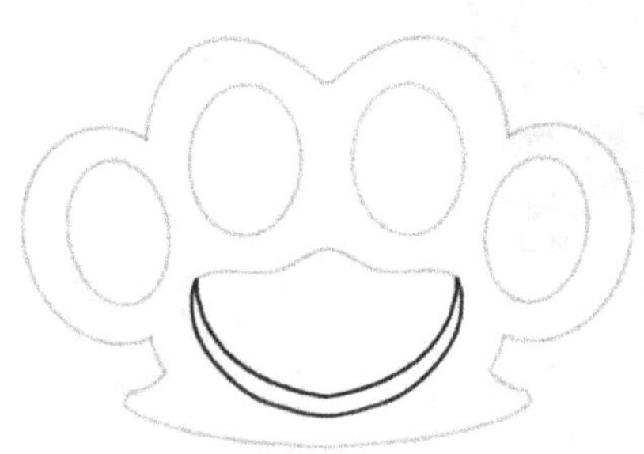

08

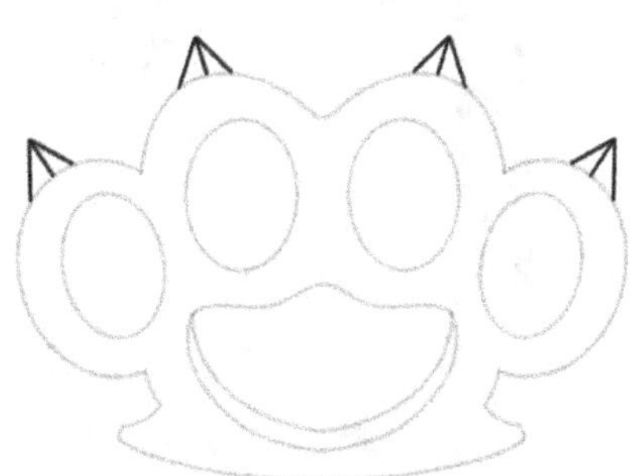

09

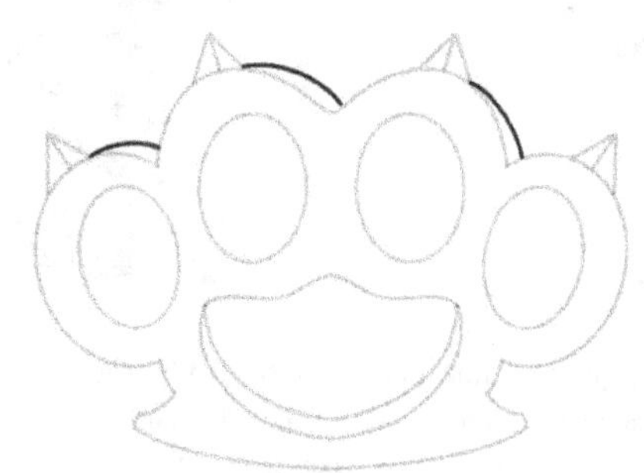

10

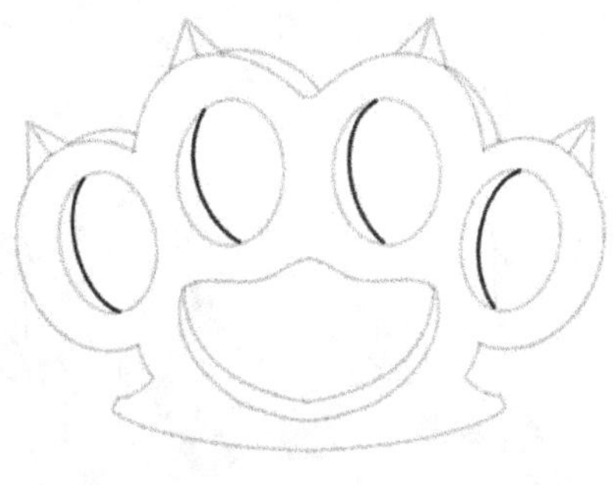

11

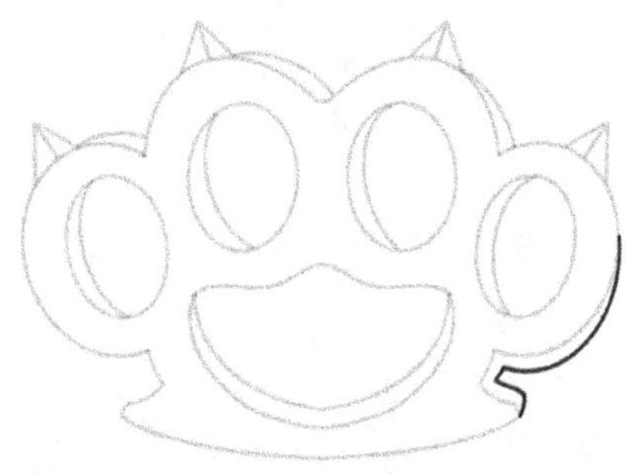

12

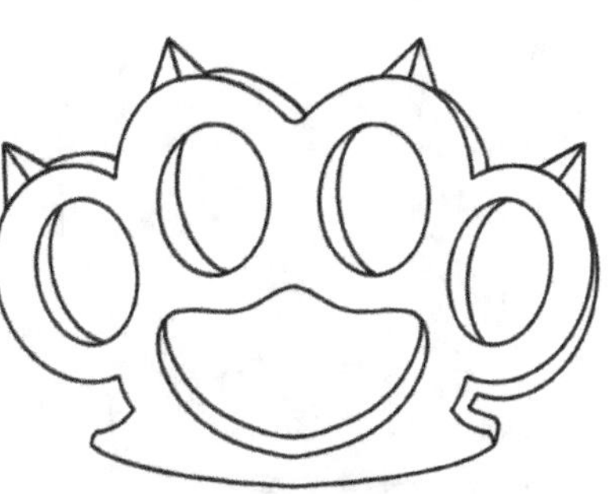

HOW TO DRAW PUNK THINGS

LEATHER JACKET

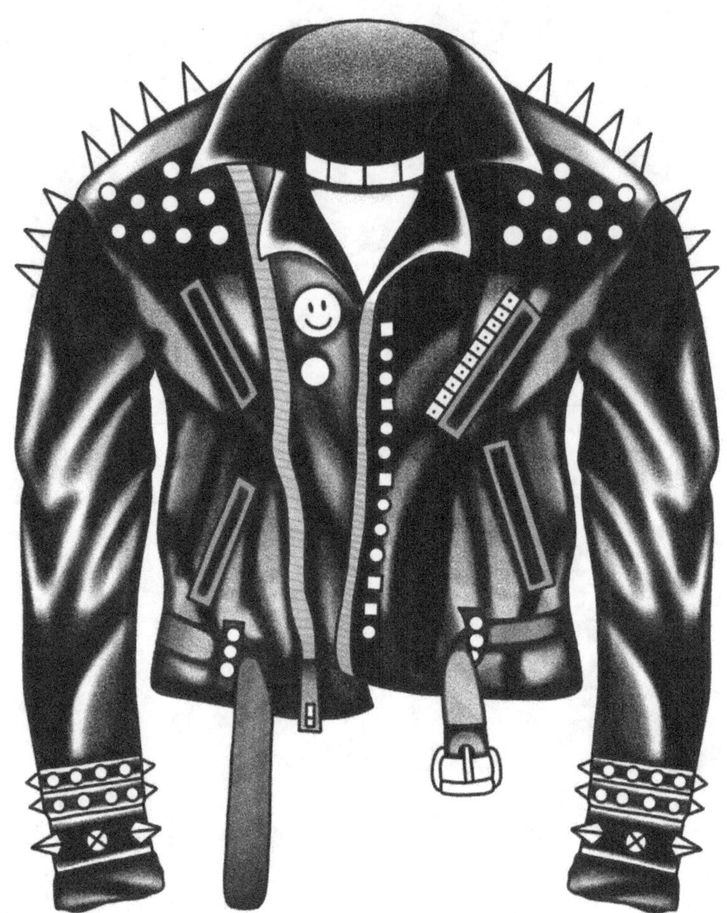

A quintessential punk icon, the leather jacket symbolises rebellion, individuality, and the unapologetic edge of alternative culture.

01

02

03

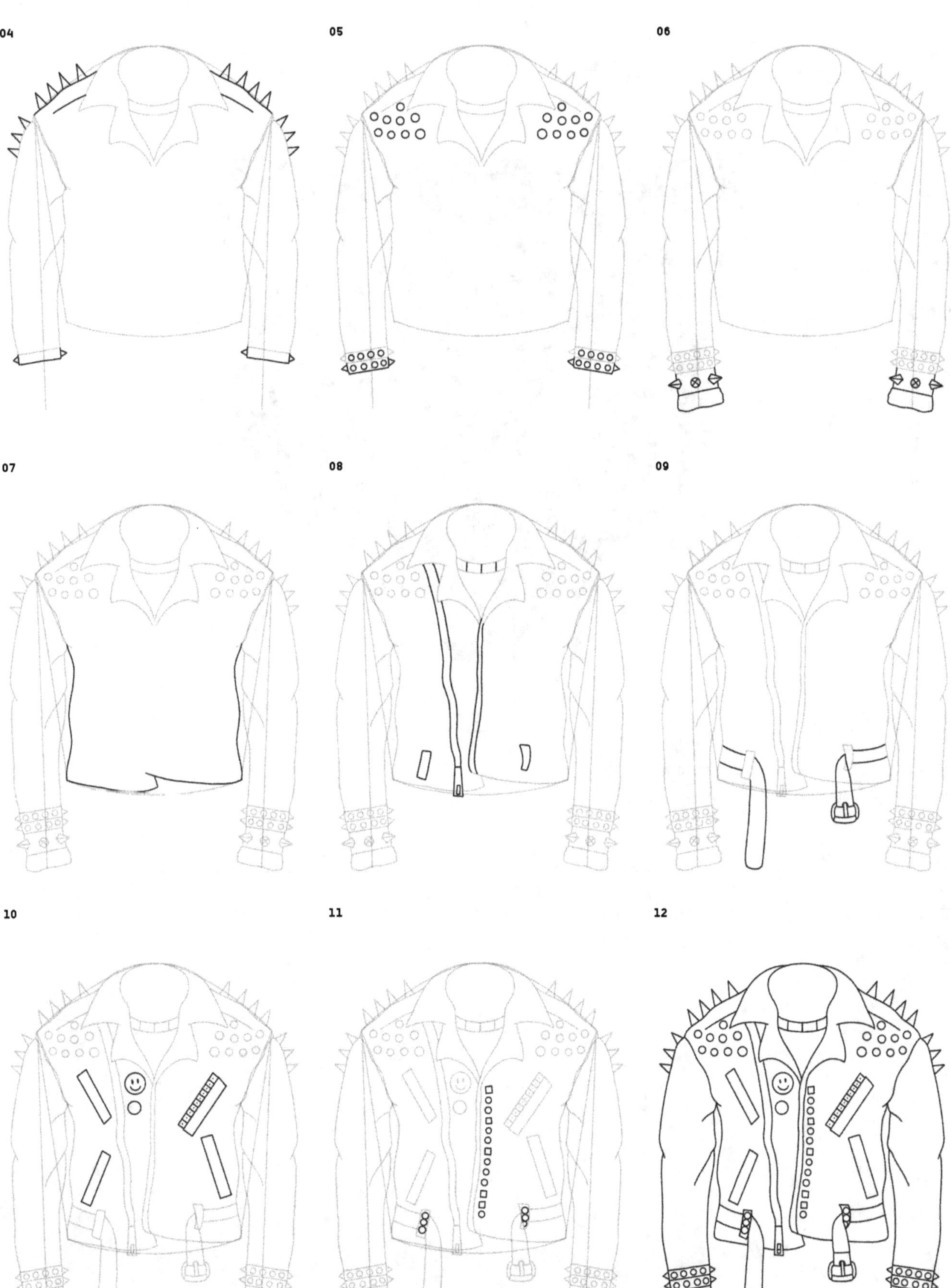

04
05
06
07
08
09
10
11
12
HOW TO DRAW PUNK THINGS

LEOPARD

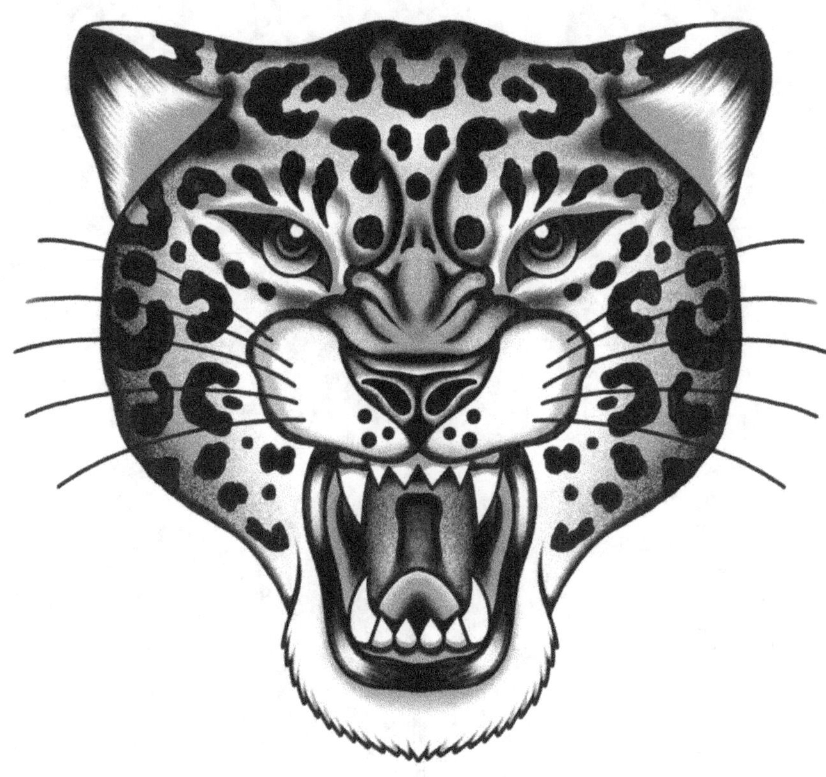

A bold emblem of wildness and defiance, the leopard represents punk's fearless embrace of nonconformity and fierce self-expression.

01   **02**   **03**

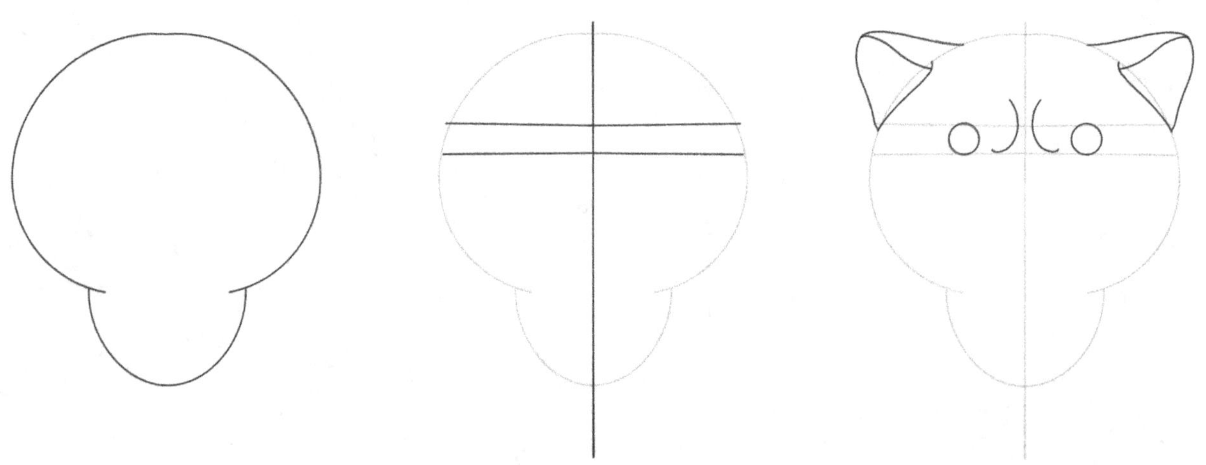

04

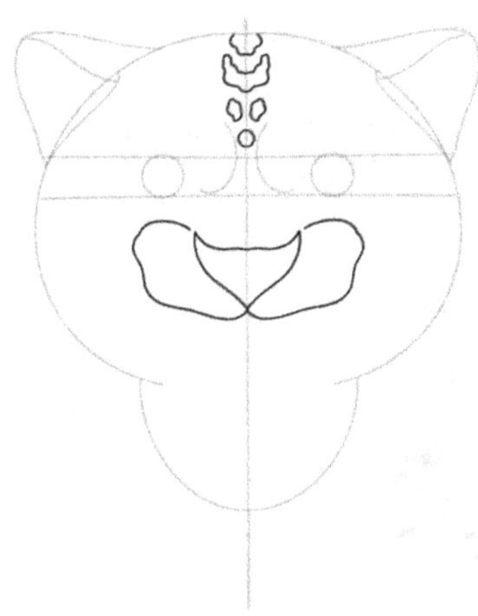

05

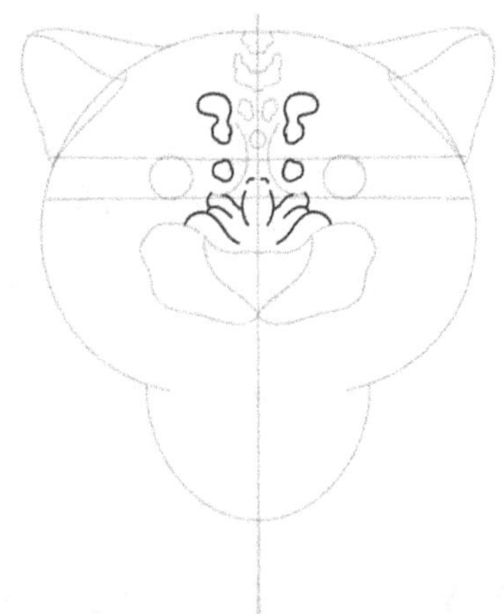

06

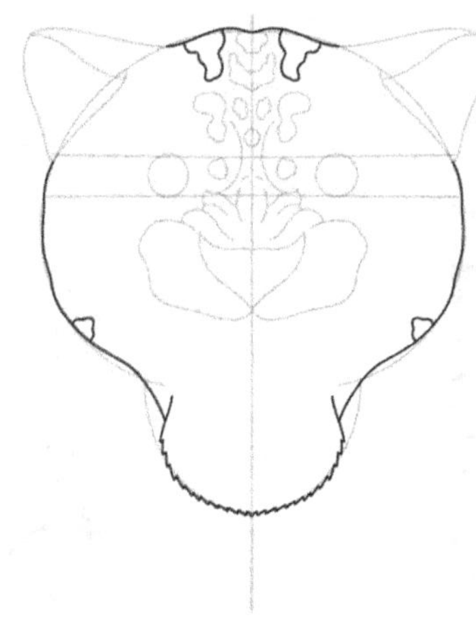

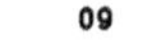

07

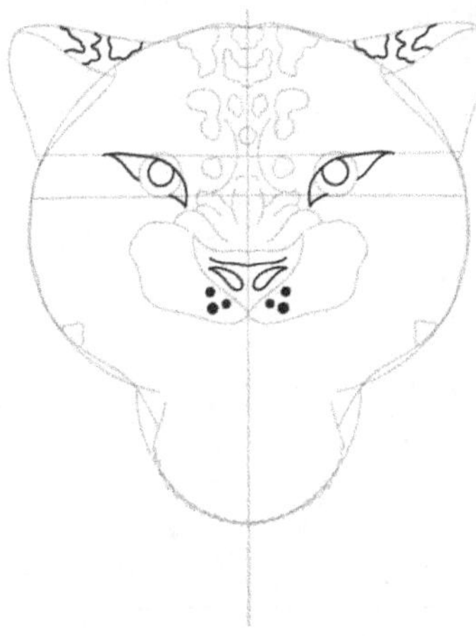

08

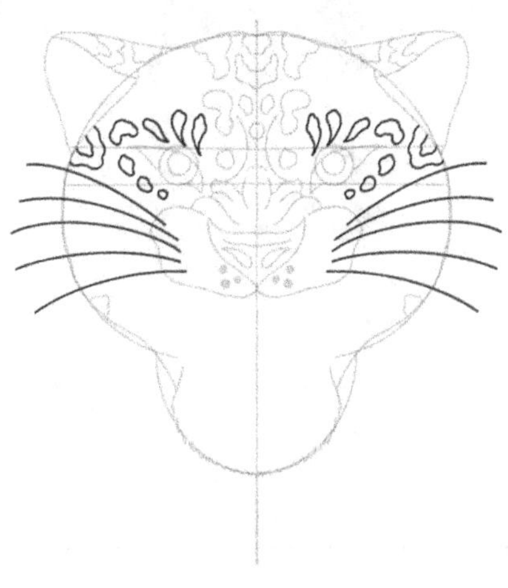

09

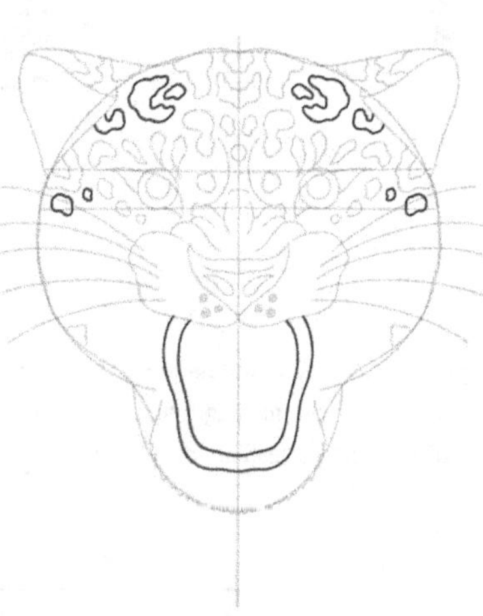

10

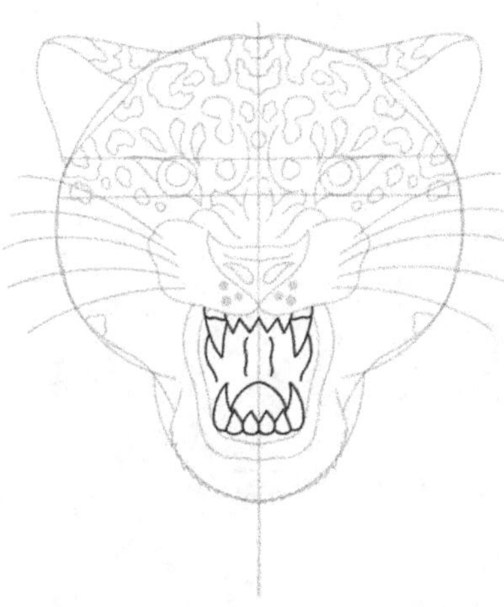

11

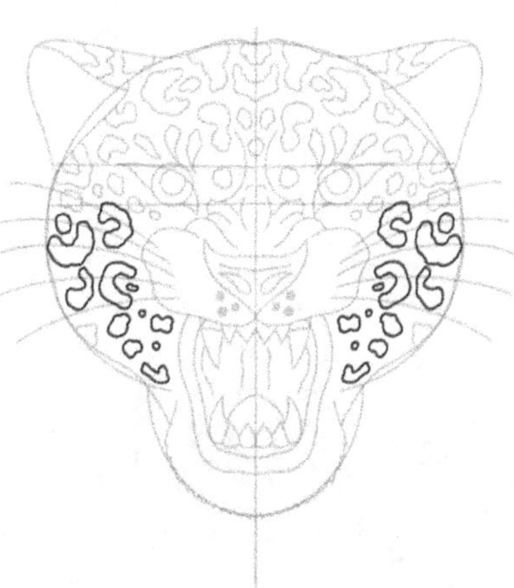

12

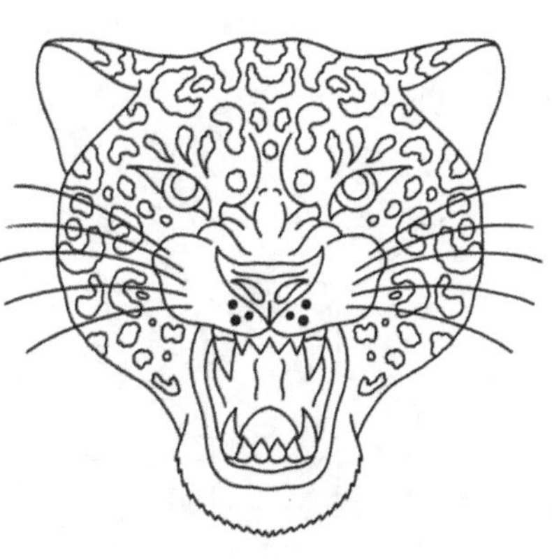

LOCK & CHAIN

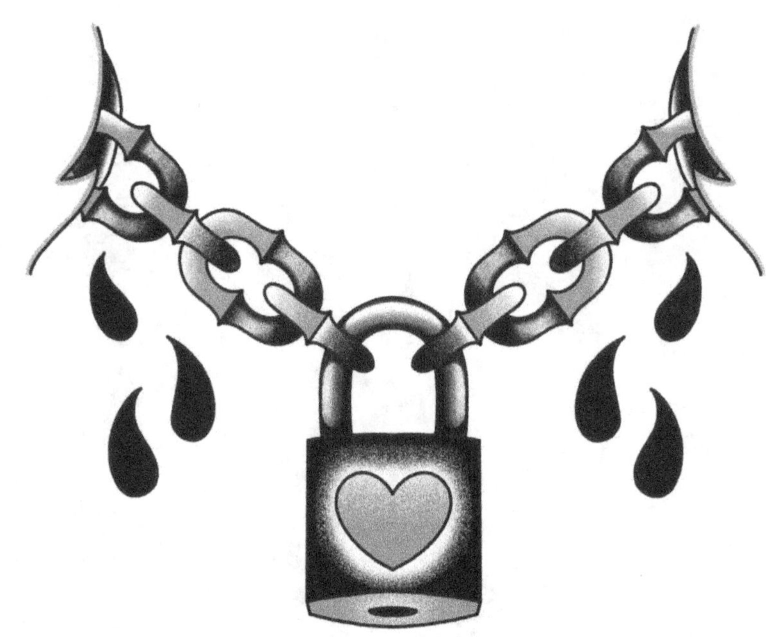

A symbol of restraint and defiance, the lock and chain reflect punk's fight against societal constraints and its resilience.

01　　　　　　　　　　　　**02**　　　　　　　　　　　　**03**

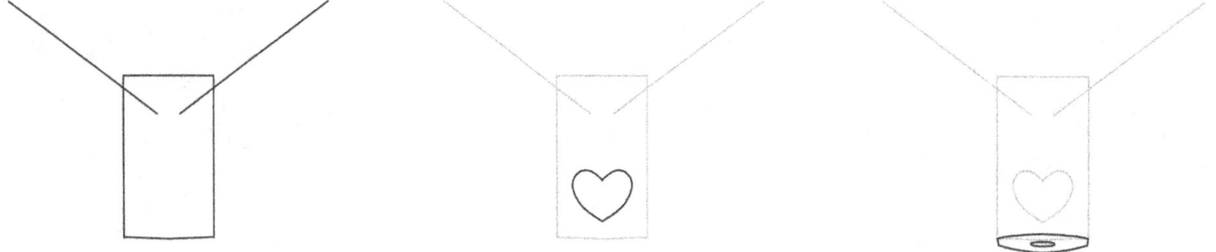

04

05

06

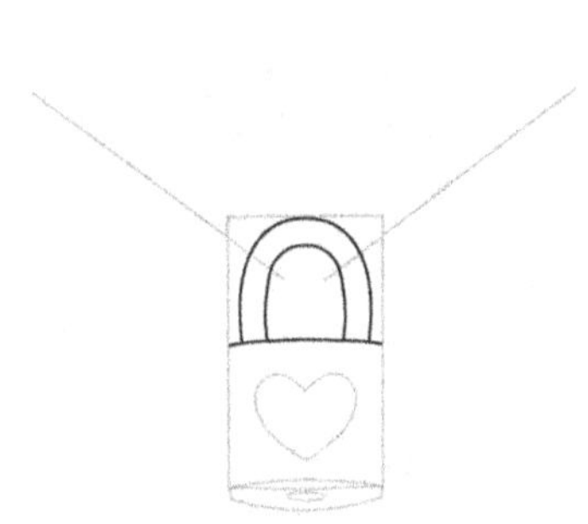

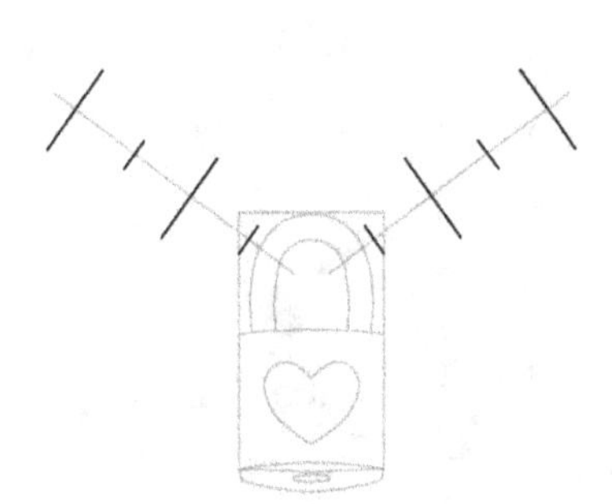

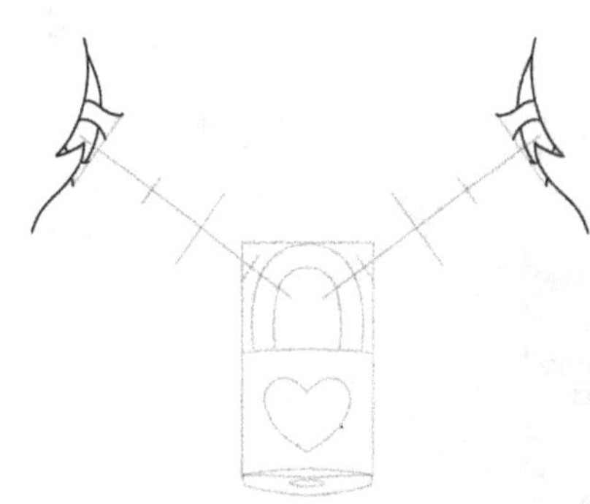

07

08

09

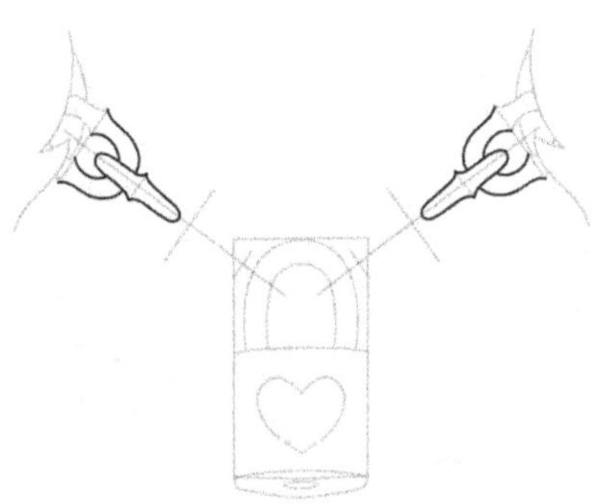

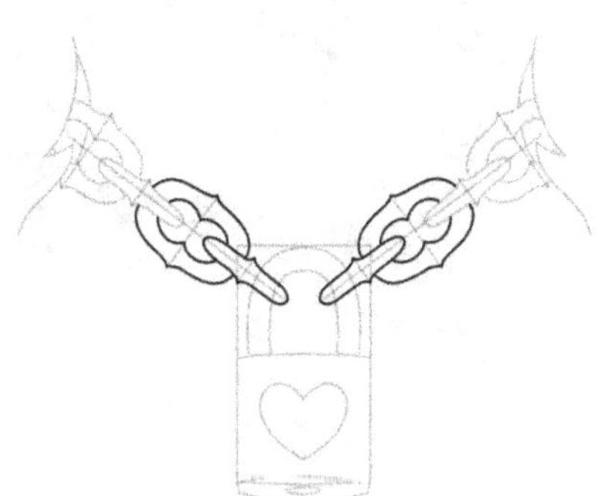

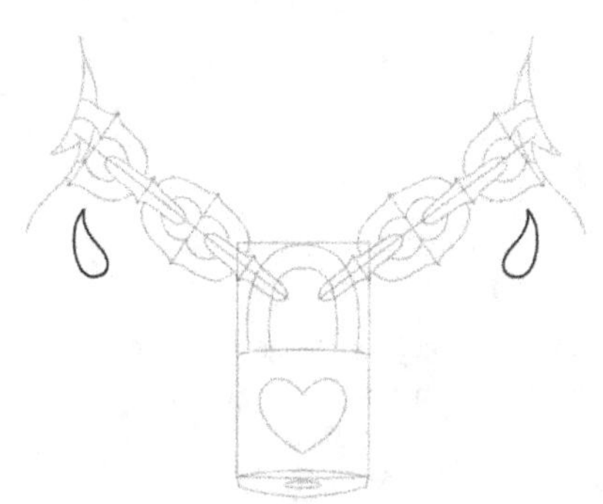

10

11

12

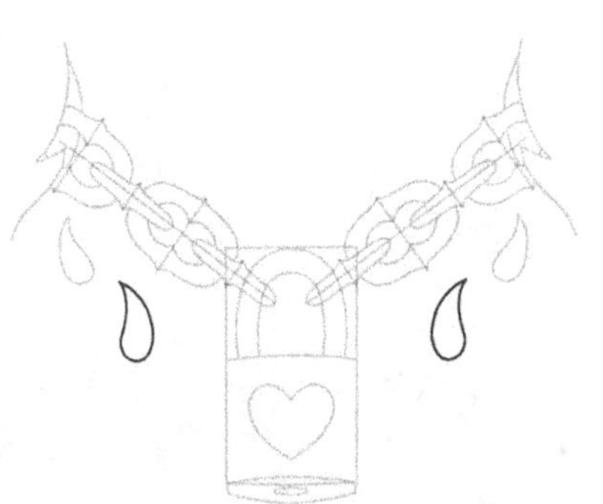

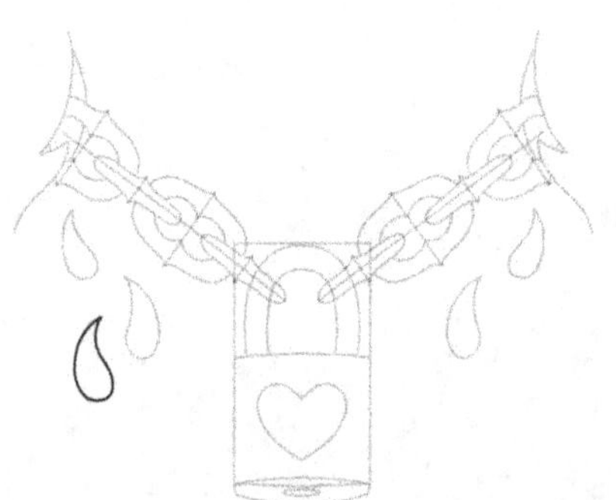

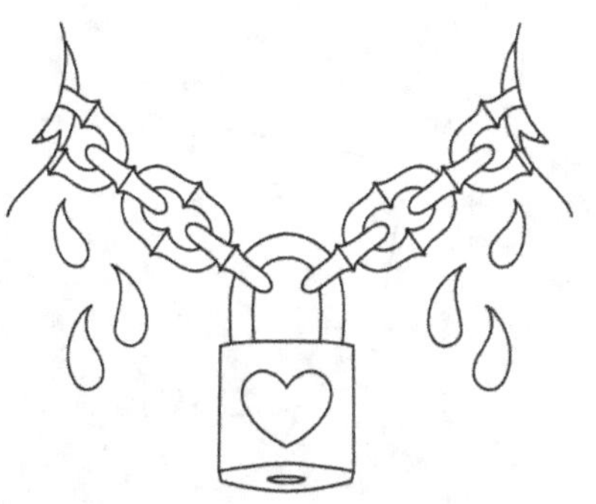

HOW TO DRAW PUNK THINGS

MATCHBOX

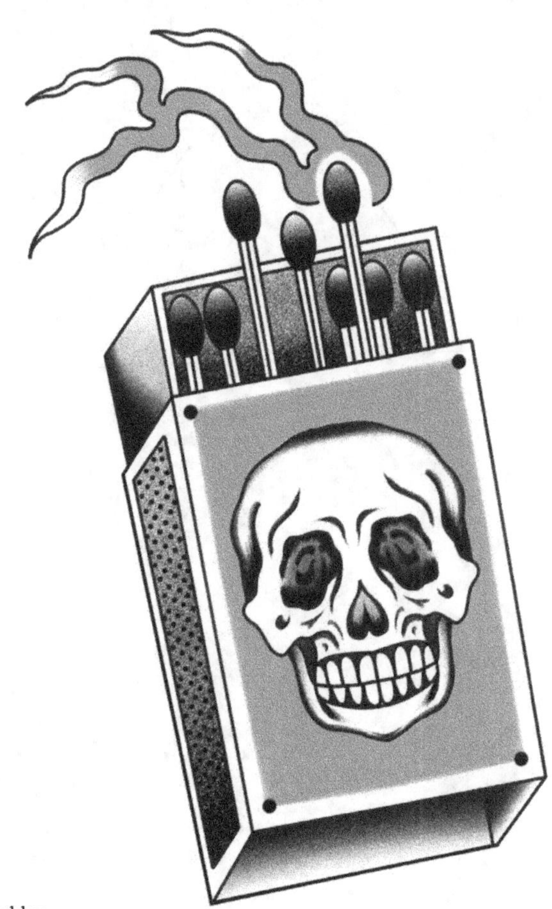

A symbol of igniting change, the matchbox
represents punk's incendiary energy.

01   **02**   **03**

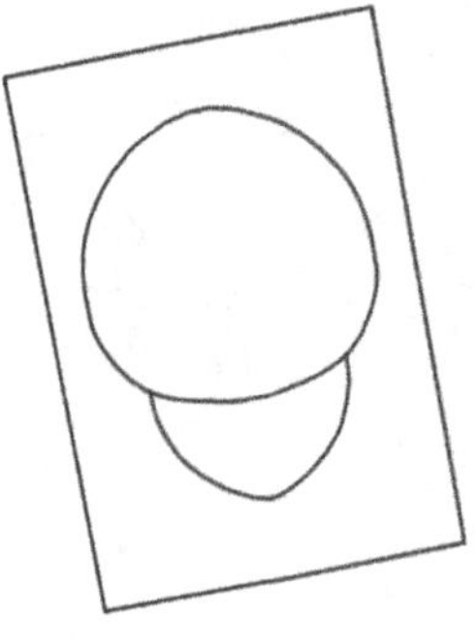

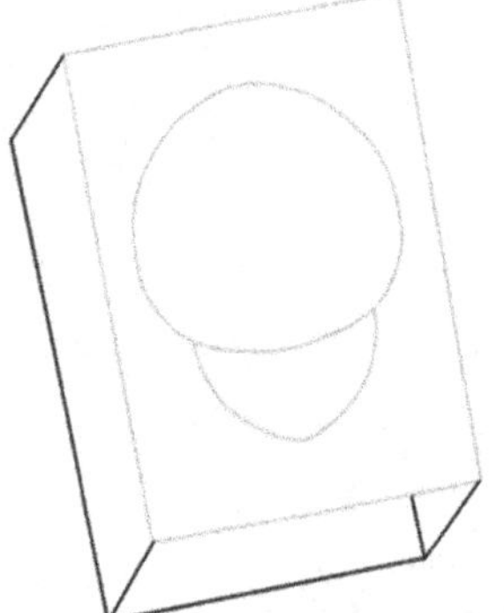

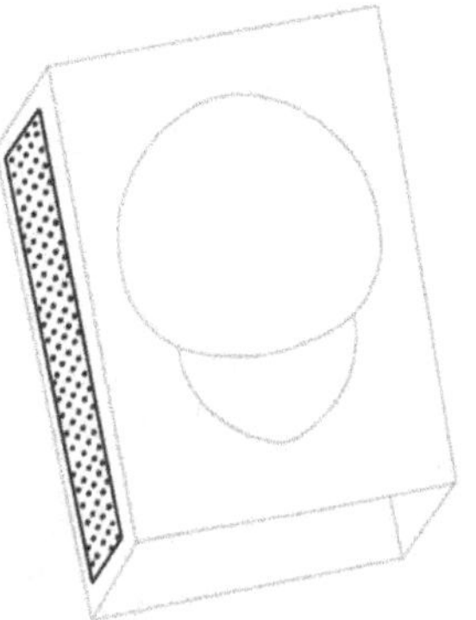

04

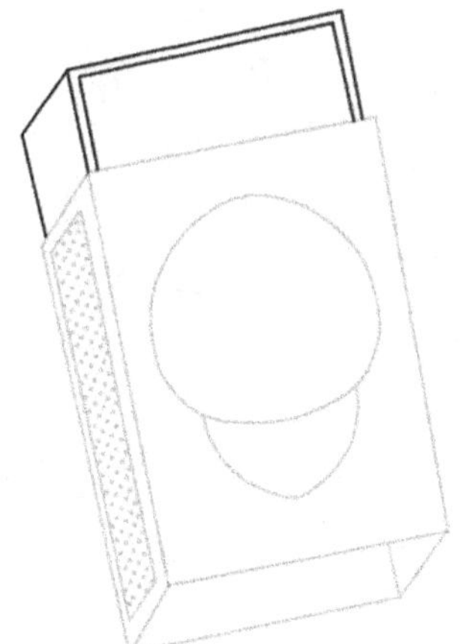

05

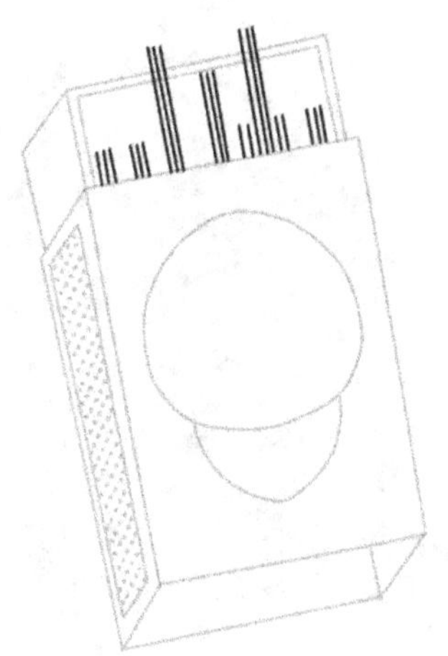

06

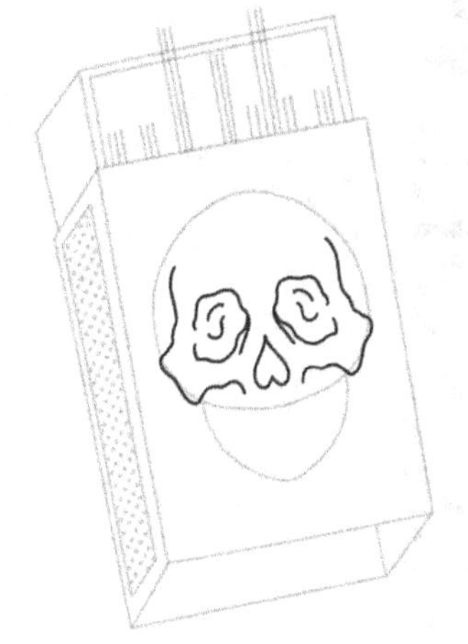

07

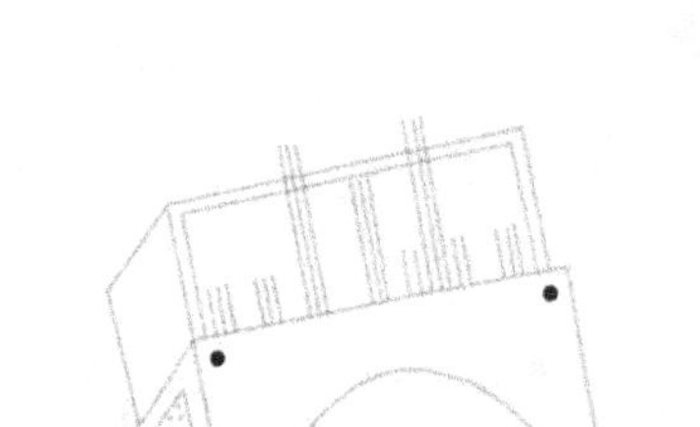

08

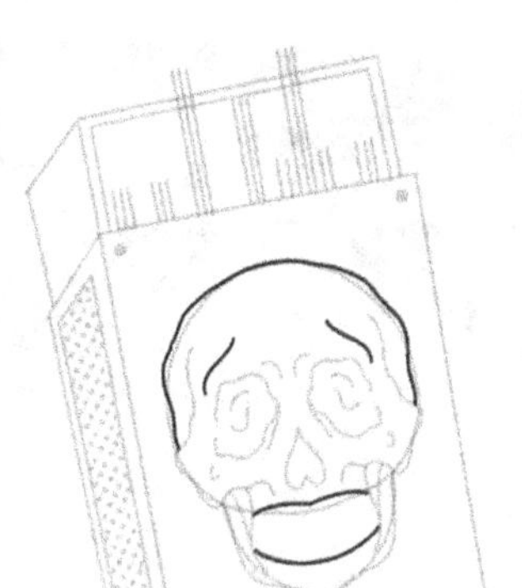

09

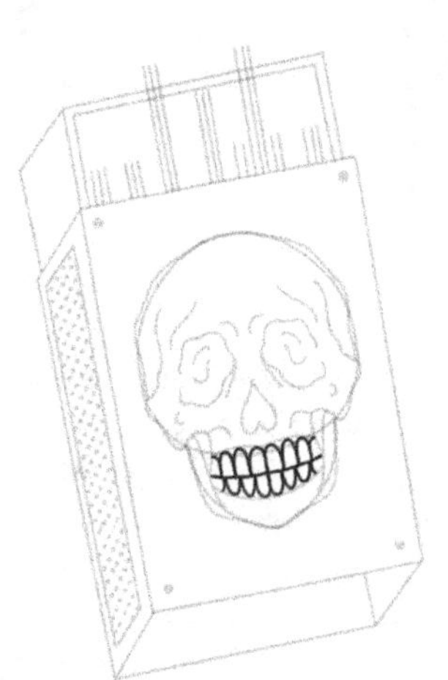

10

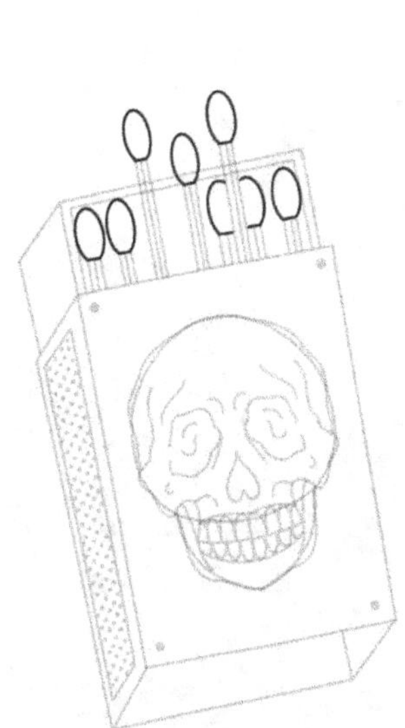

11

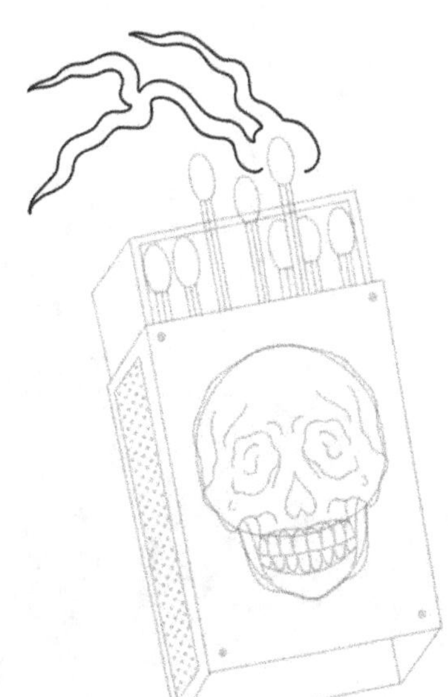

12

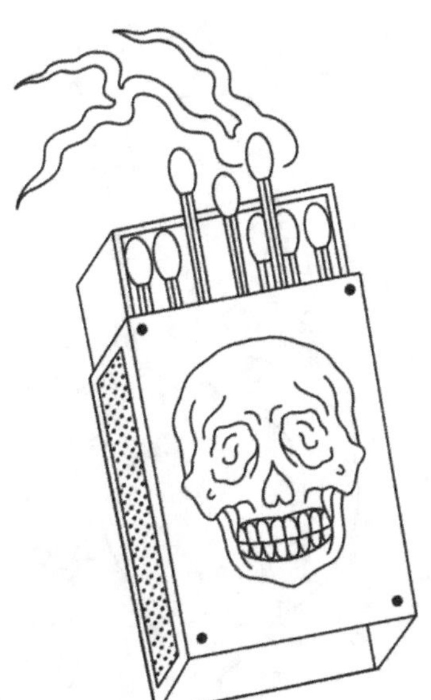

HOW TO DRAW PUNK THINGS

ROSE & MICROPHONE

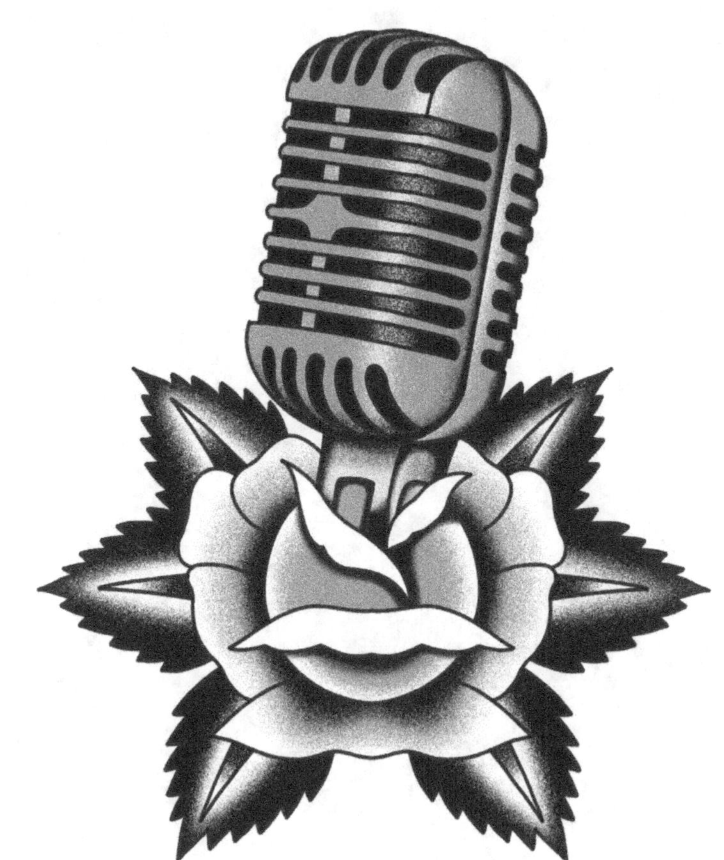

A voice for the voiceless, the rose and microphone symbolises punk's power to amplify marginalised voices and spread rebellious messages.

01

02

03

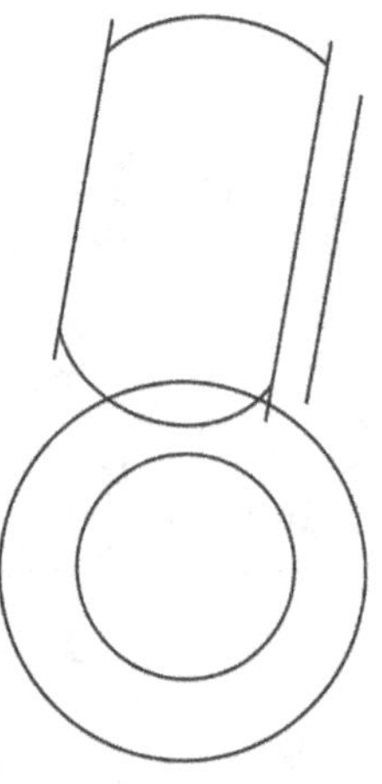

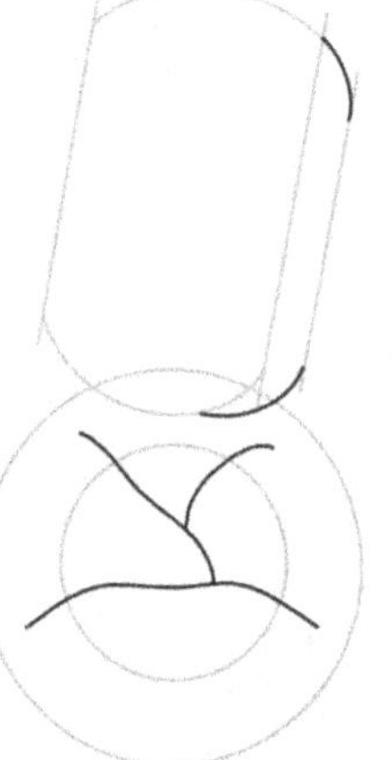

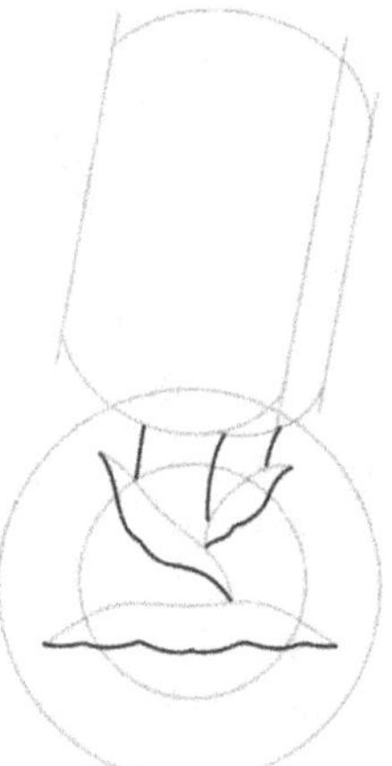

04

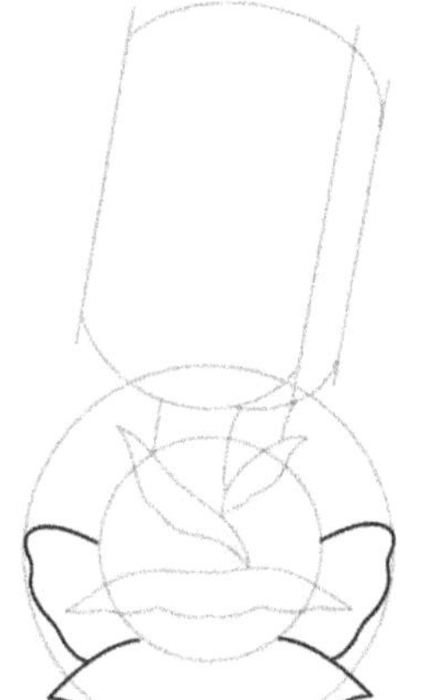

05

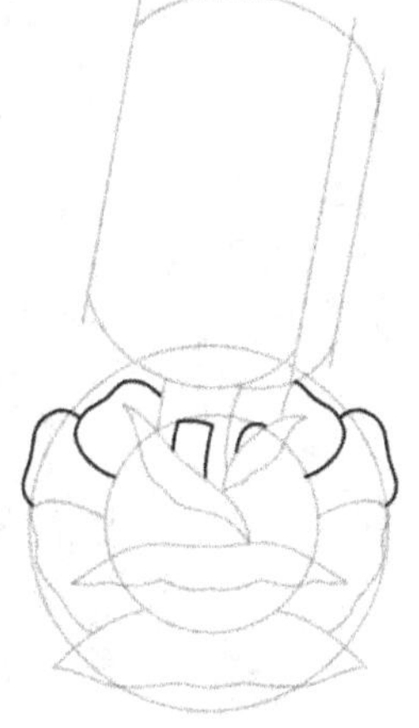

06

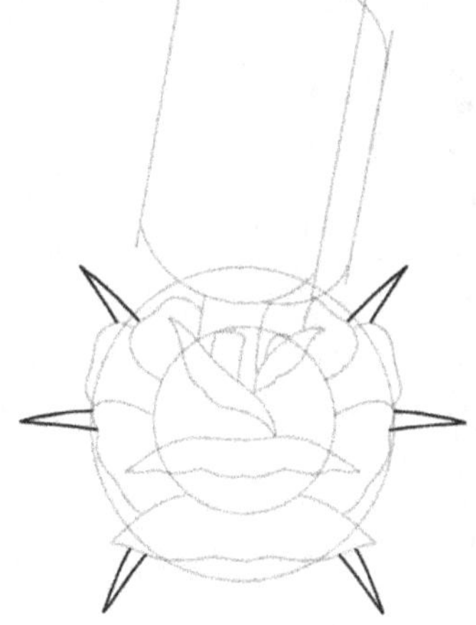

07

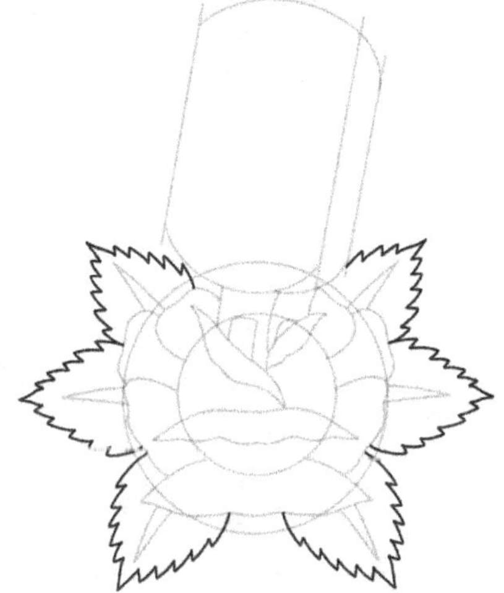

08

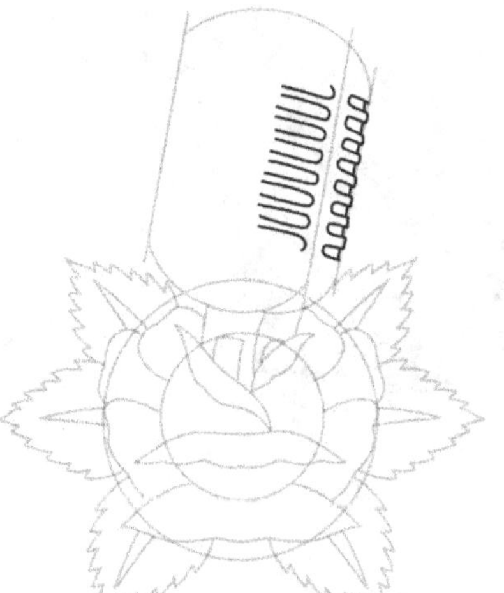

09

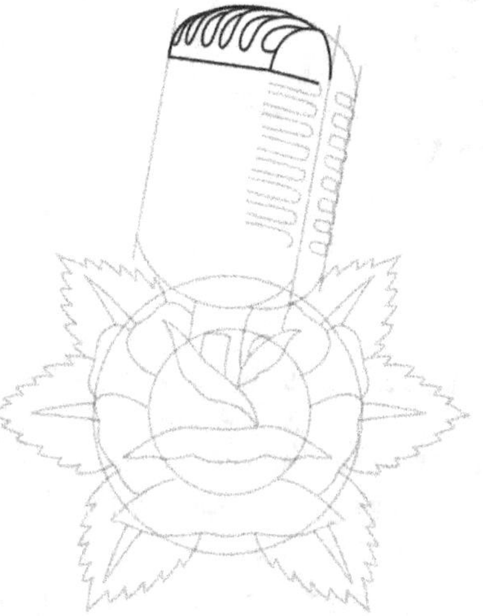

10

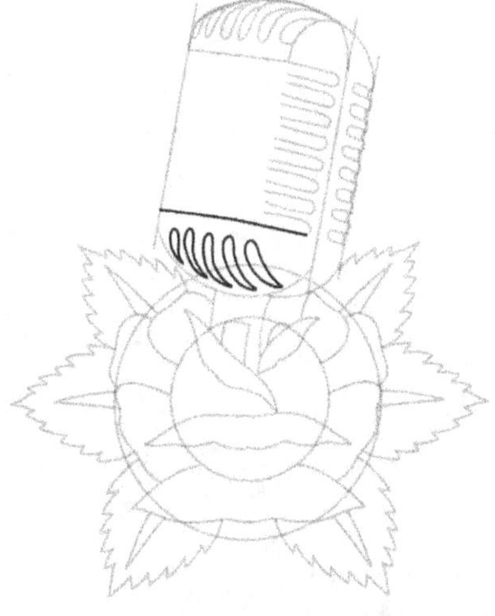

11

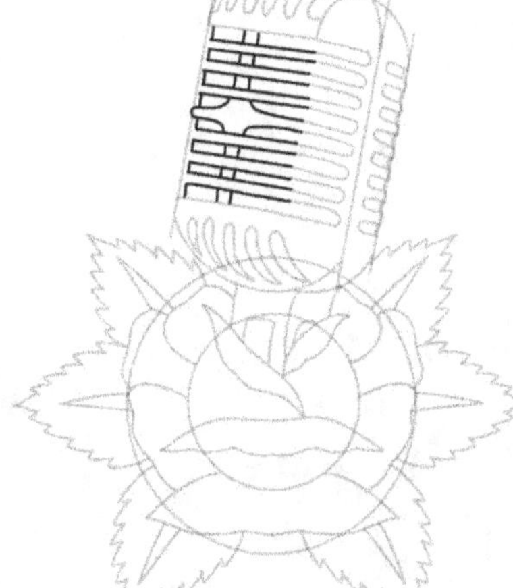

12

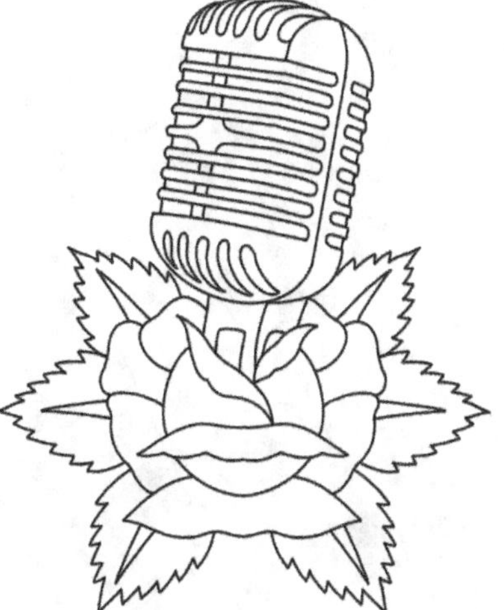

MOLOTOV COCKTAIL

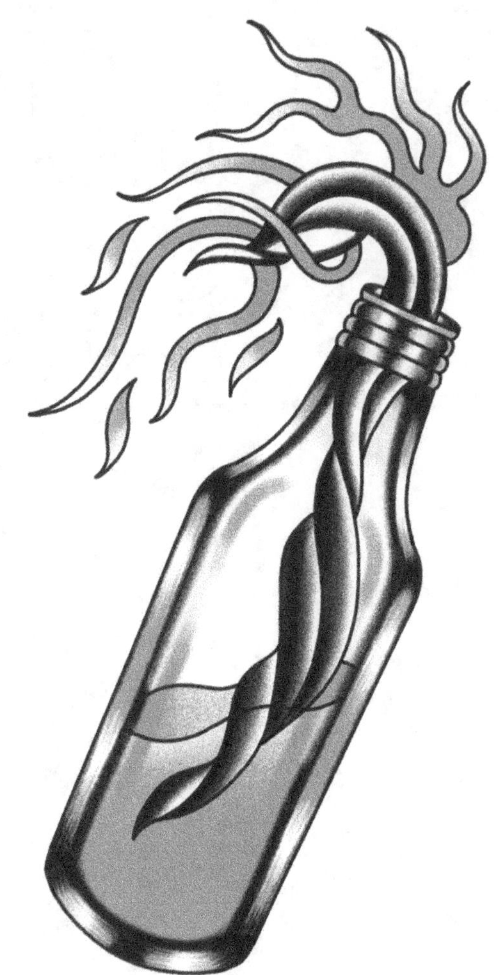

In punk culture, the Molotov cocktail symbolises radical defiance and anti-establishment sentiment, reflecting the movement's embrace of direct action and rebellion against oppressive systems.

01

02

03

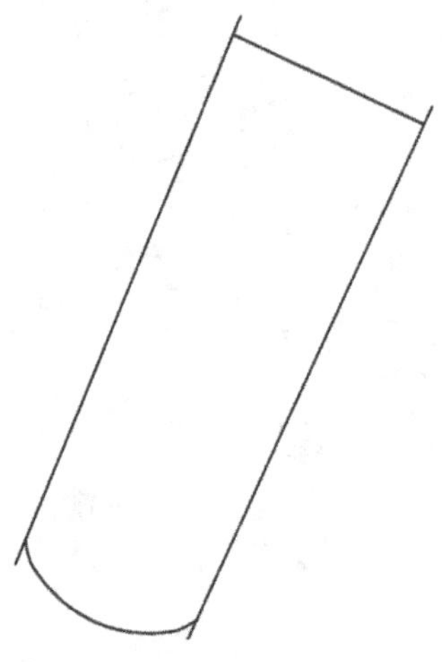

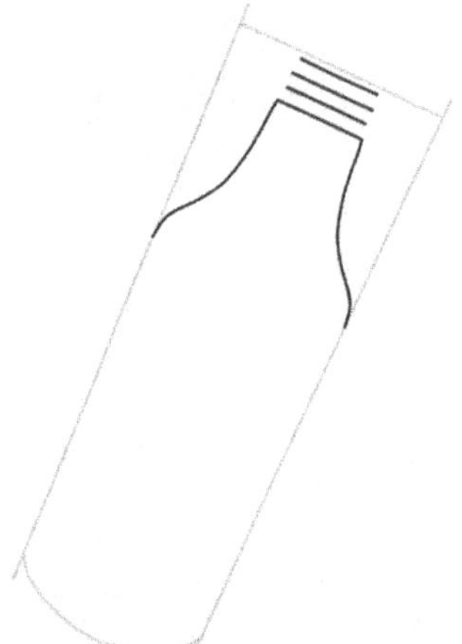

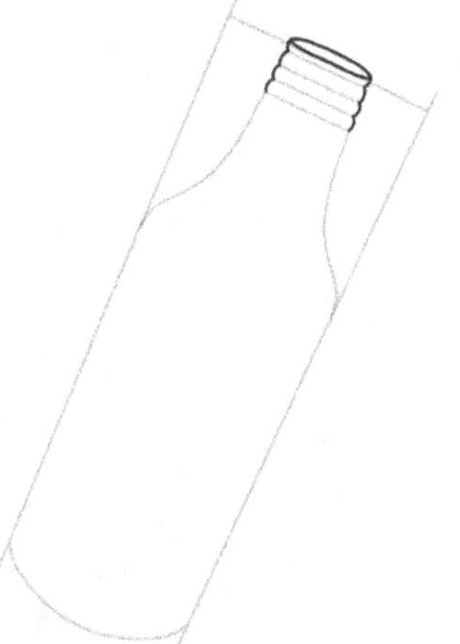

04

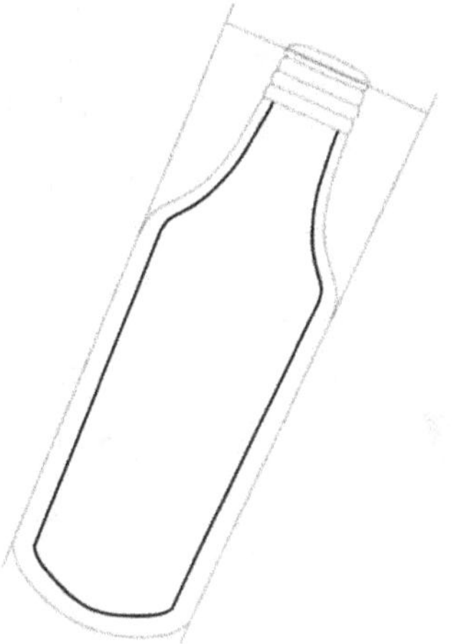

05

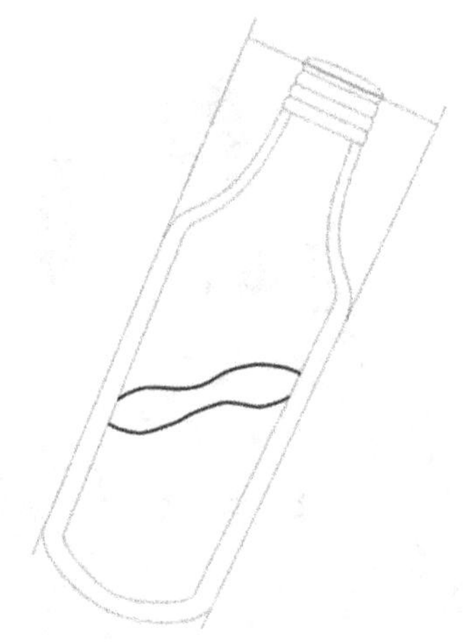

06

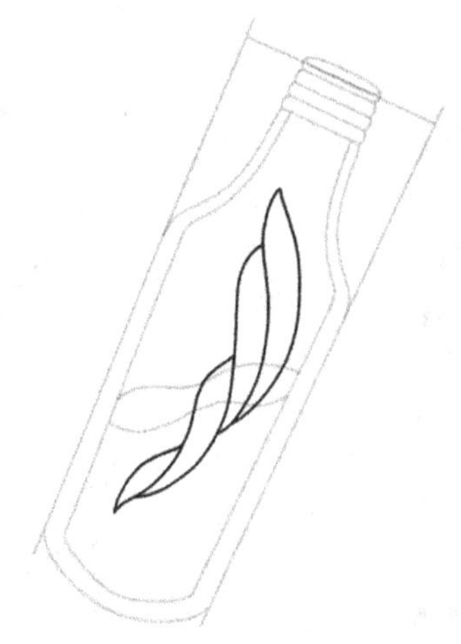

07

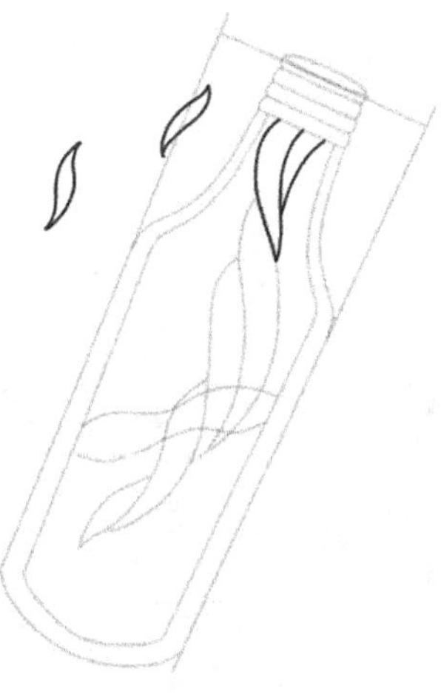

08

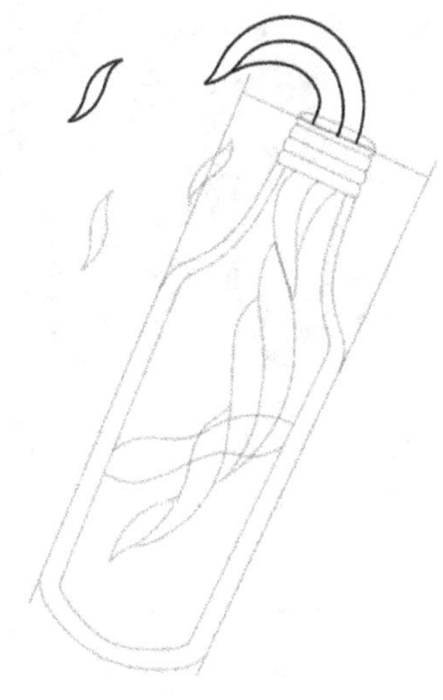

09

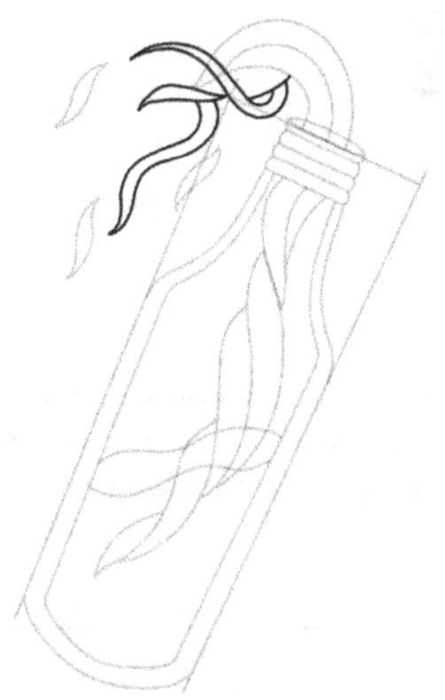

10

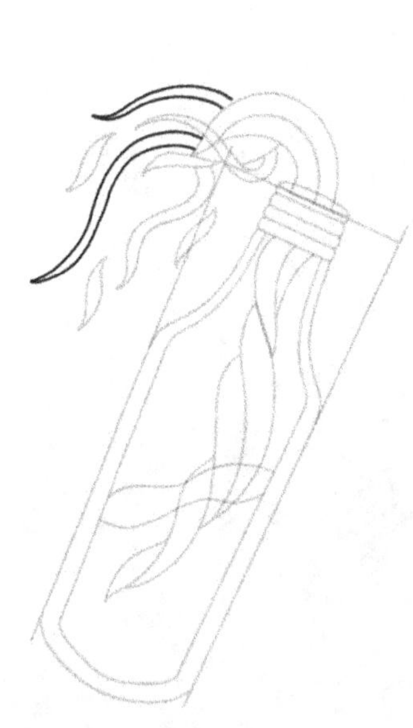

11

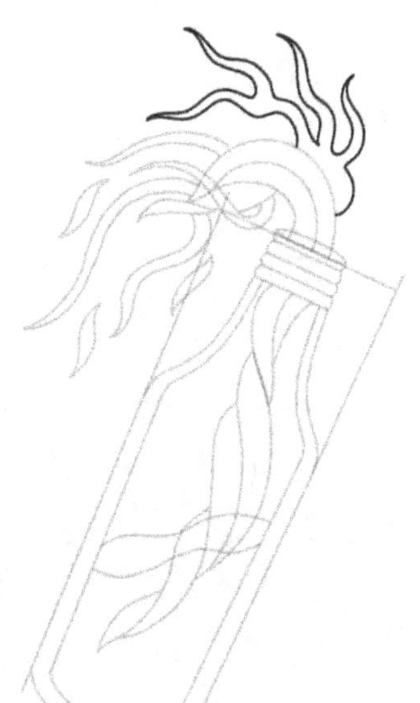

12

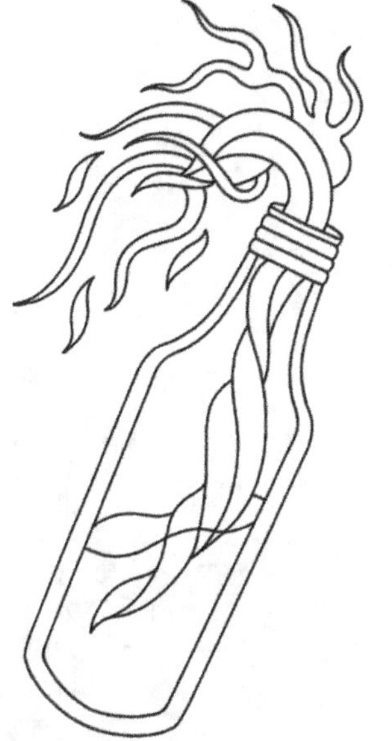

PRAYING HANDS

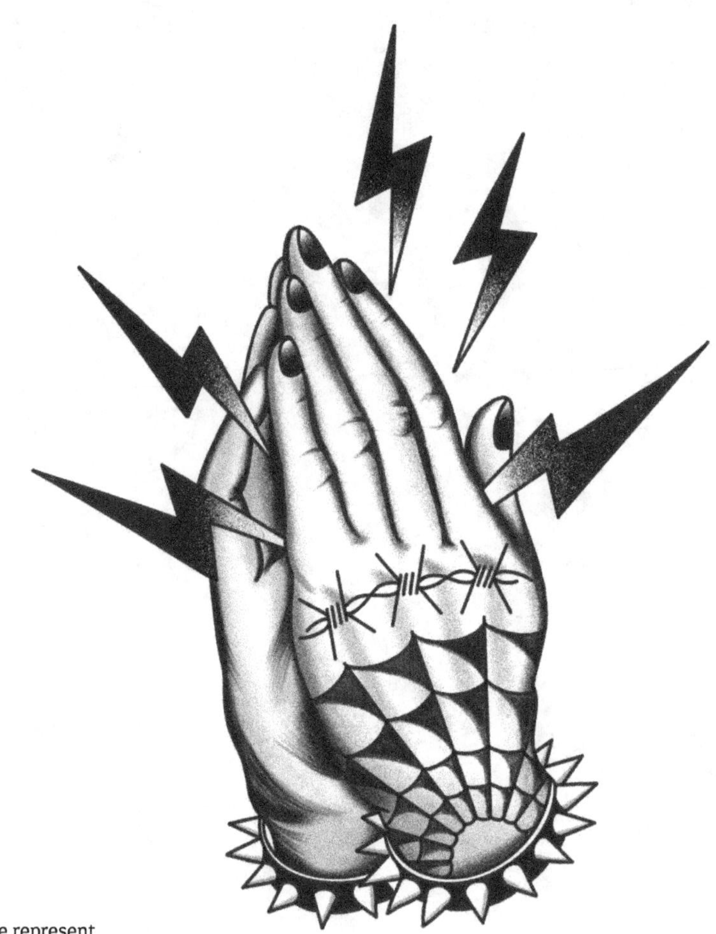

Praying hands in punk culture represent hope, defiance, or a provocative critique of traditional beliefs and authority.

01

02

03

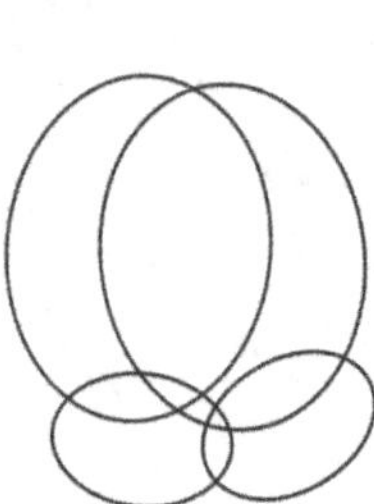

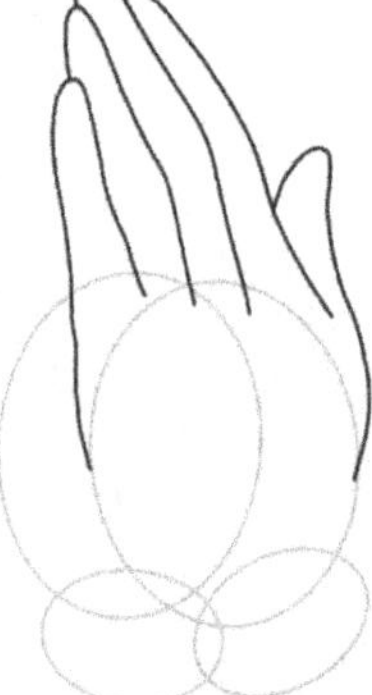

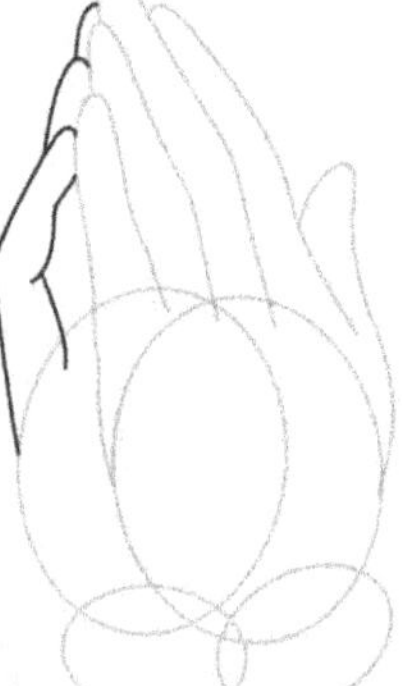

04

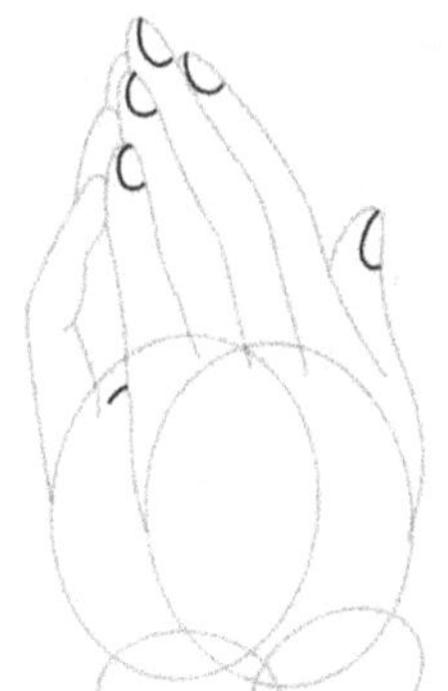

05

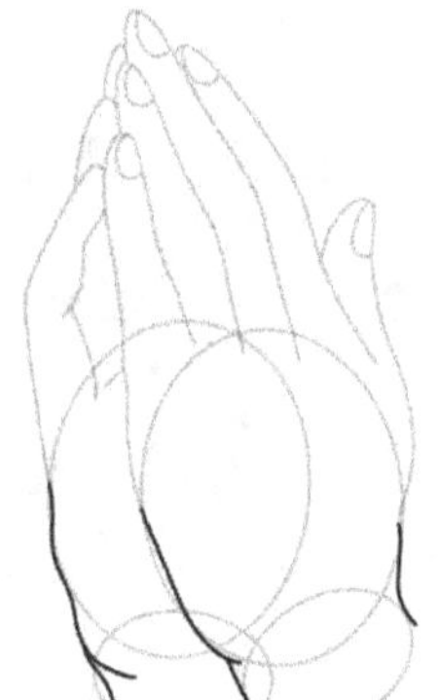

06

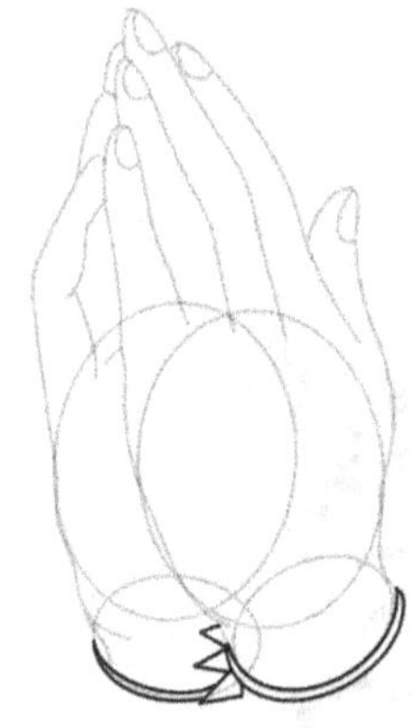

07

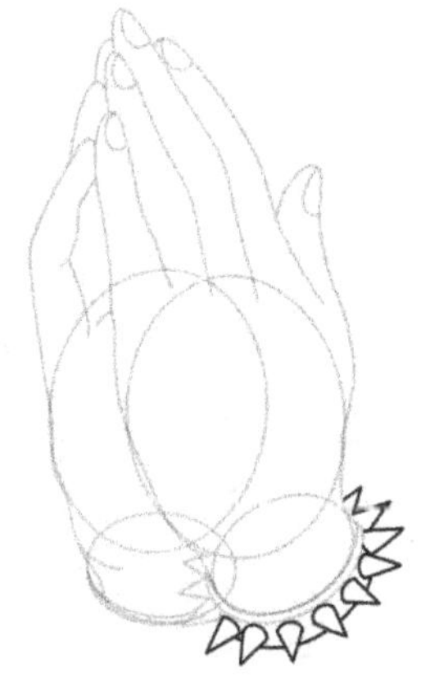

08

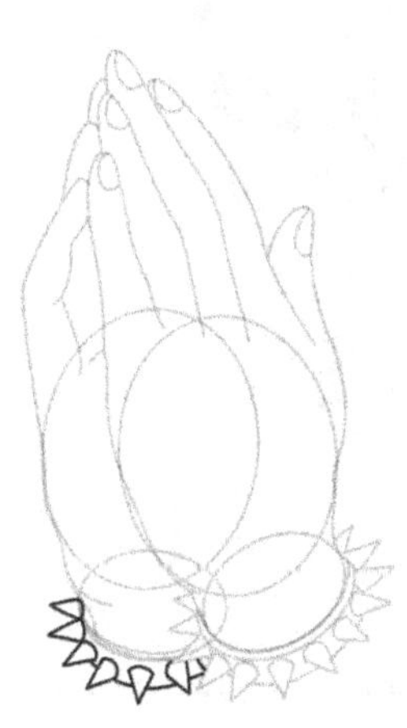

09

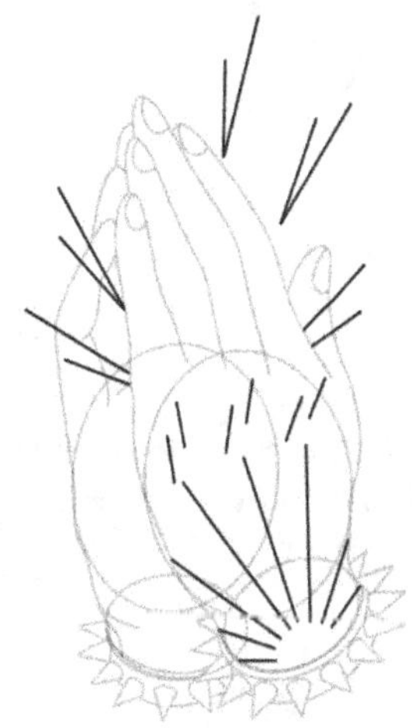

10

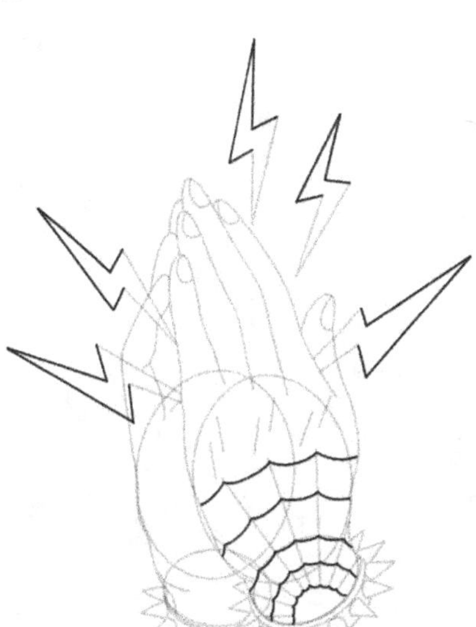

11

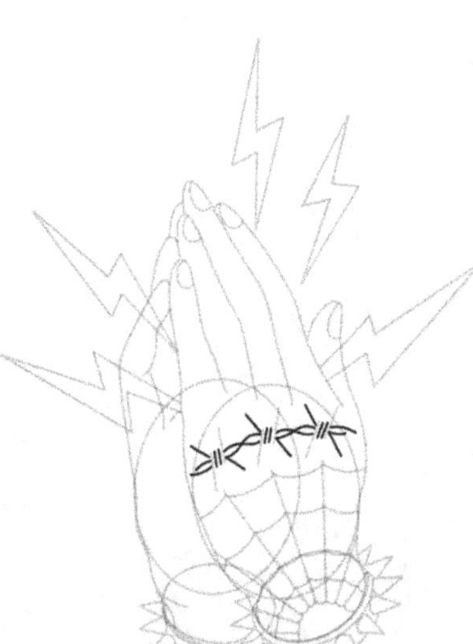

12

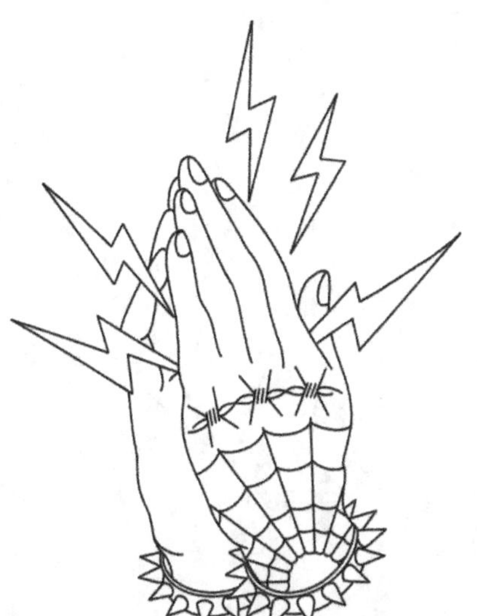

HOW TO DRAW PUNK THINGS

SKEELTON HAND SMOKING

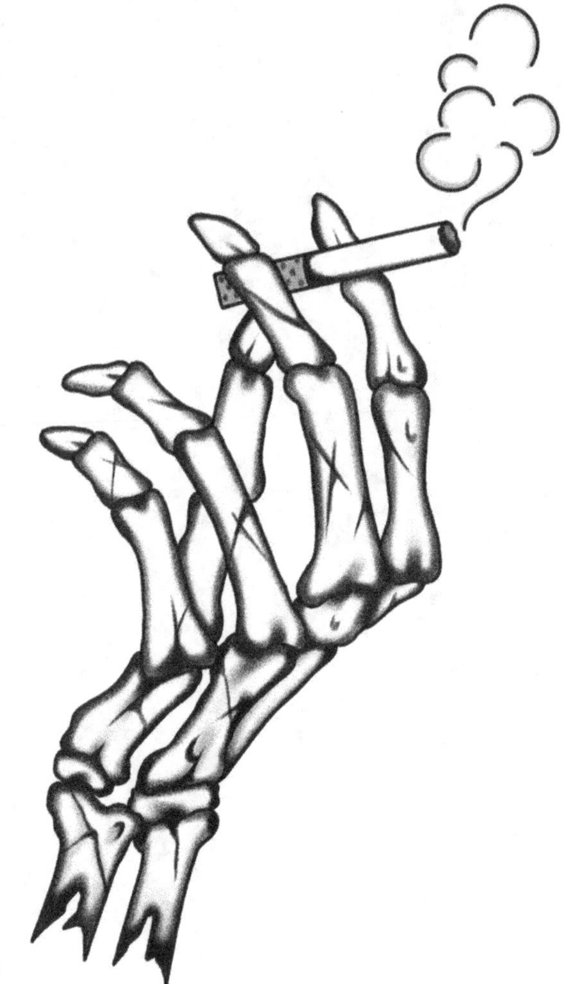

A rebellious icon, the smoking skeleton hand embodies punk's carefree attitude.

01

02

03

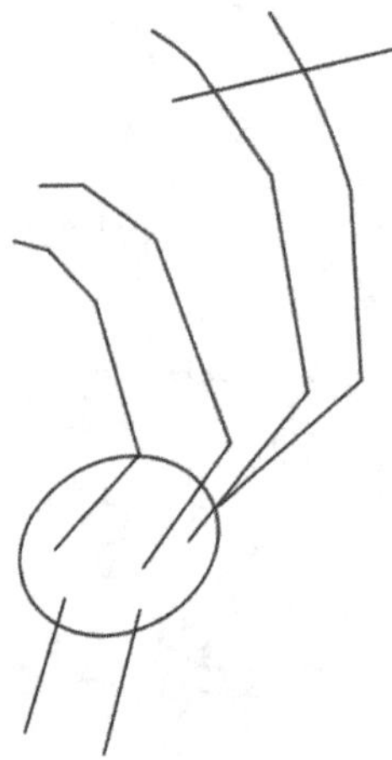

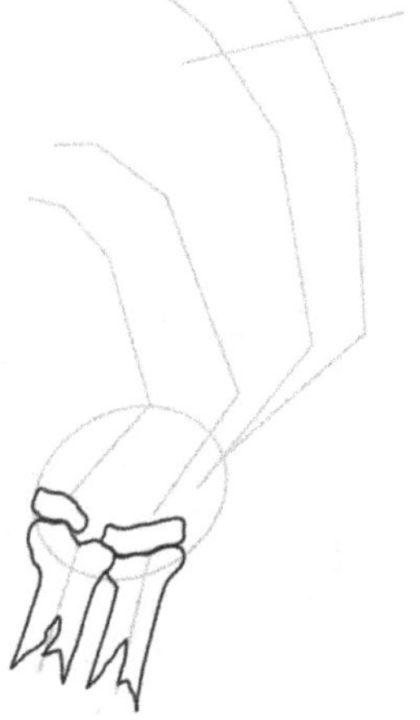

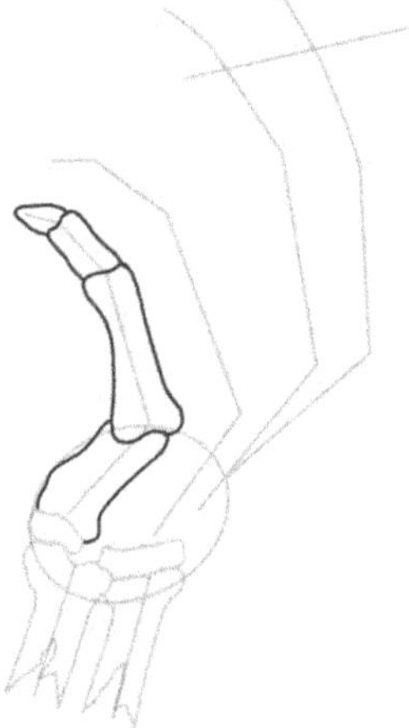

04

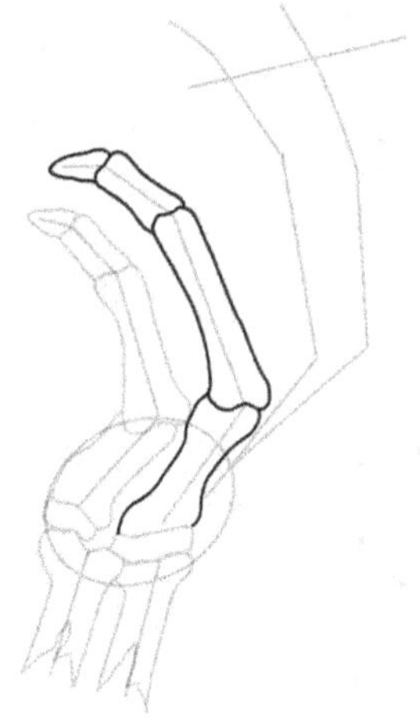

05

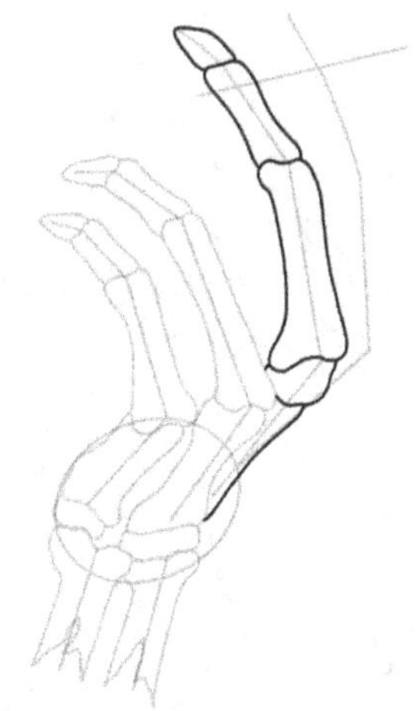

06

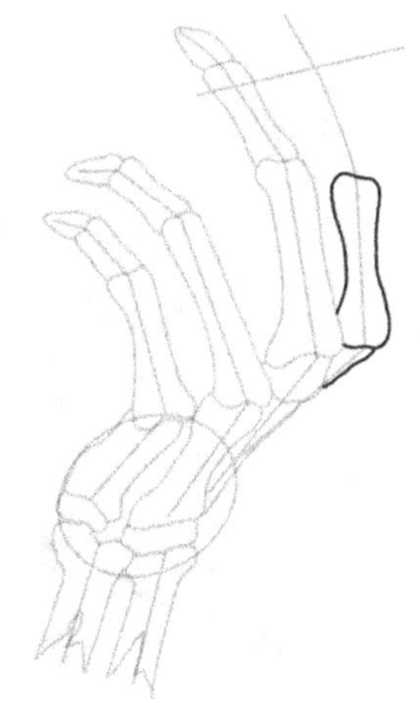

07

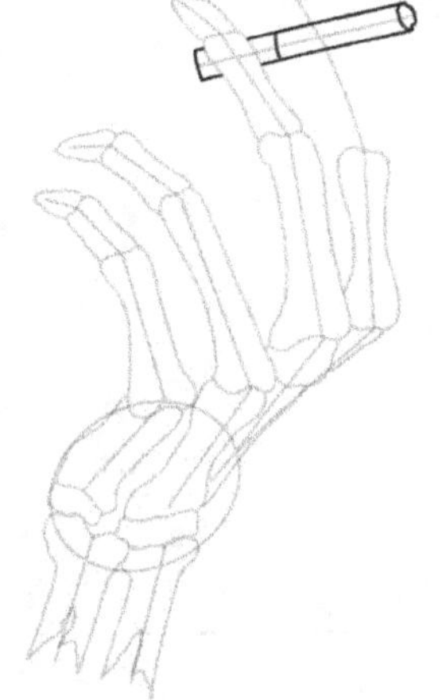

08

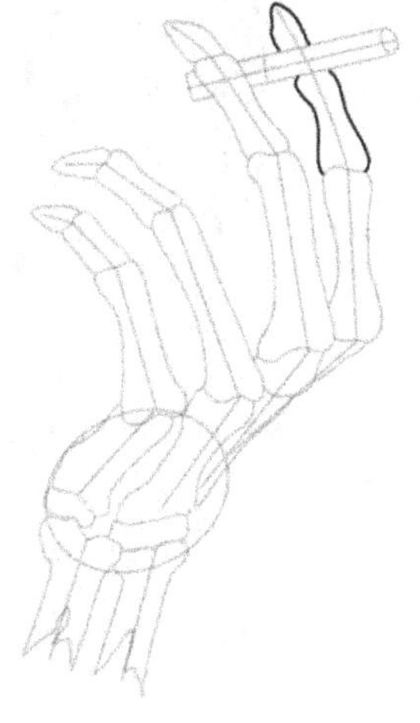

09

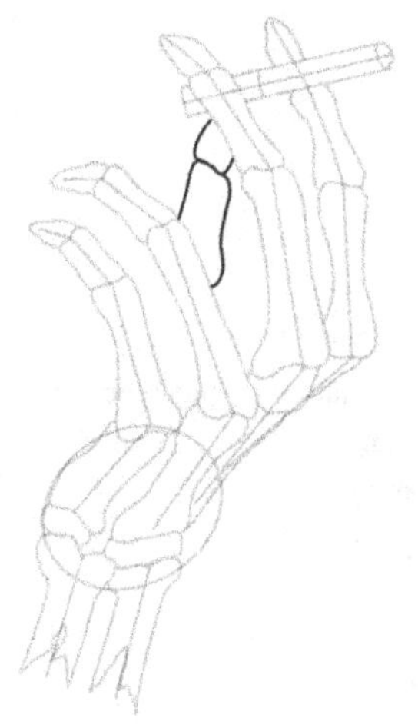

10

11

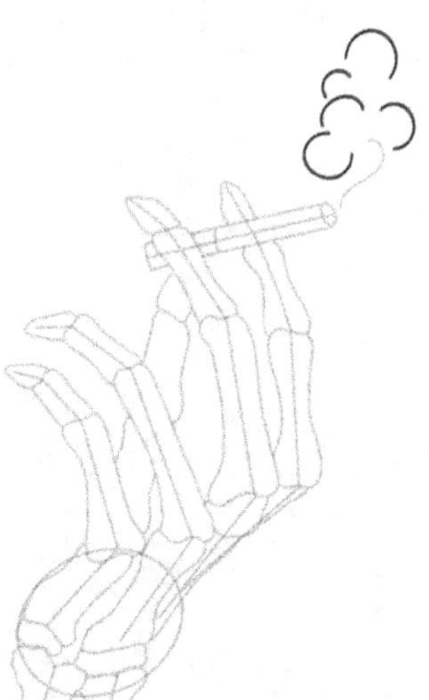

12

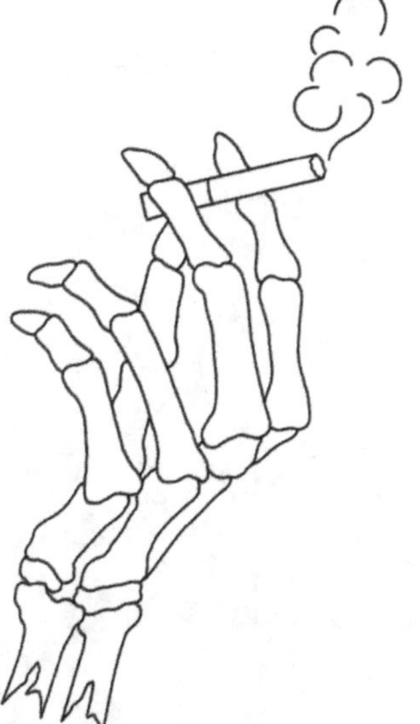

HOW TO DRAW PUNK THINGS

PUNK ROCK KNUCKLES

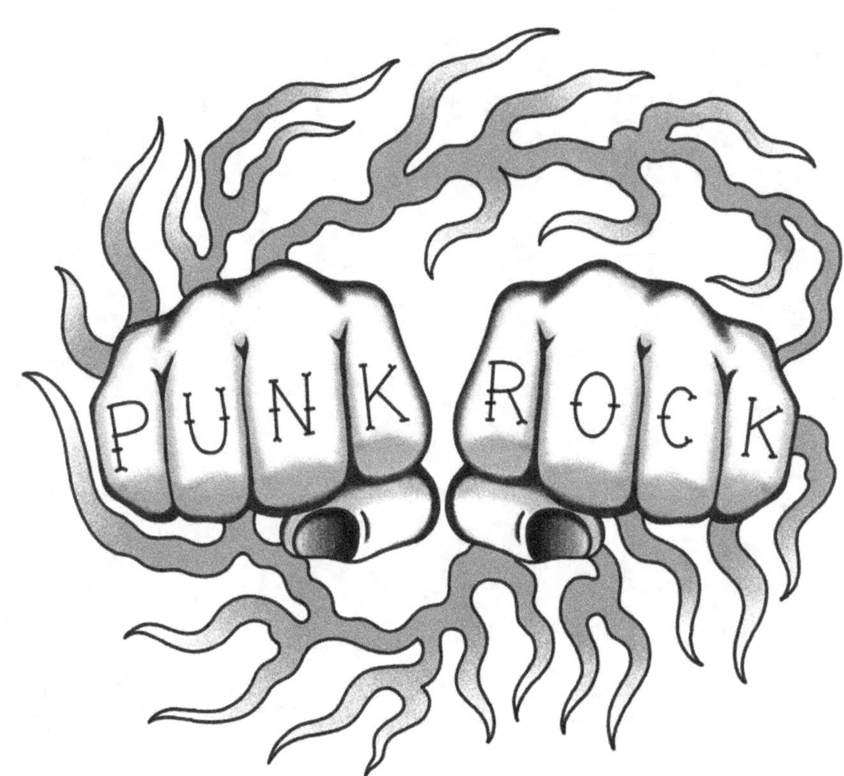

A badge of commitment, punk rock knuckles symbolise punk culture's unity, strength, and defiant identity.

01

02

03

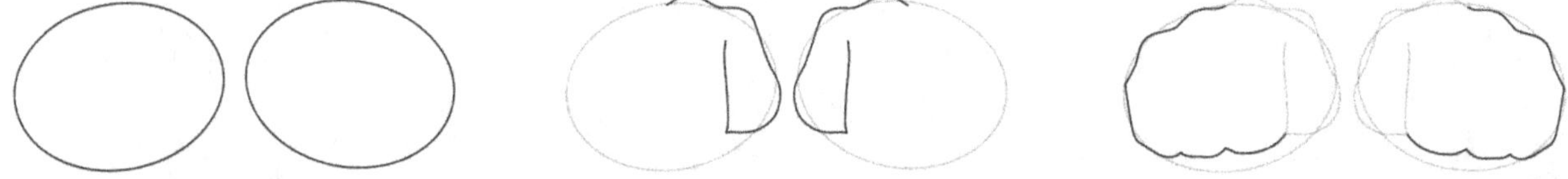

04

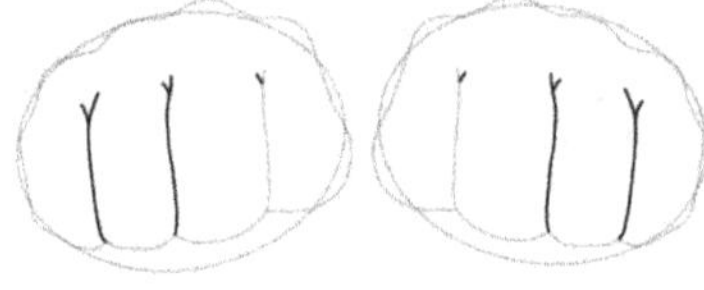

05

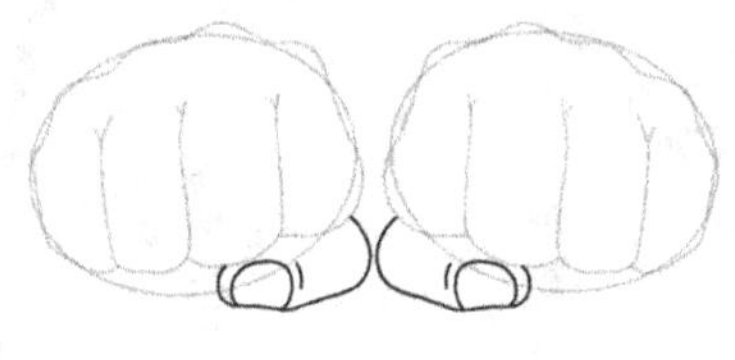

06

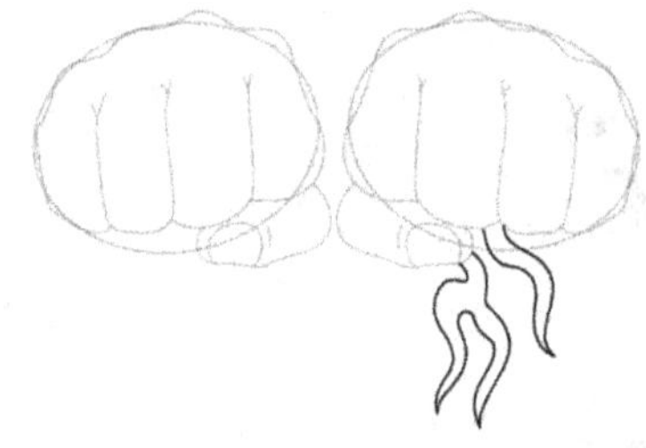

07

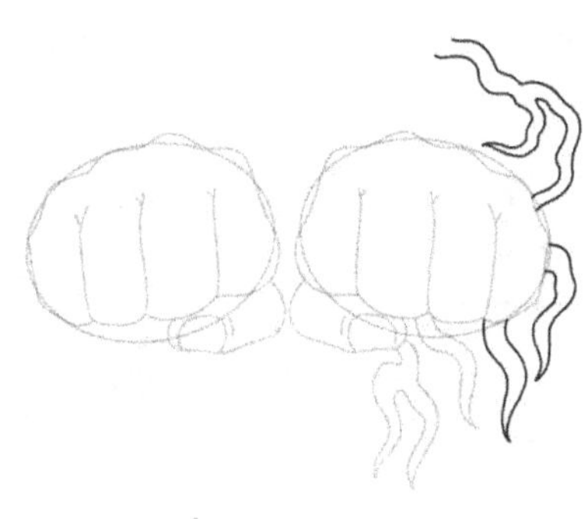

08

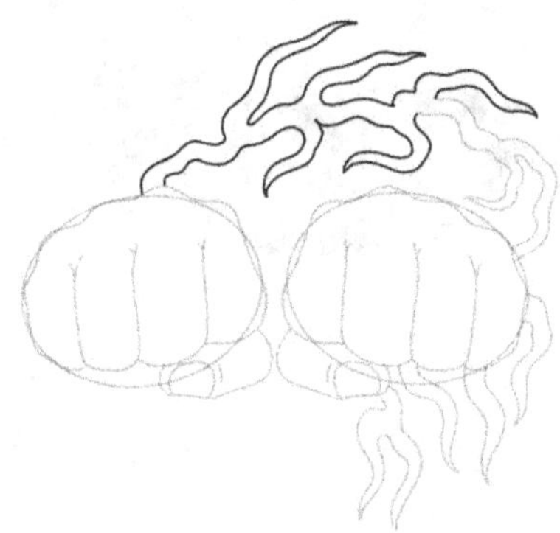

09

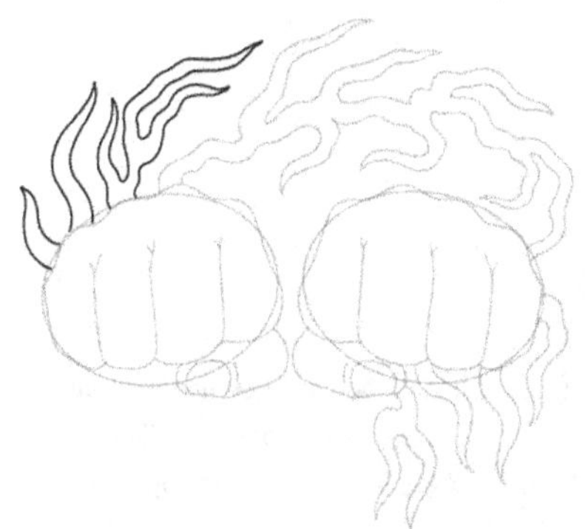

10

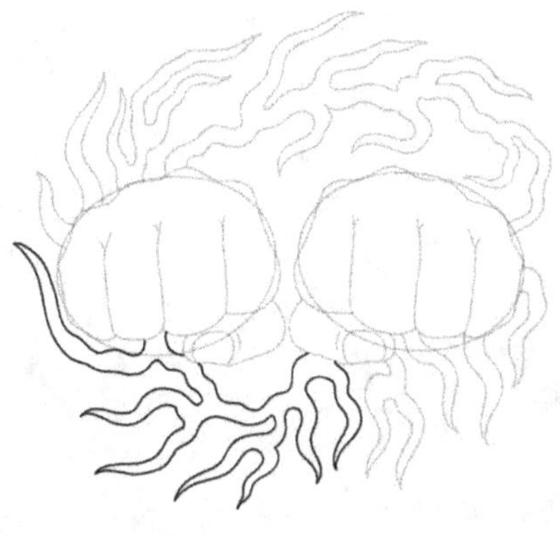

11

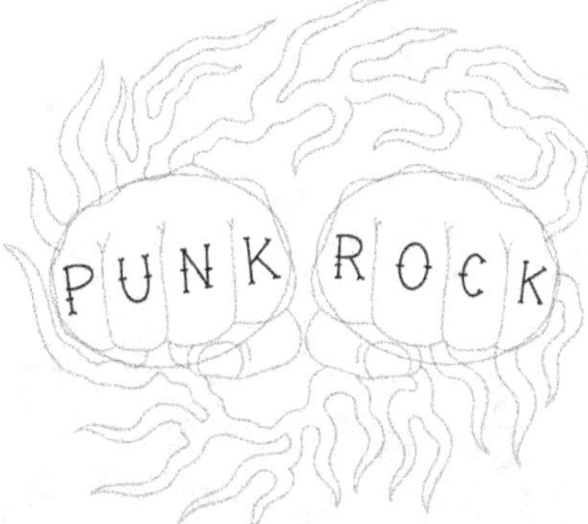

12

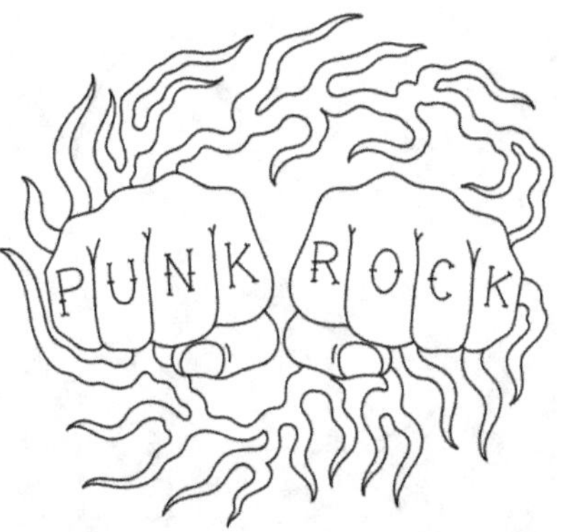

HOW TO DRAW PUNK THINGS

RAISED FIST

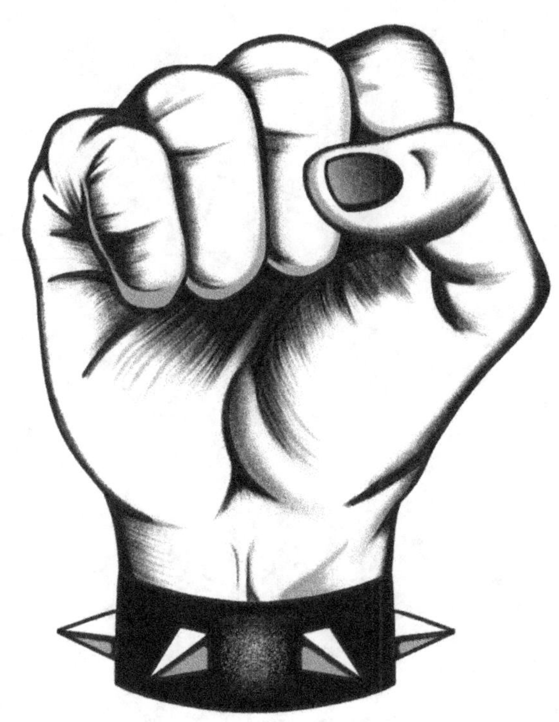

A universal symbol of resistance, the raised
fist embodies punk's spirit of rebellion,
solidarity, and fighting against oppression.

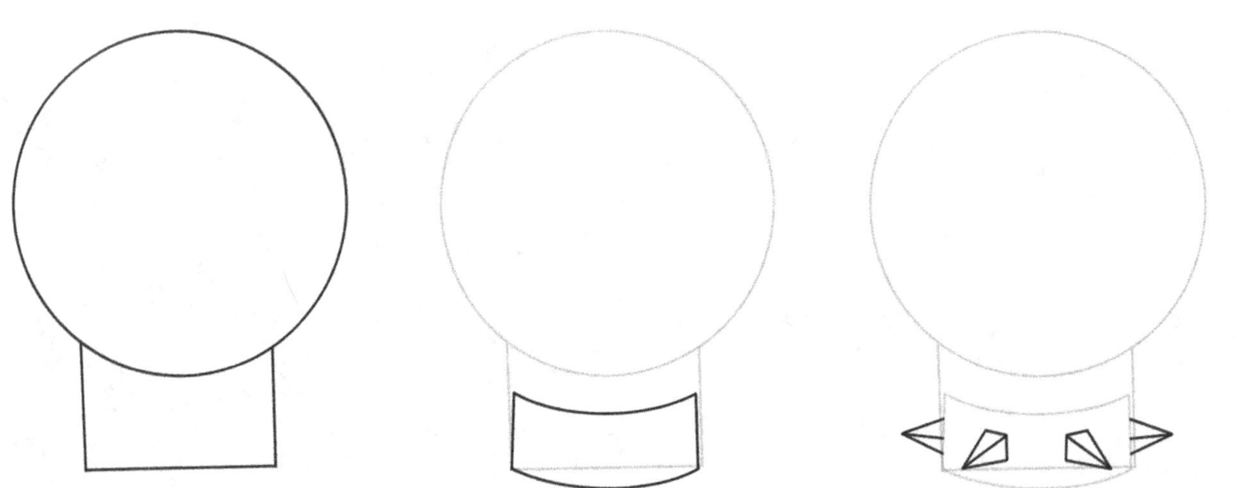

01

02

03

04

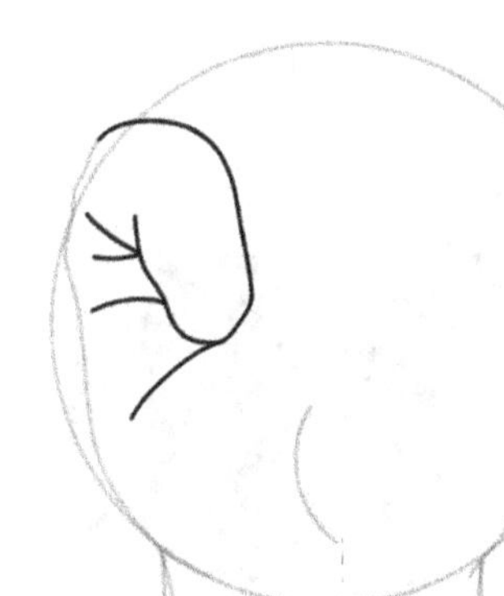

05

06

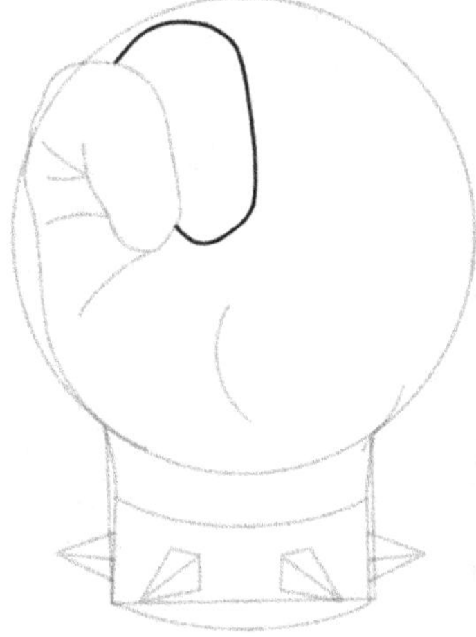

07

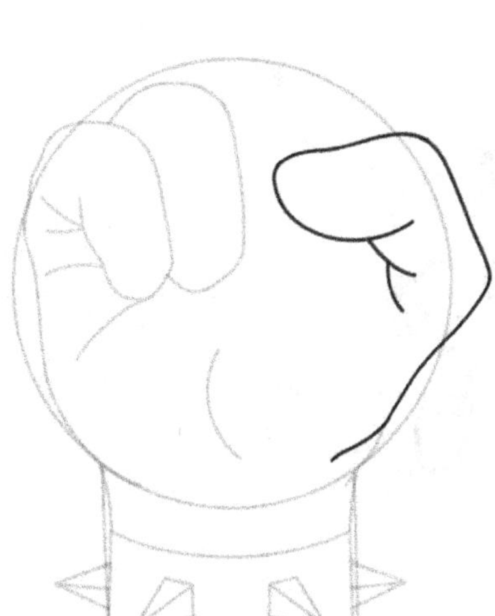

08

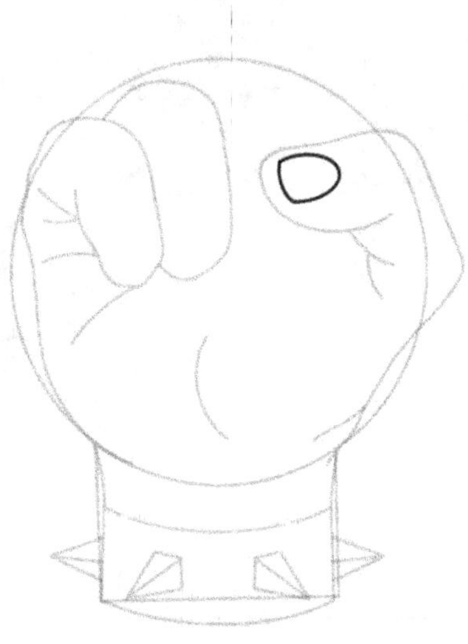

09

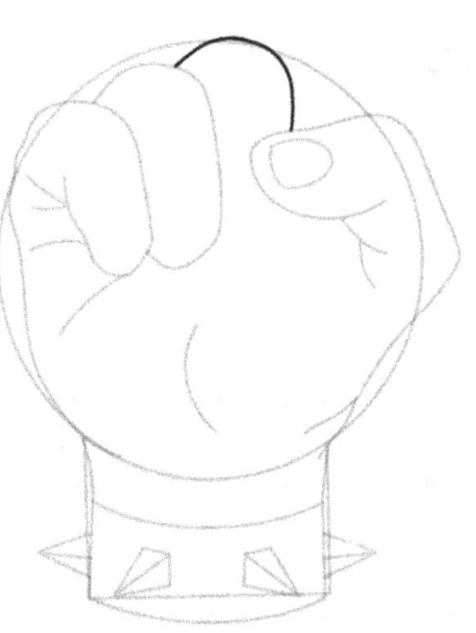

10

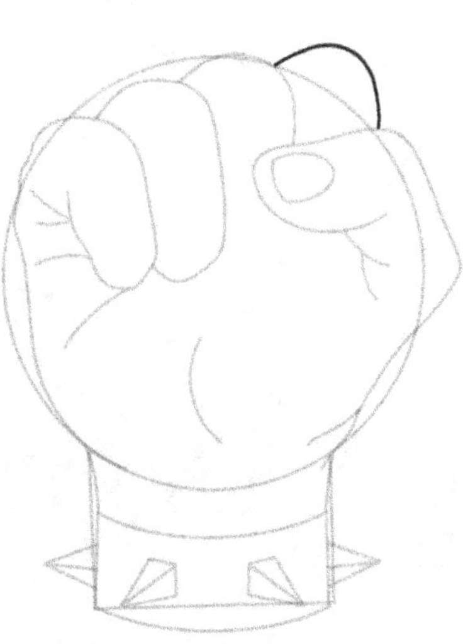

11

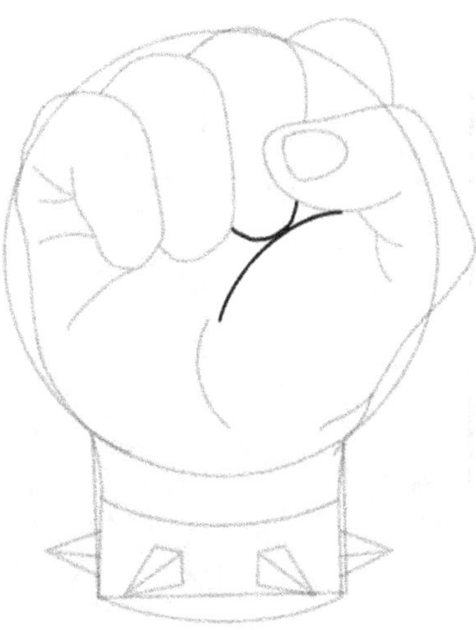

12

RAZOR BLADE

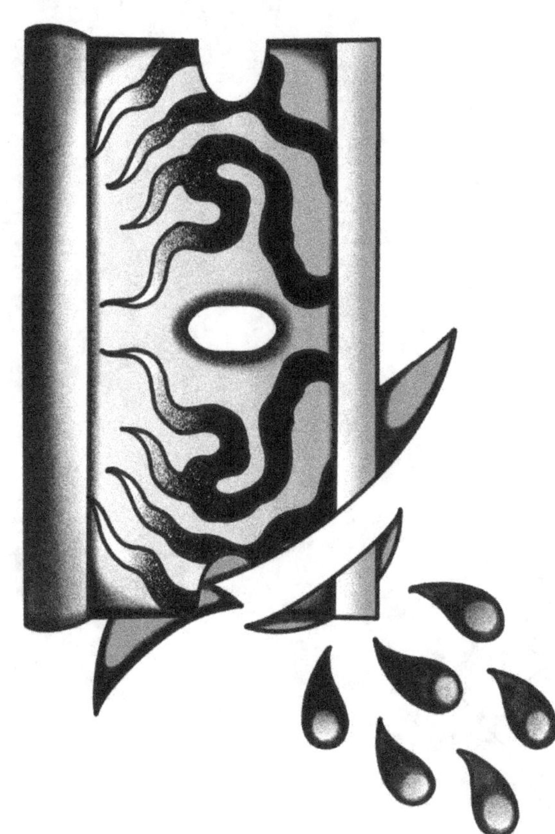

A symbol of raw edge and danger, the razor reflects punk's sharp defiance and refusal to conform to polished societal expectations.

01

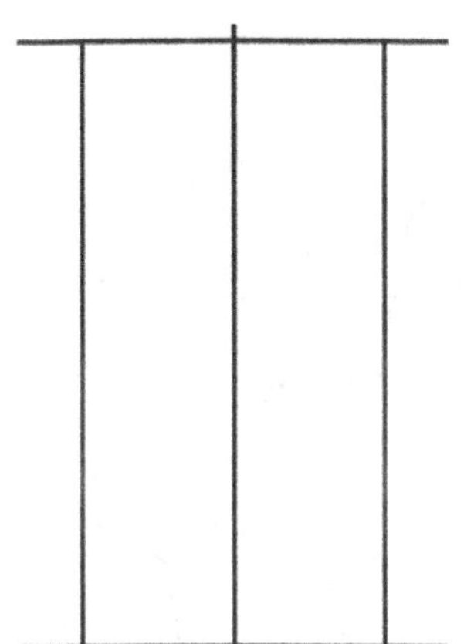

02

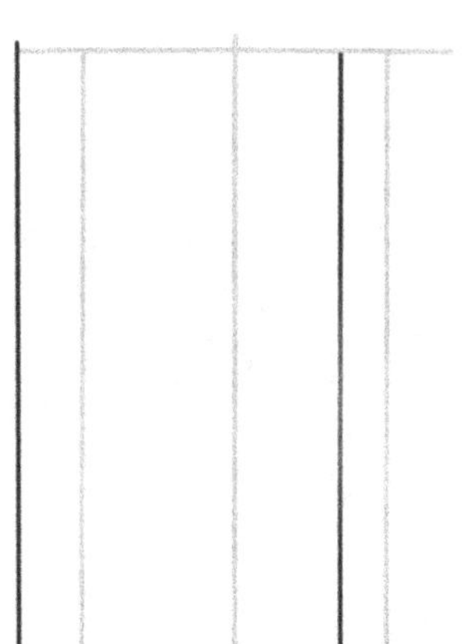

03

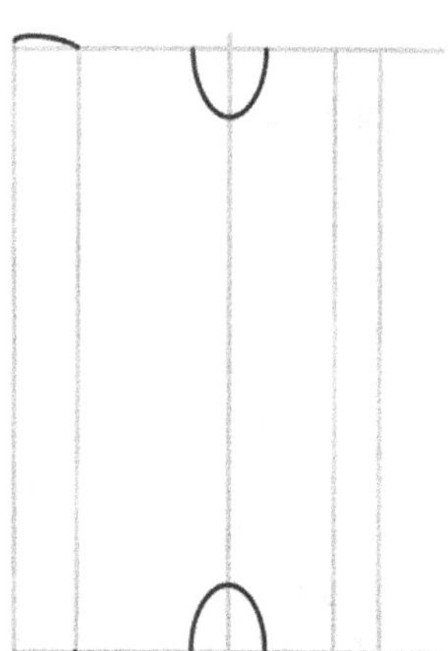

04

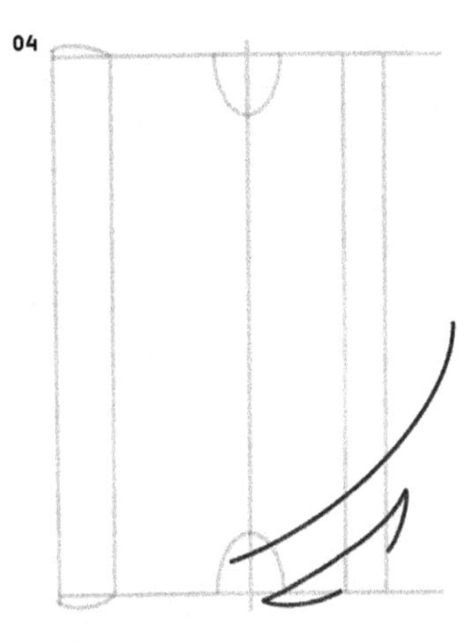

05

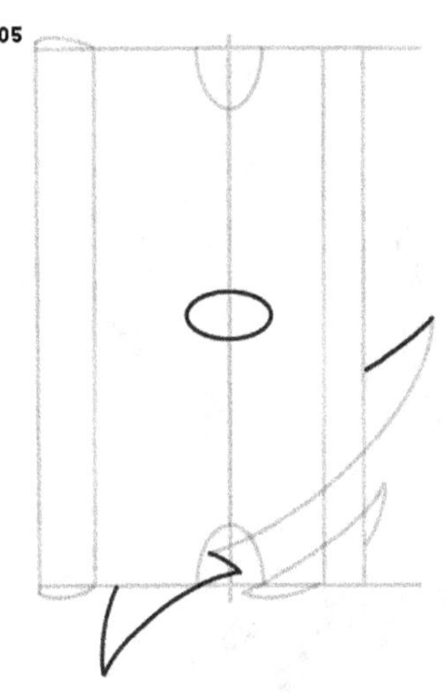

06

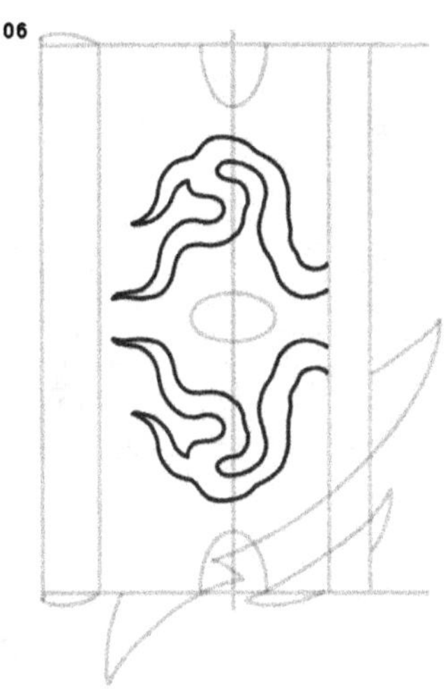

07

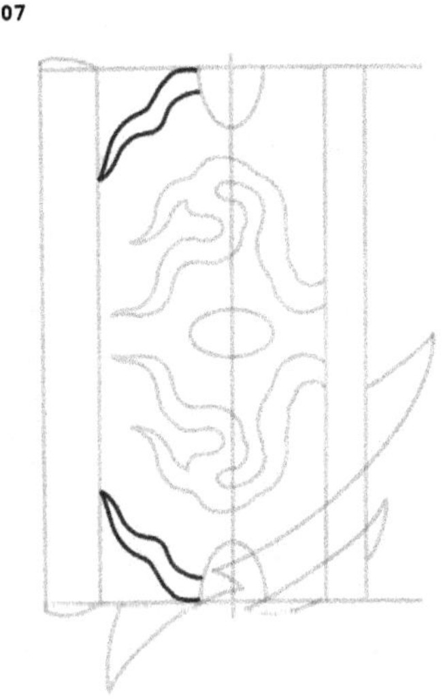

08

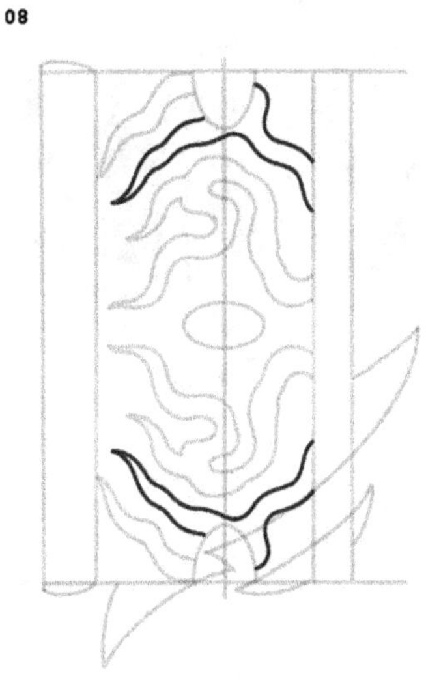

09

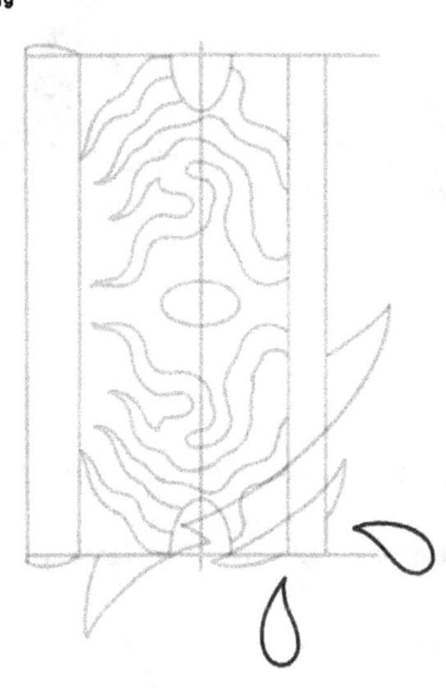

10

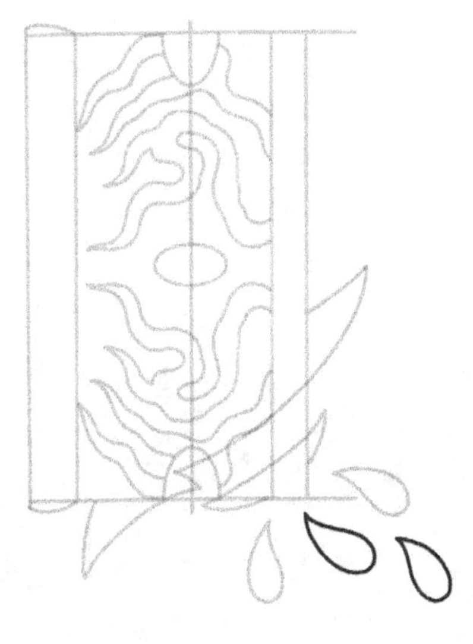

11

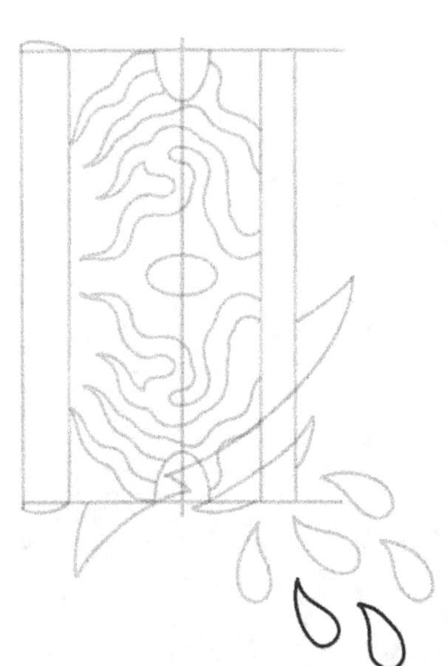

12

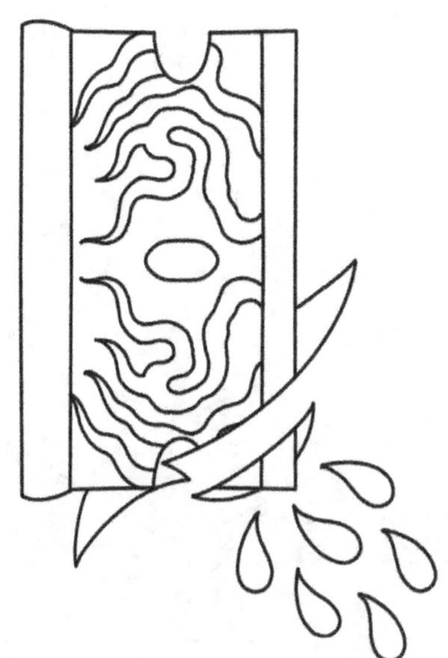

RECORD PLAYER

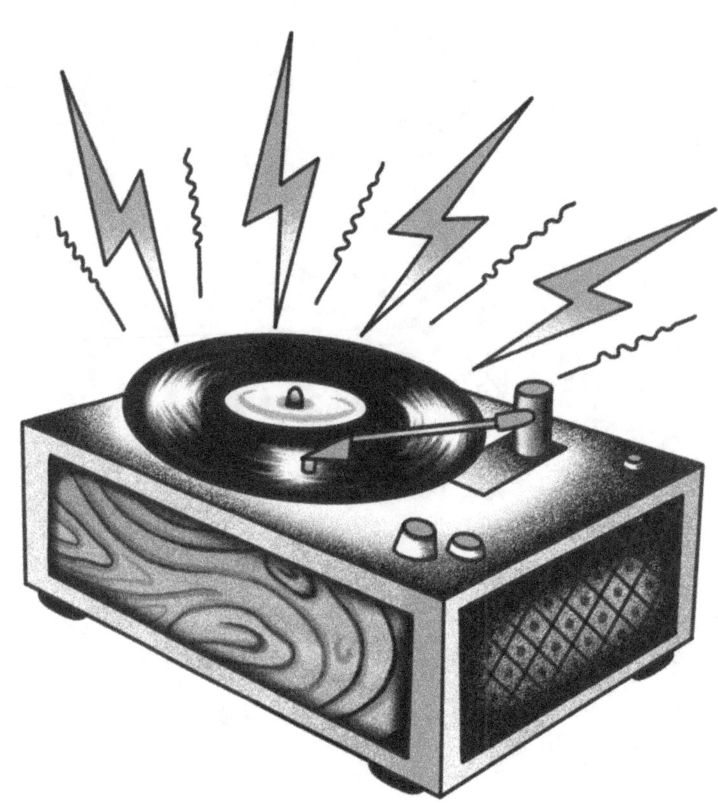

A nostalgic nod to the roots of punk, the
record player symbolises the analogue,
authentic connection to music and rebellion.

01

02

03

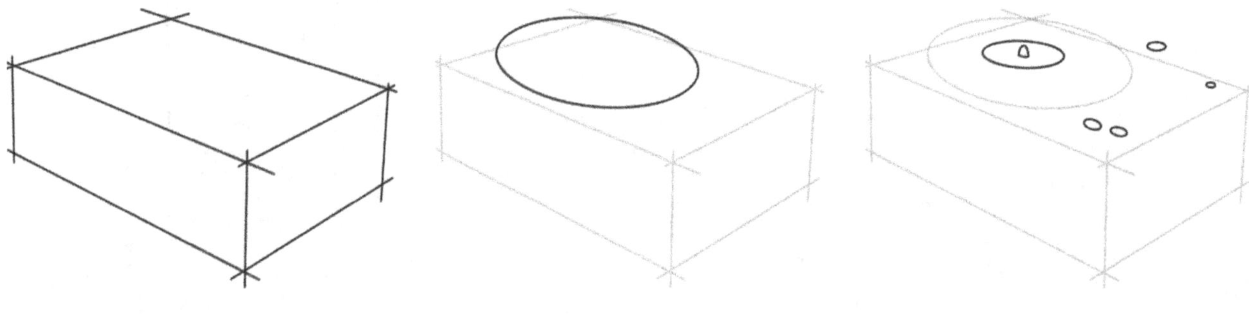

04

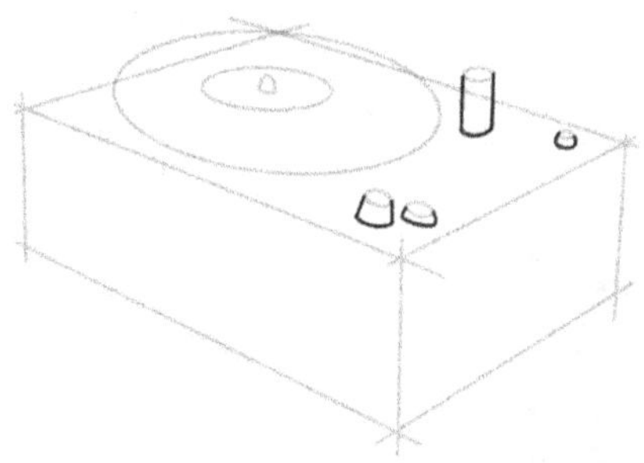

05

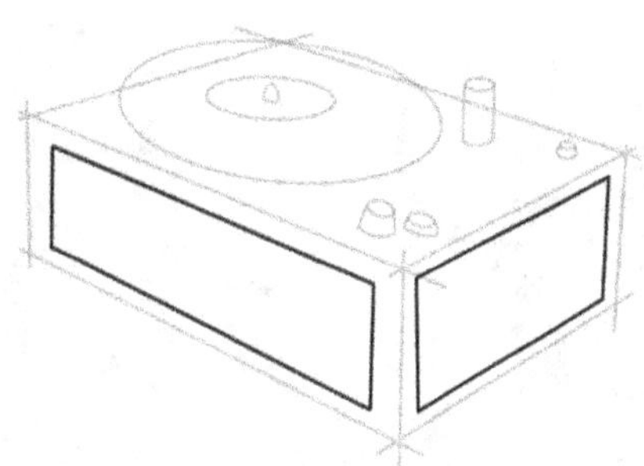

06

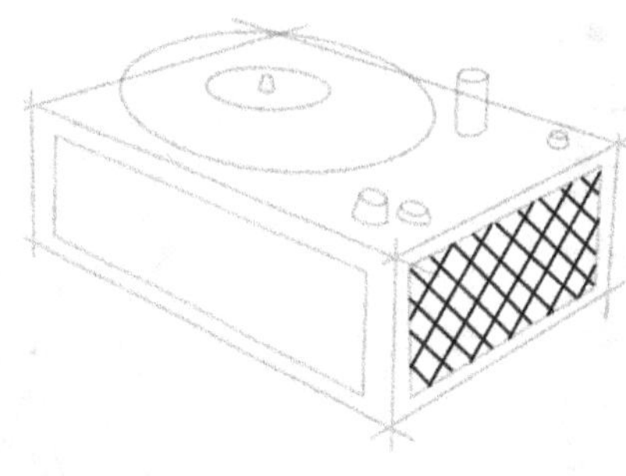

07

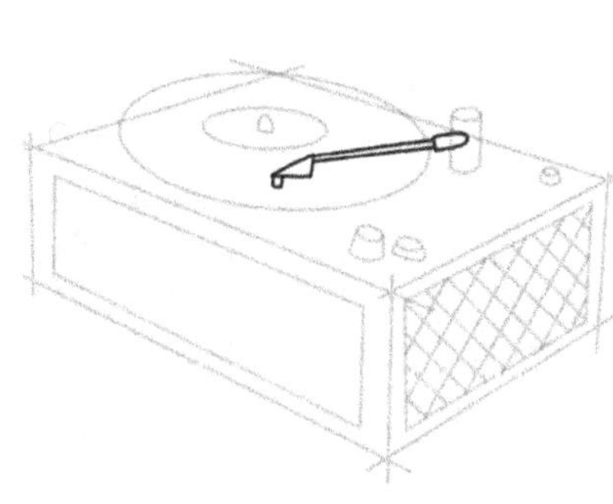

08

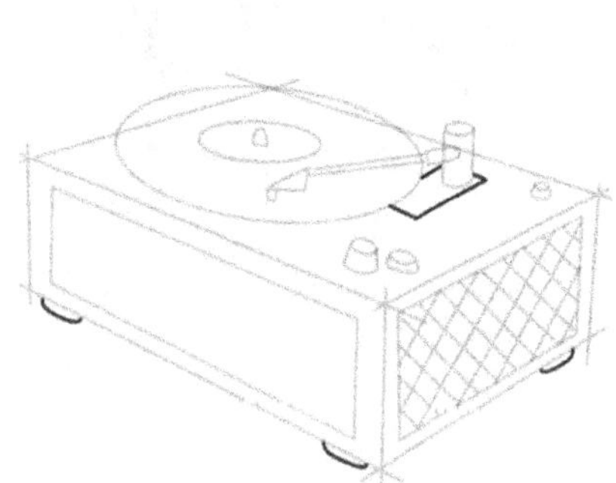

09

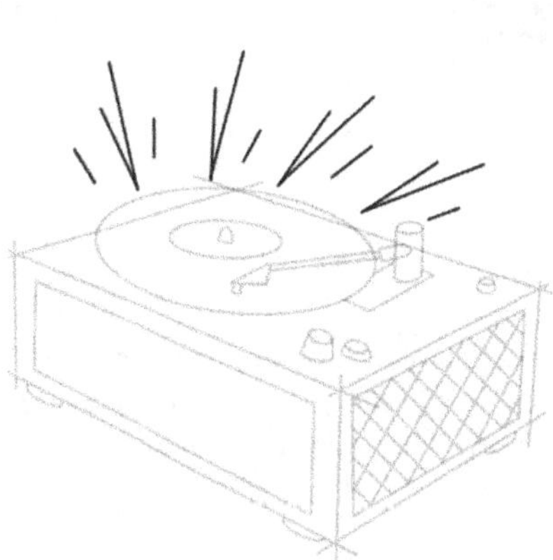

10

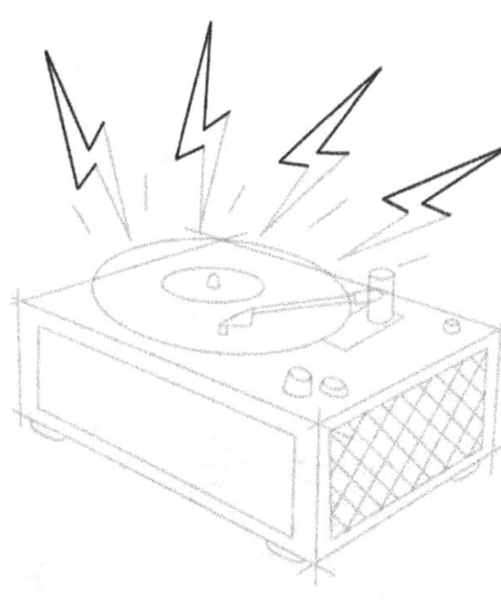

11

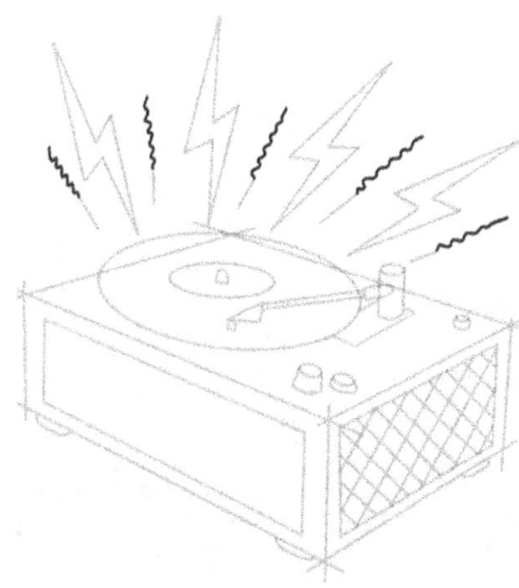

12

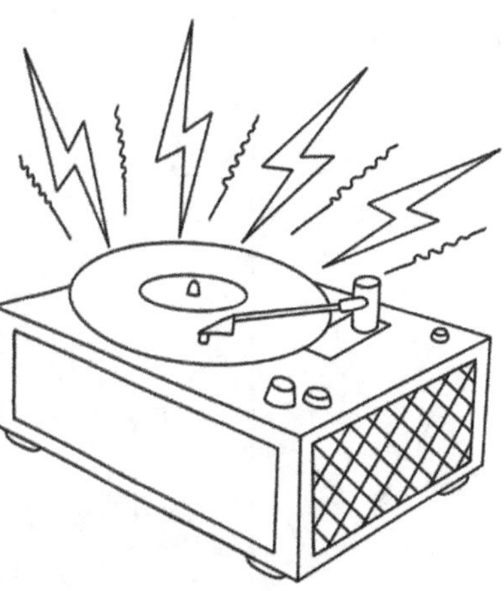

HOW TO DRAW PUNK THINGS

RIBCAGE HEART

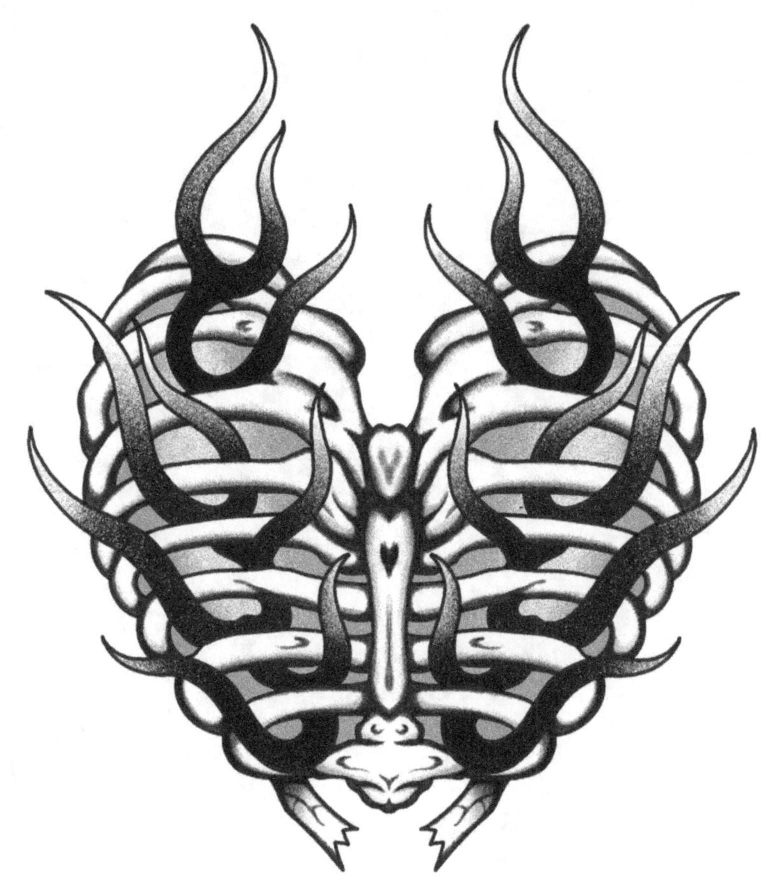

A raw symbol of exposed emotion and resilience, the ribcage heart represents punk's embrace of vulnerability as a form of strength and defiance.

01

02

03

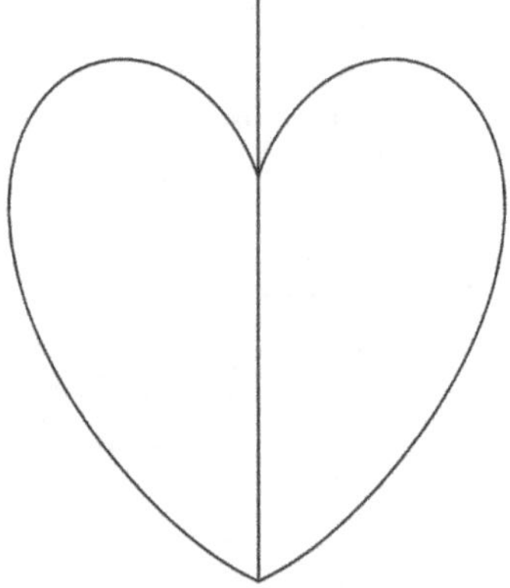

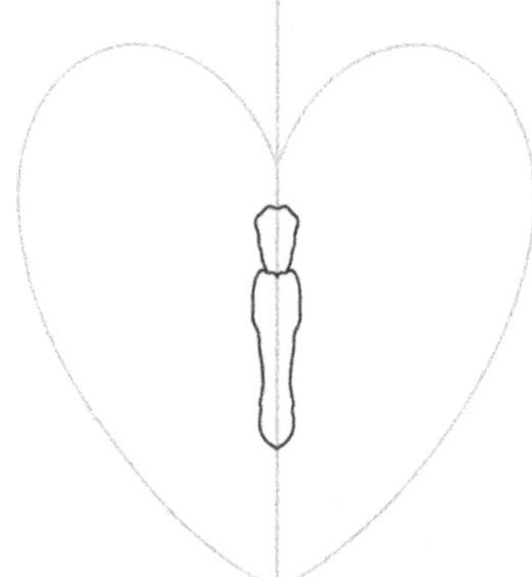

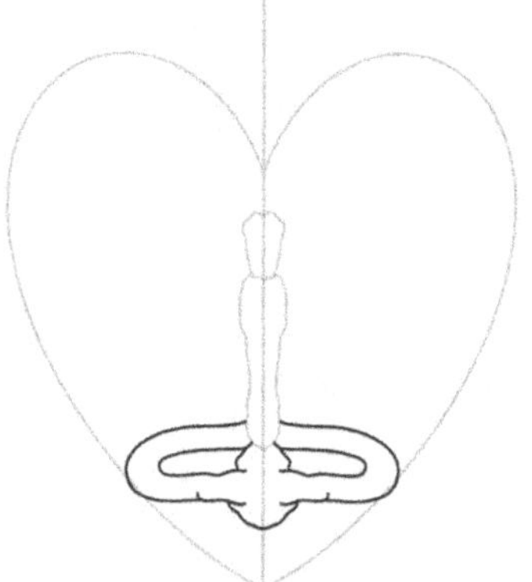

04

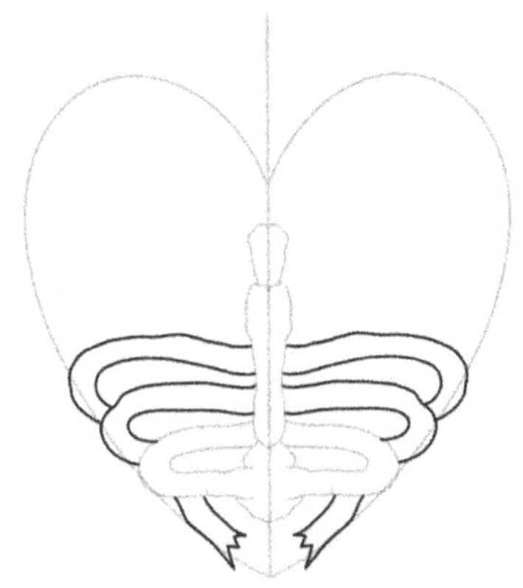

05

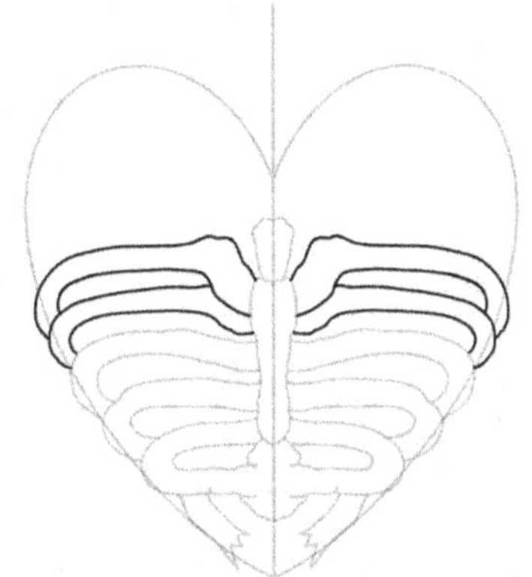

06

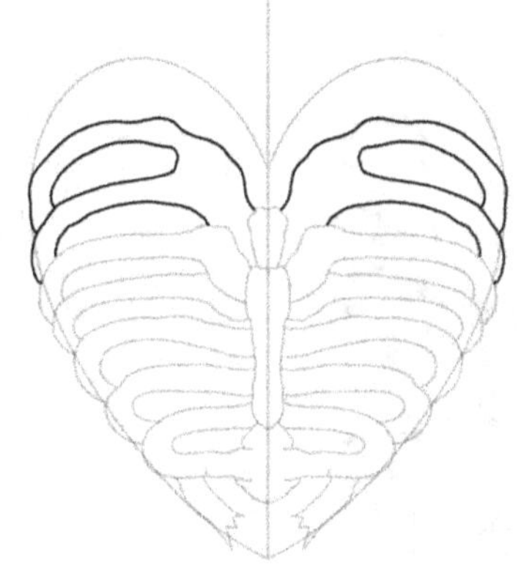

07

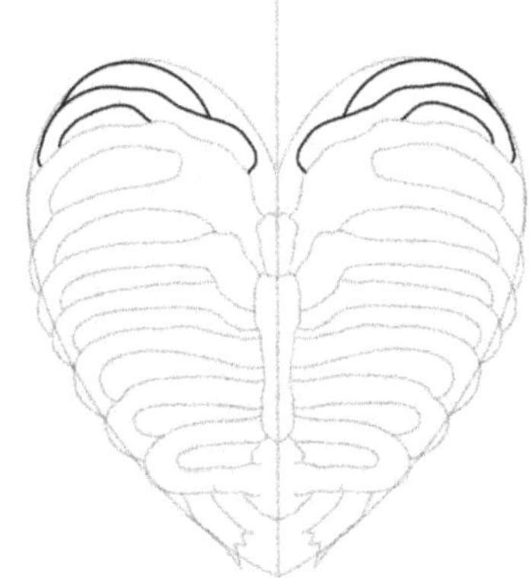

08

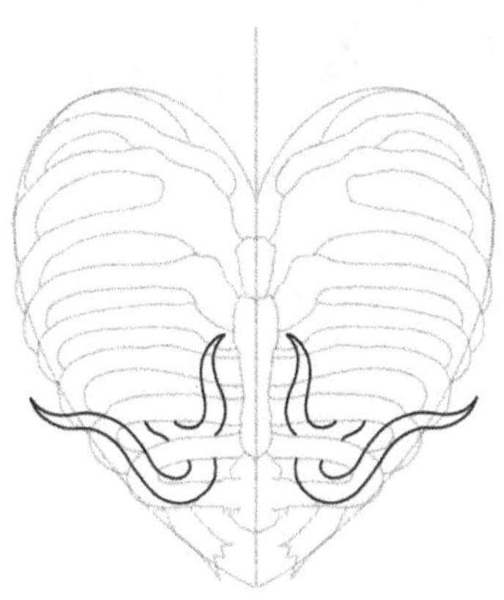

09

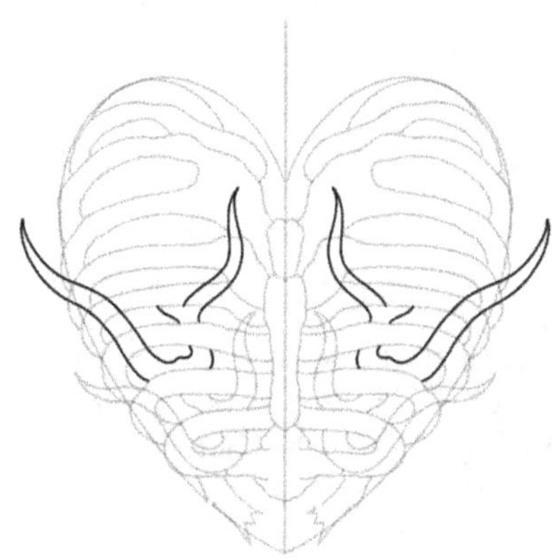

10

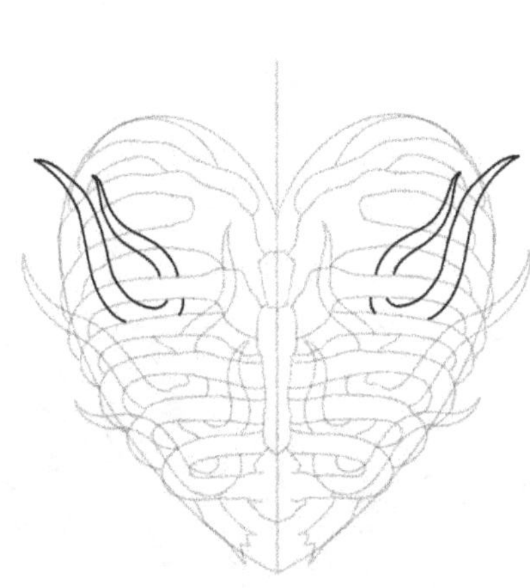

11

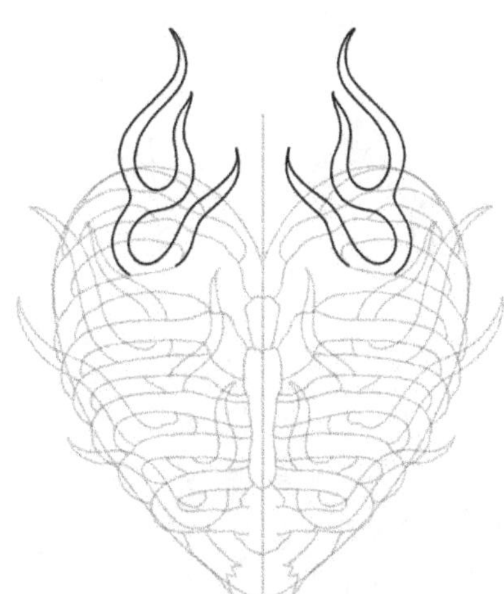

12

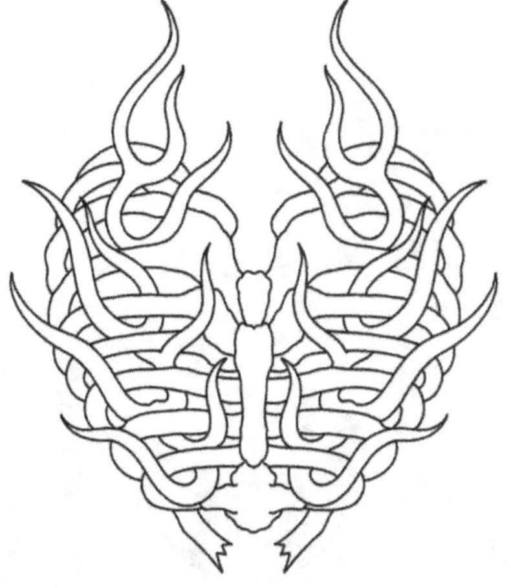

HOW TO DRAW PUNK THINGS

'ROCK ON' SKELETON HAND

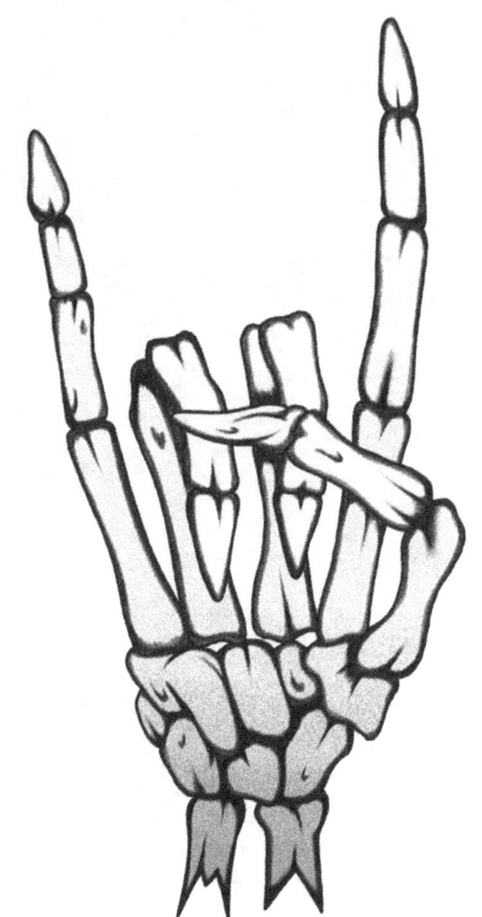

A gesture of solidarity and celebration, the 'rock on' skeleton hand symbolises punk's enduring connection to music and rebellion.

01   **02**   **03**

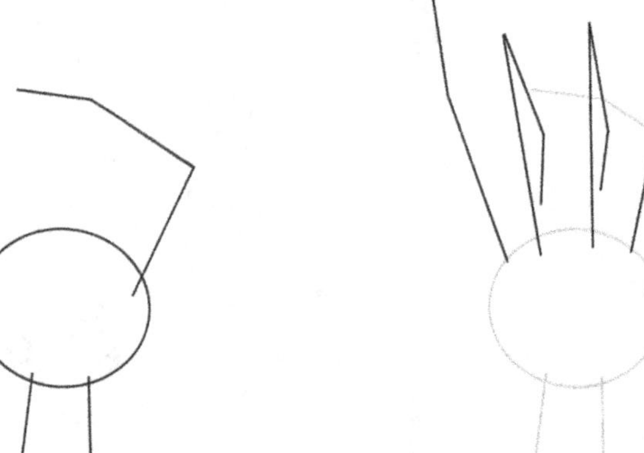

04

05

06

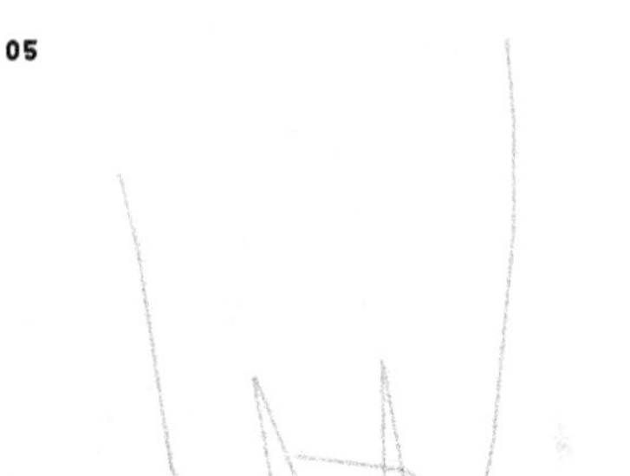

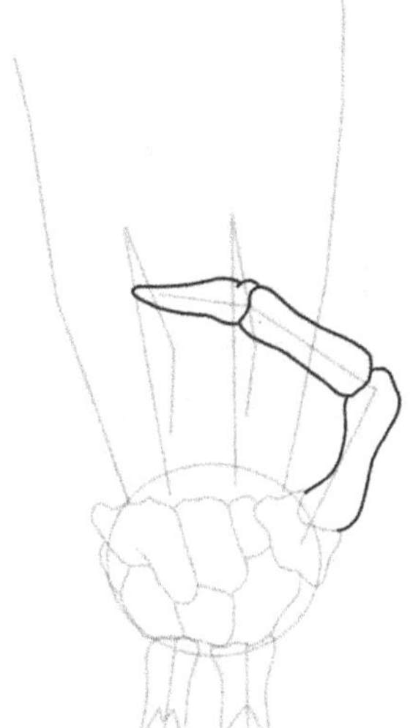

07

08

09

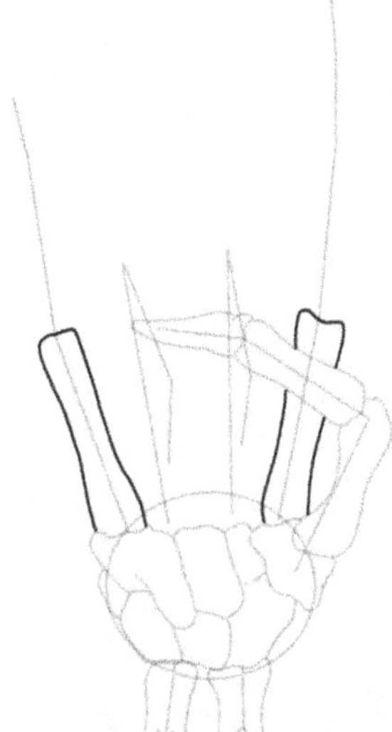

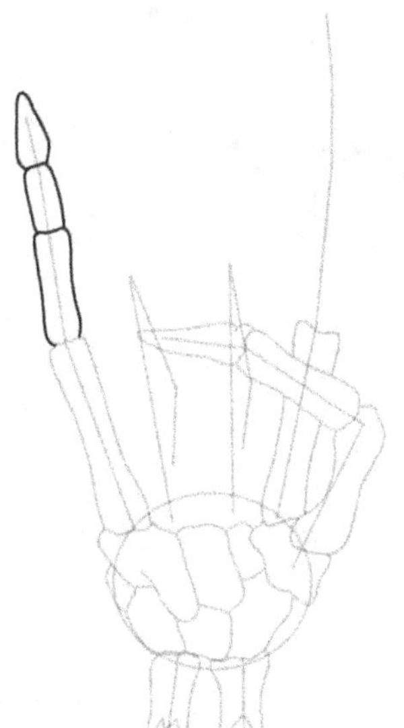

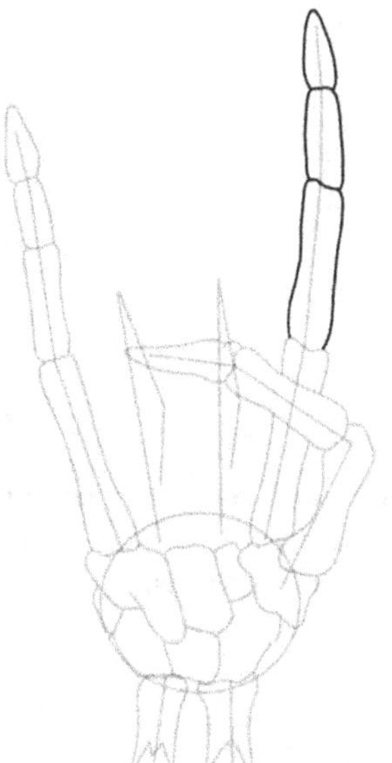

10

11

12

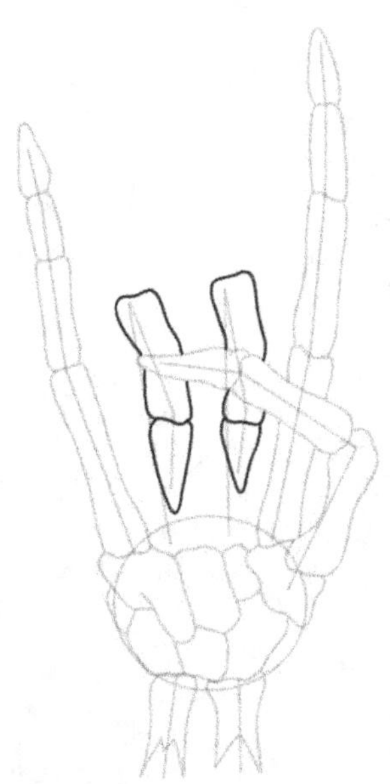

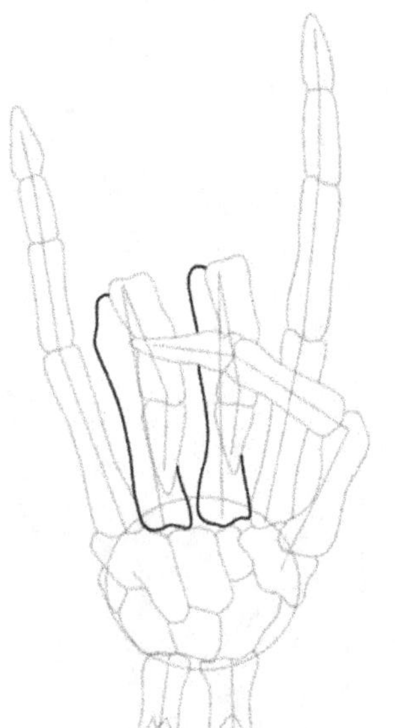

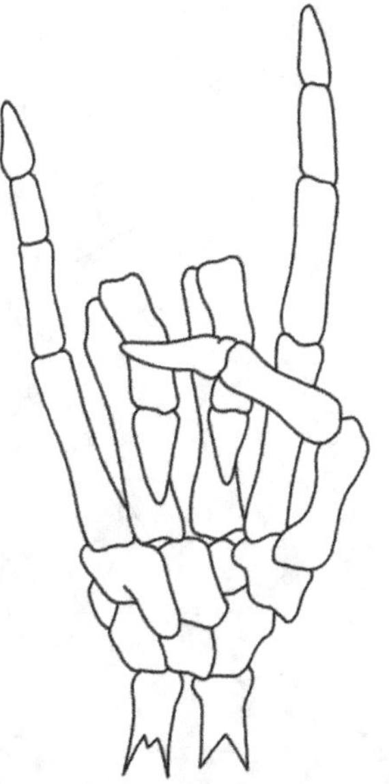

HOW TO DRAW PUNK THINGS

SAFETY PIN

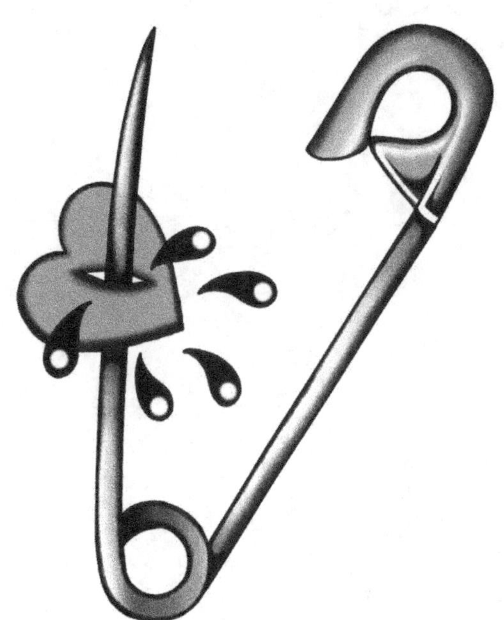

A cornerstone of DIY punk culture, the safety pin symbolises self-reliance, rebellion, and a bold statement of individuality.

01   **02**   **03**

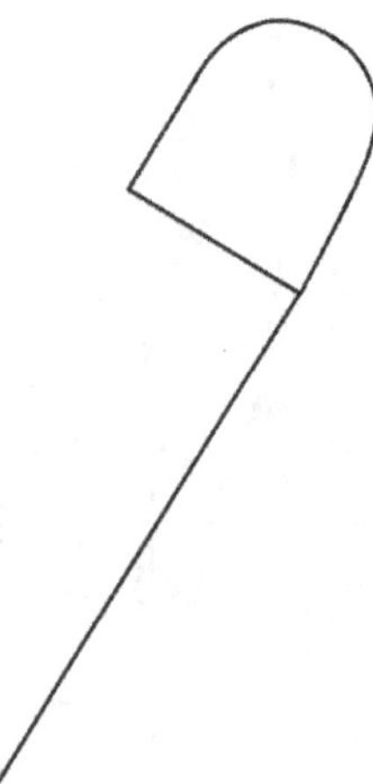

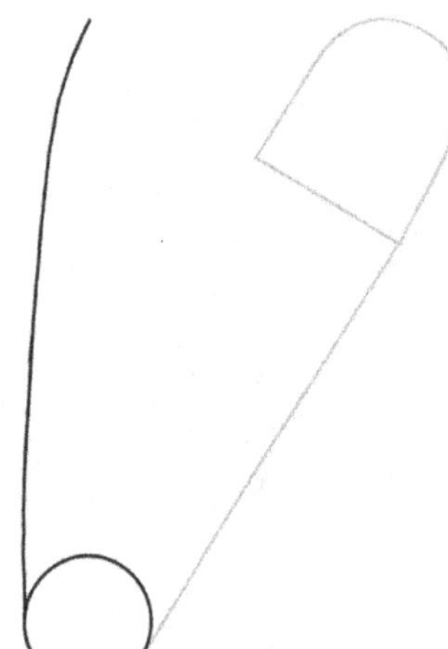

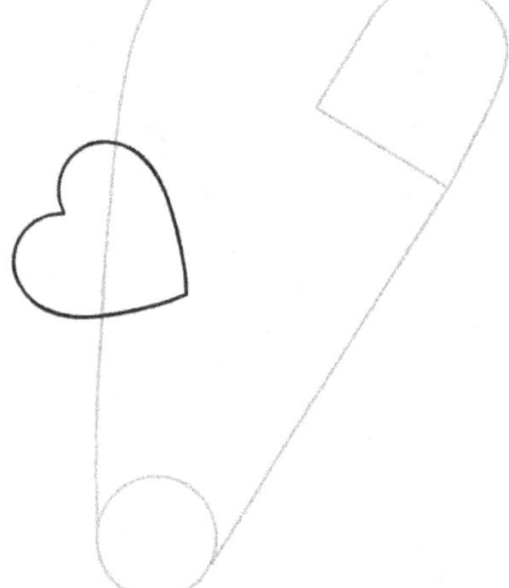

04

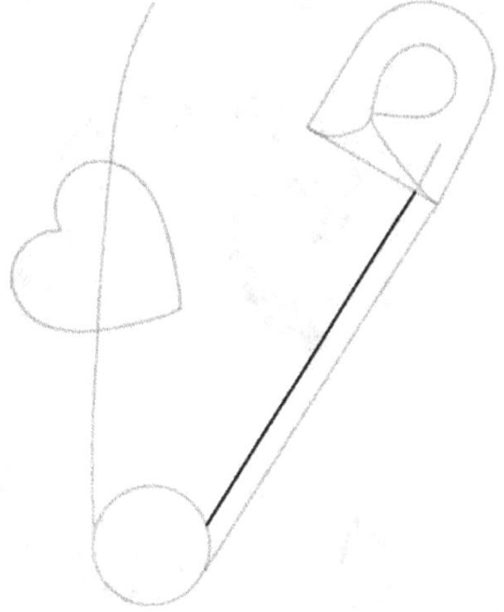

05

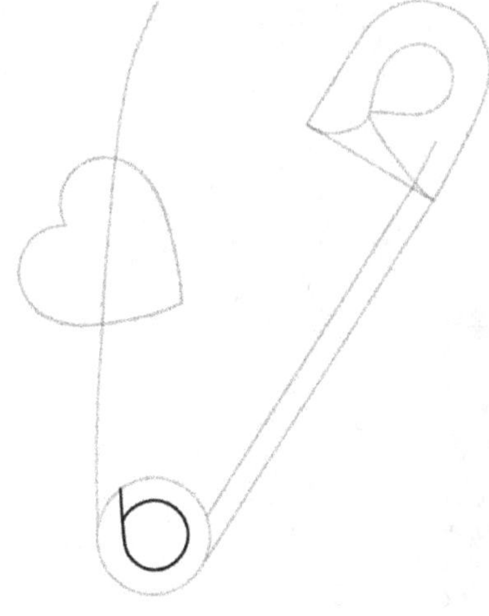

06

07

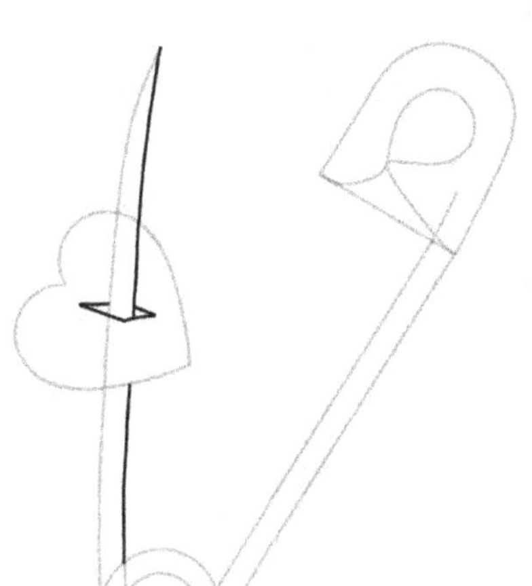

08

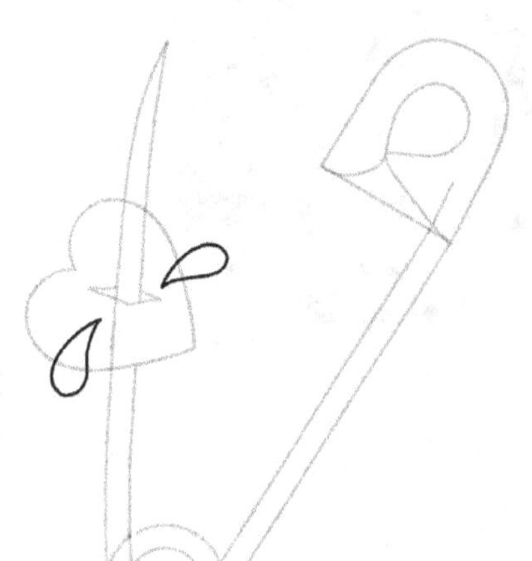

09

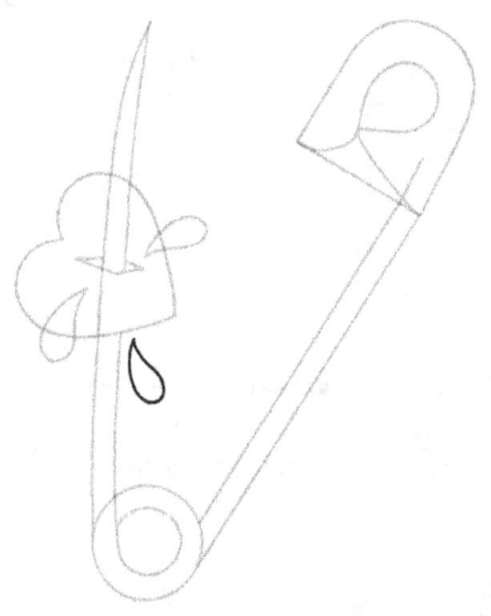

10

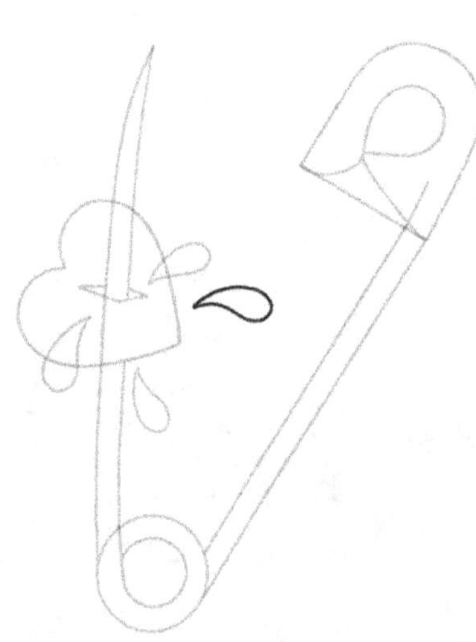

11

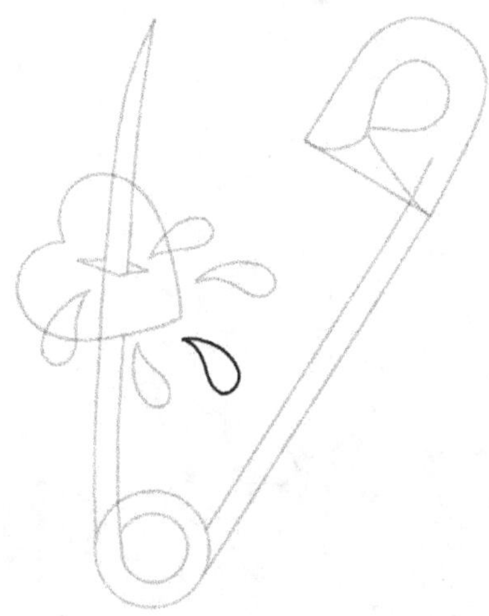

12

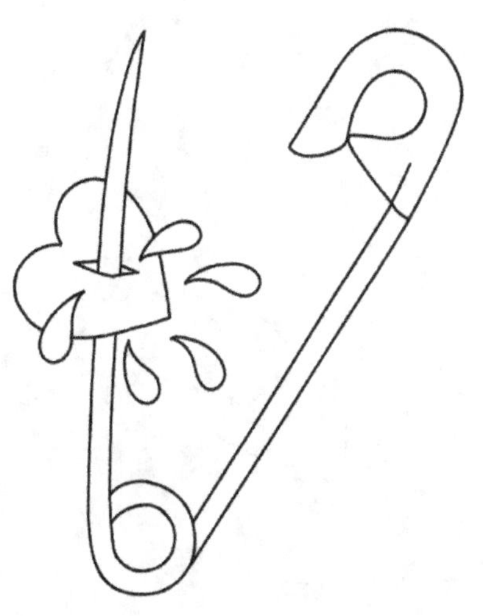

HOW TO DRAW PUNK THINGS

SCORPION

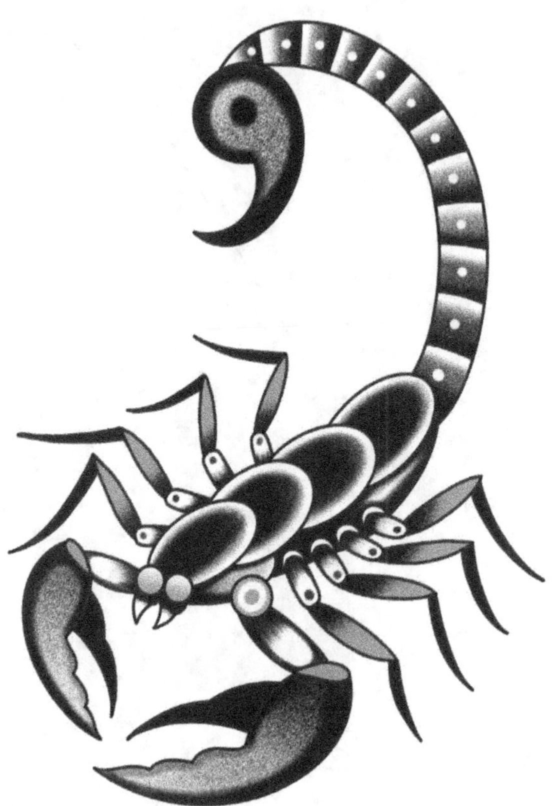

Representing danger and resilience, the
scorpion symbolises punk's fierce attitude and
readiness to strike when provoked.

01

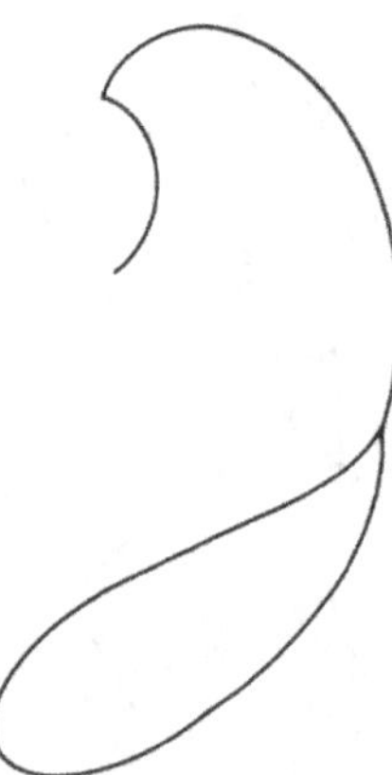

02

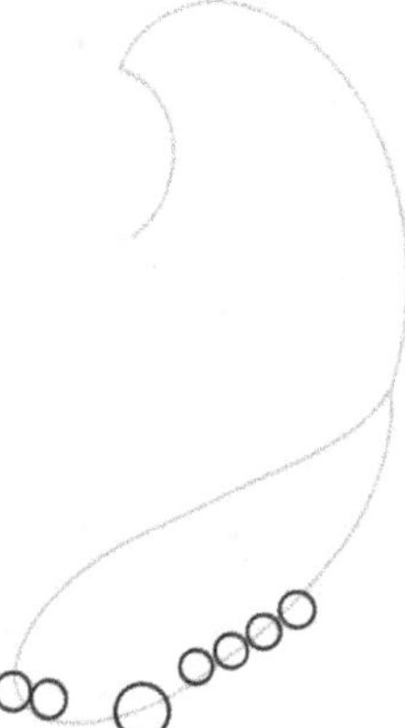

03

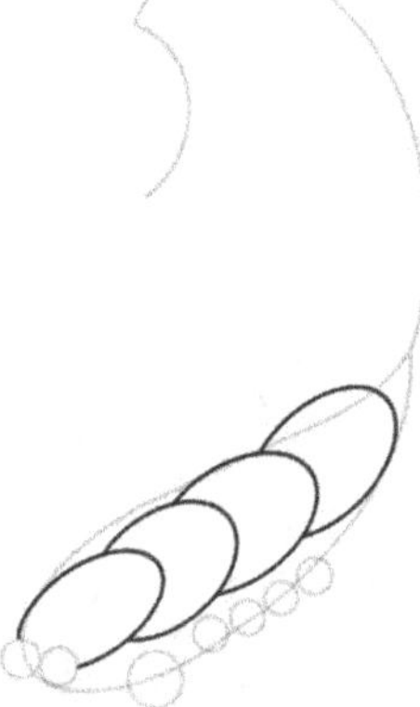

04

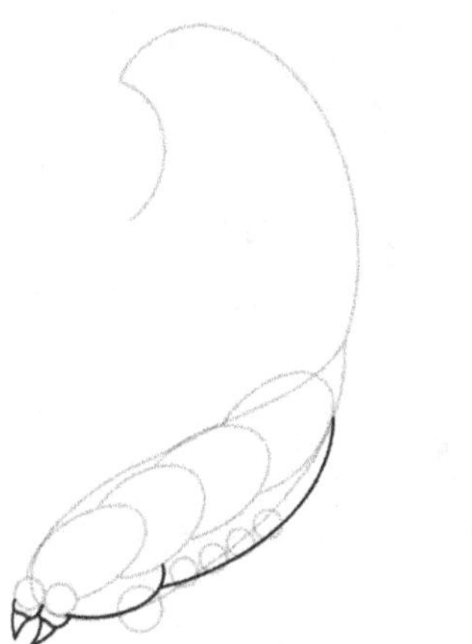

05

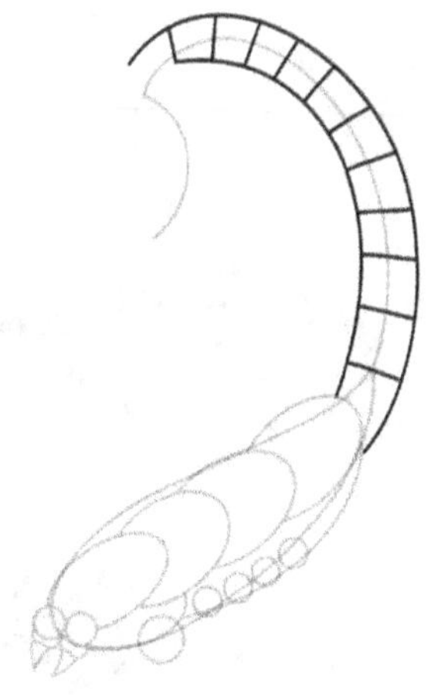

06

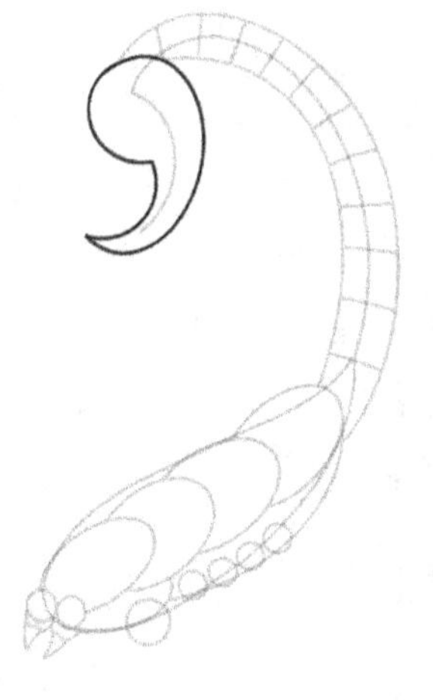

07

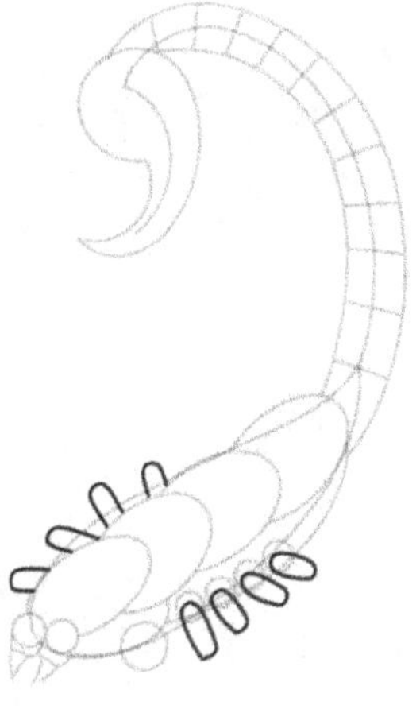

08

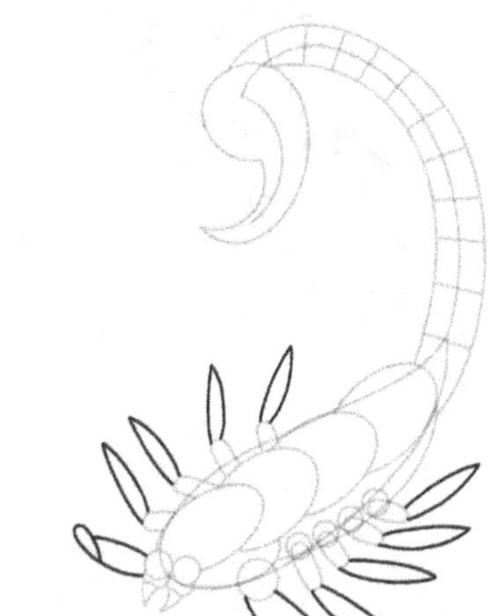

09

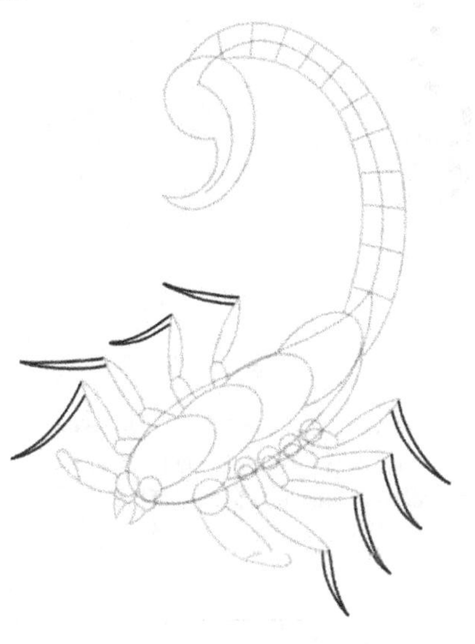

10

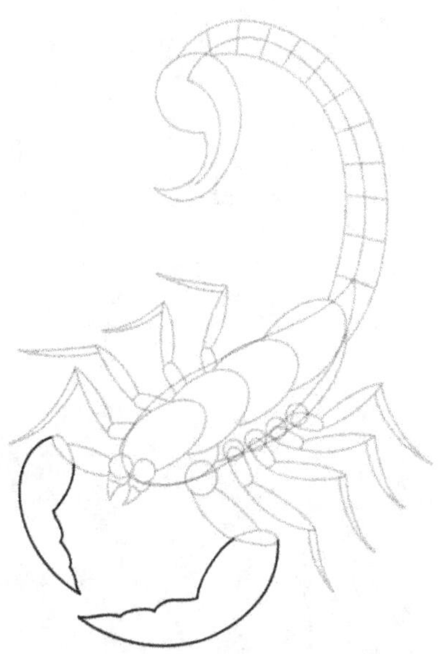

11

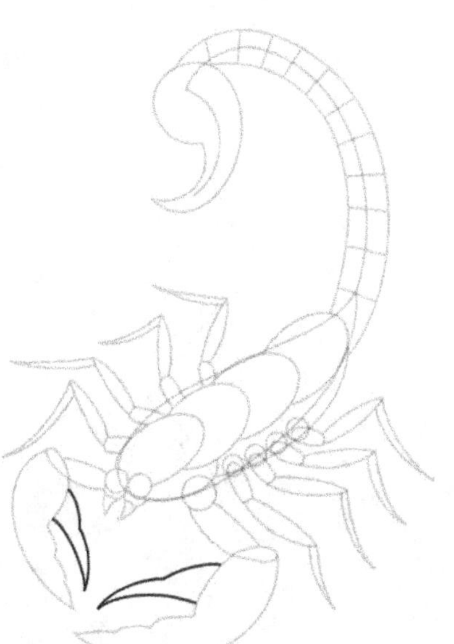

12

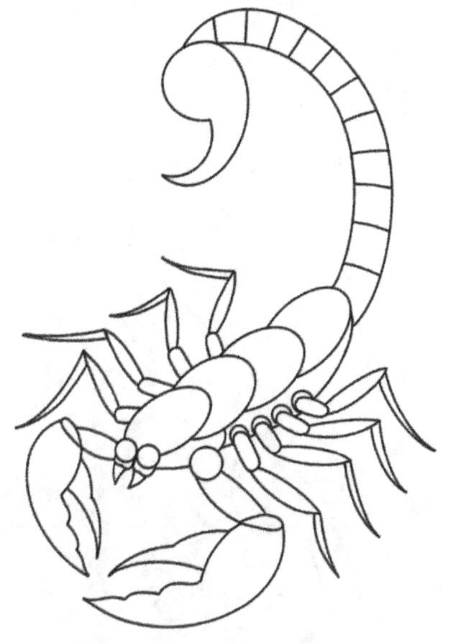

DEAD MAN'S DEAL

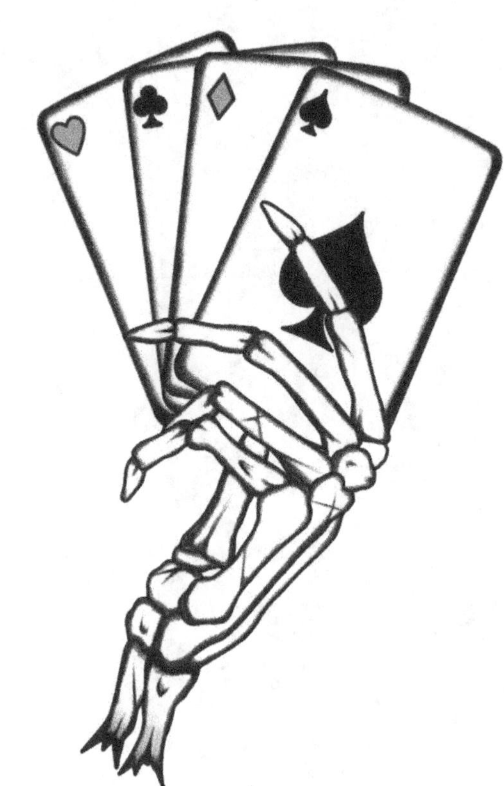

A symbol of calculated risk and embracing mortality, this icon reflects punk's fearless approach to life and rejection of fate.

01

02

03

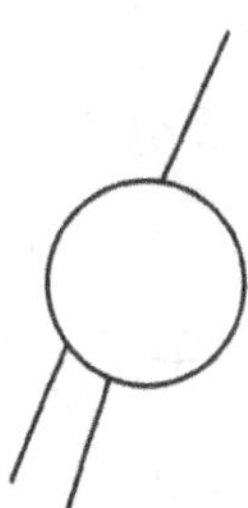

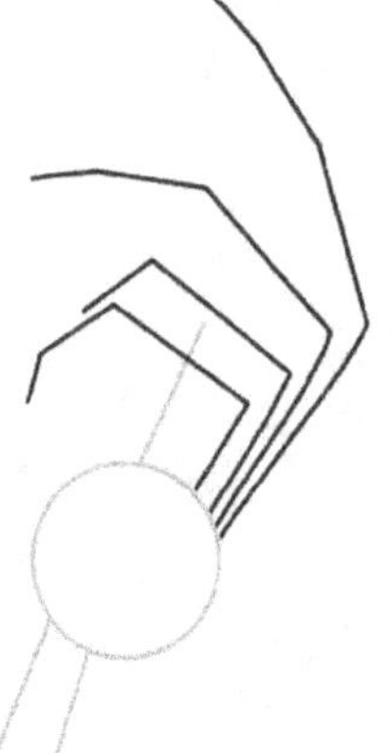

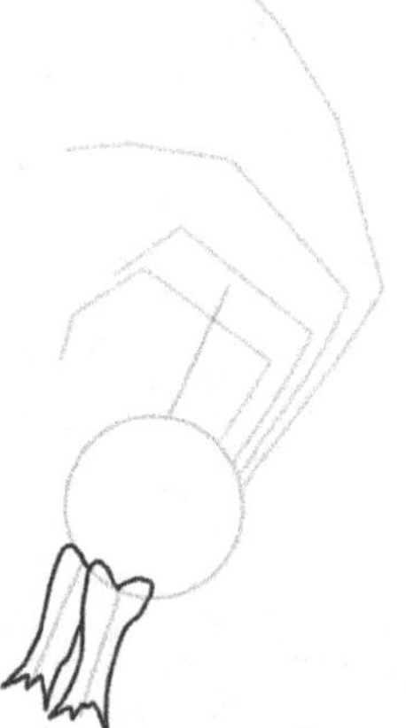

04

05

06

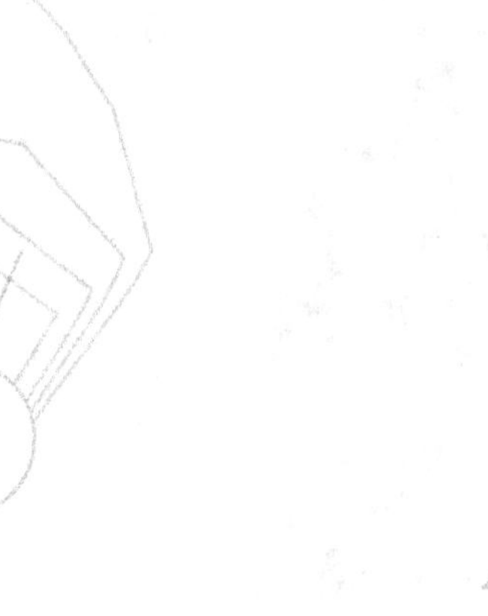
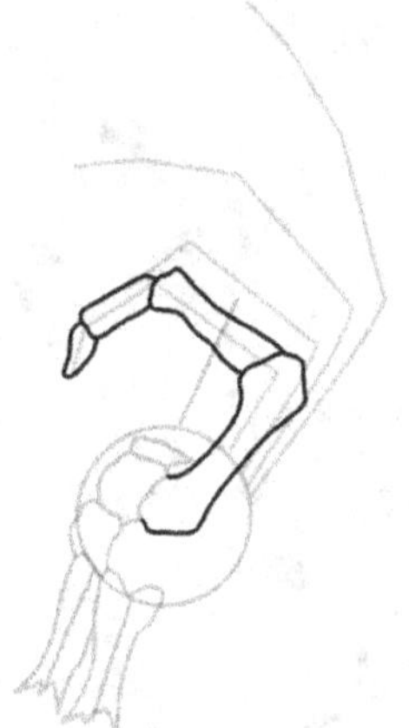
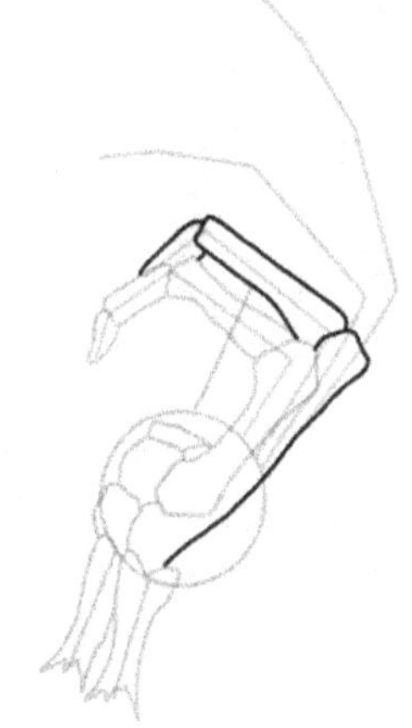

07

08

09

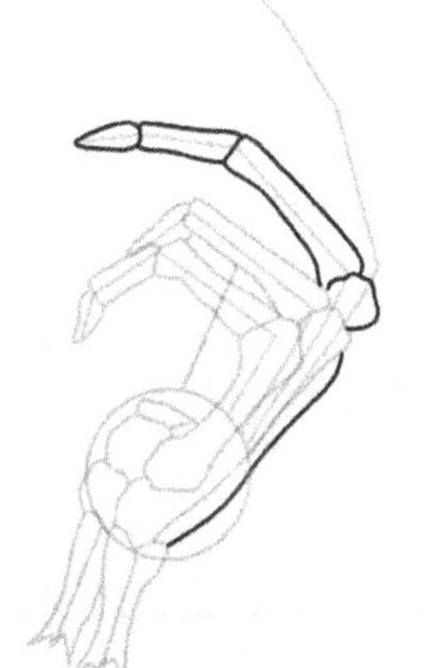
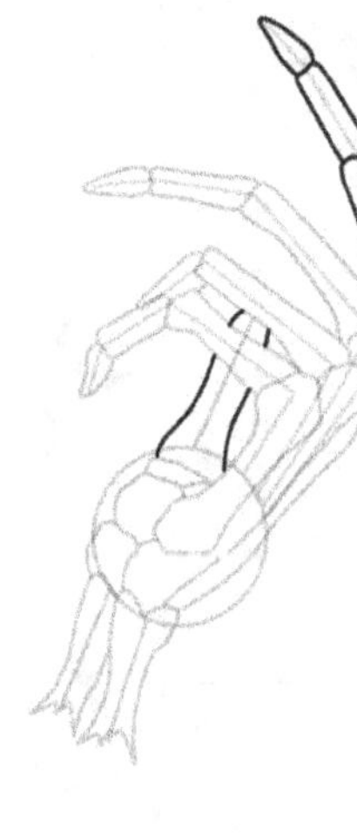
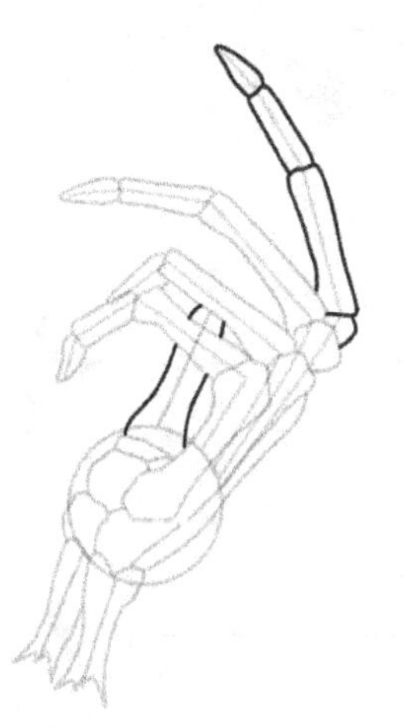

10

11

12

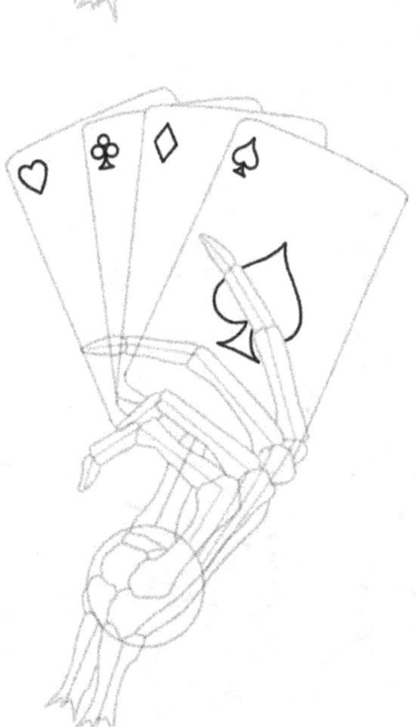
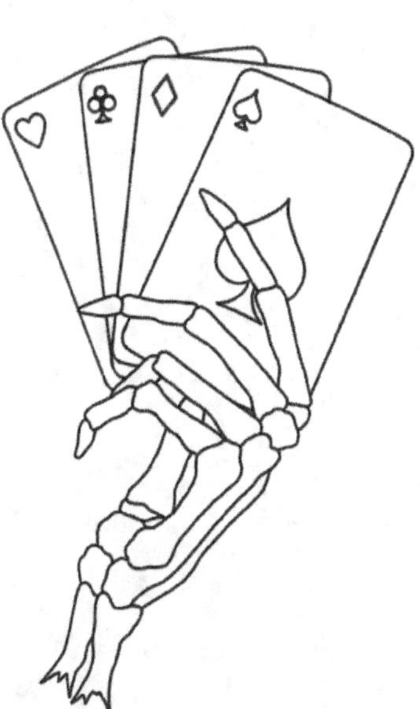

SKULL & CROSSBONES

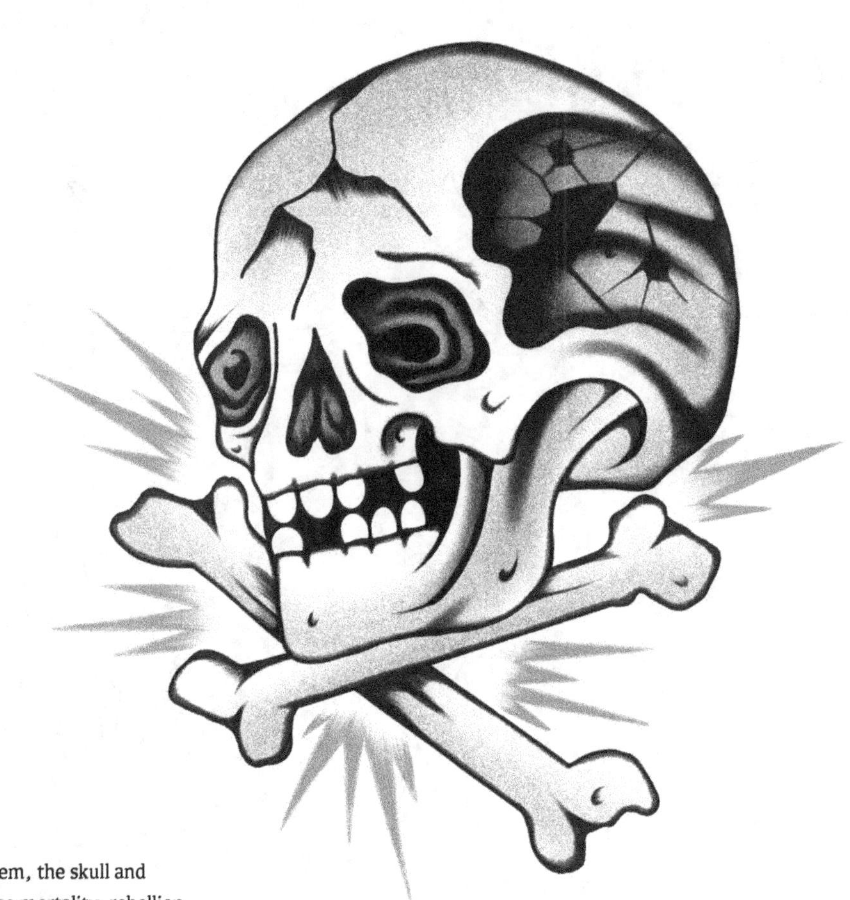

A classic punk emblem, the skull and crossbones symbolise mortality, rebellion, and defiance against authority.

01

02

03

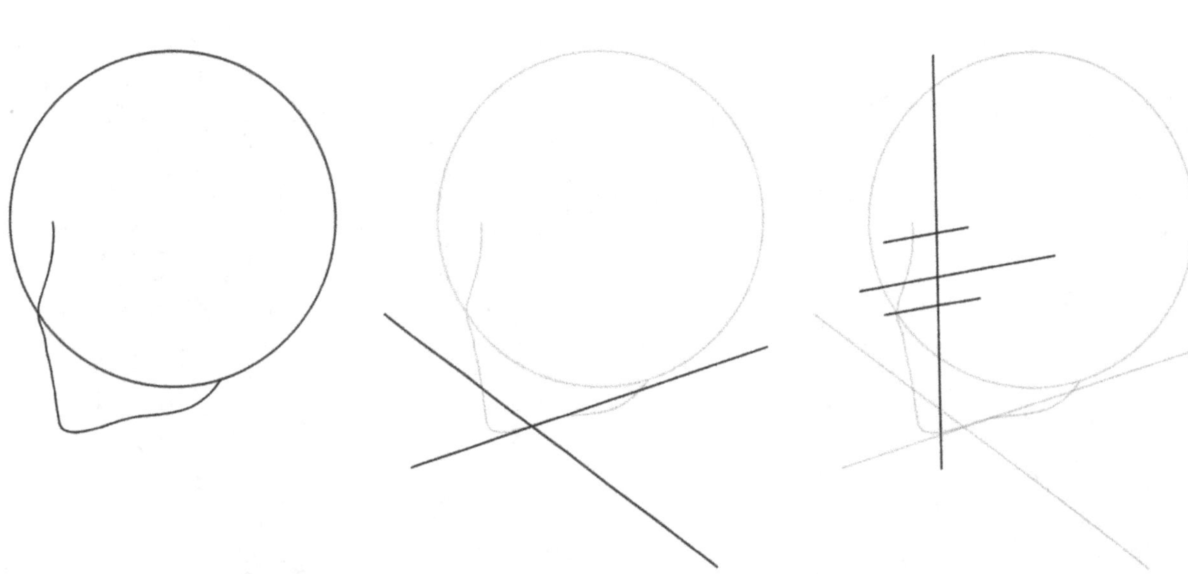

04

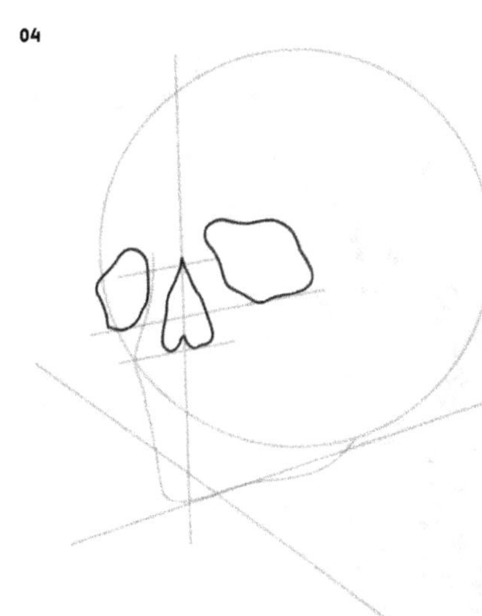

05

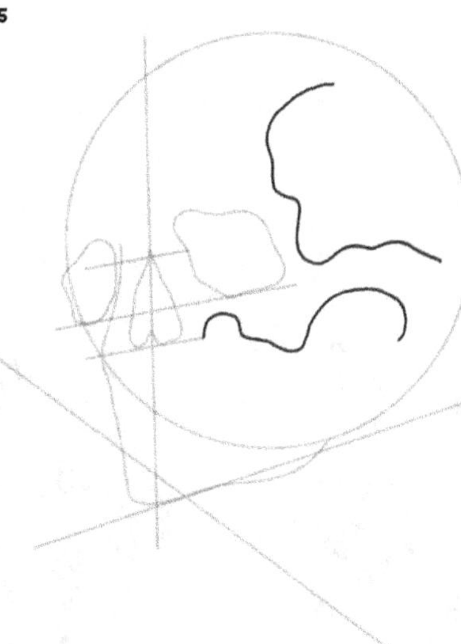

06

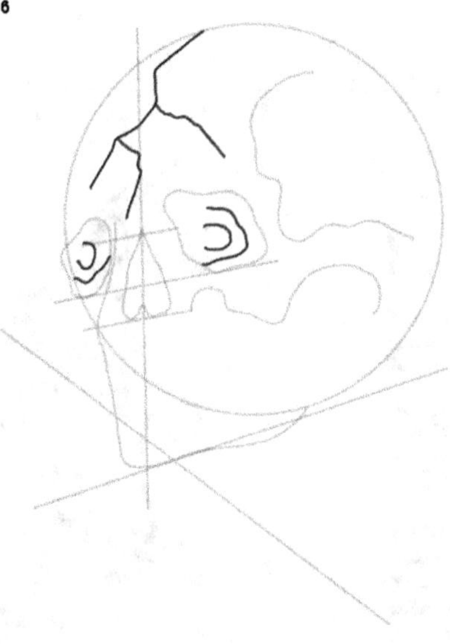

07

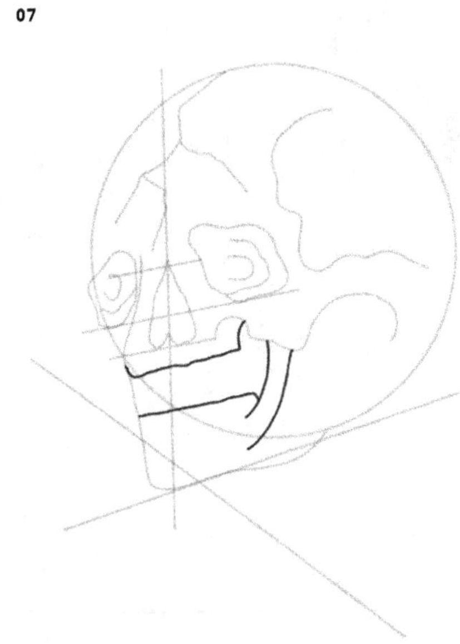

08

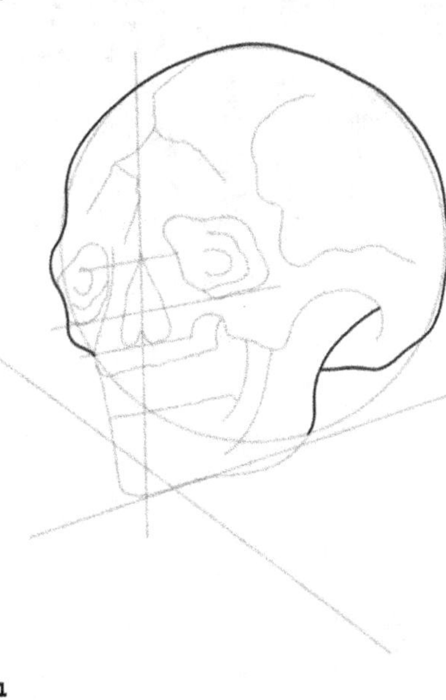

09

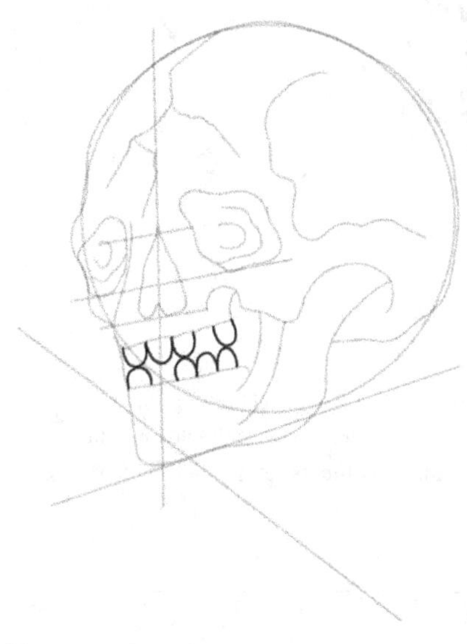

10

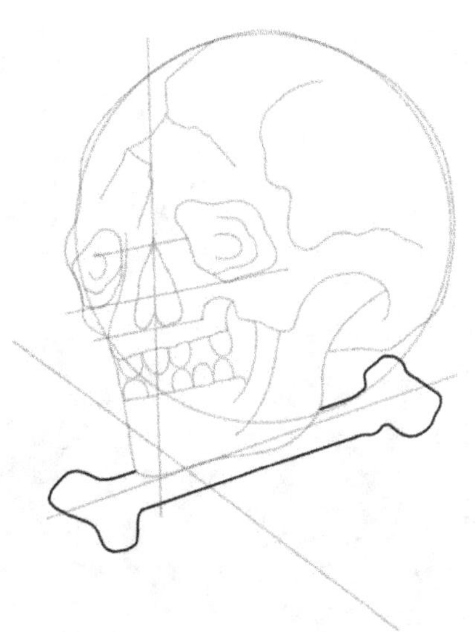

11

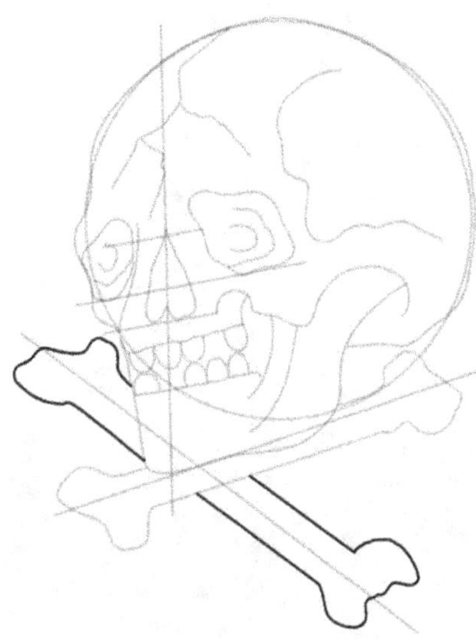

12

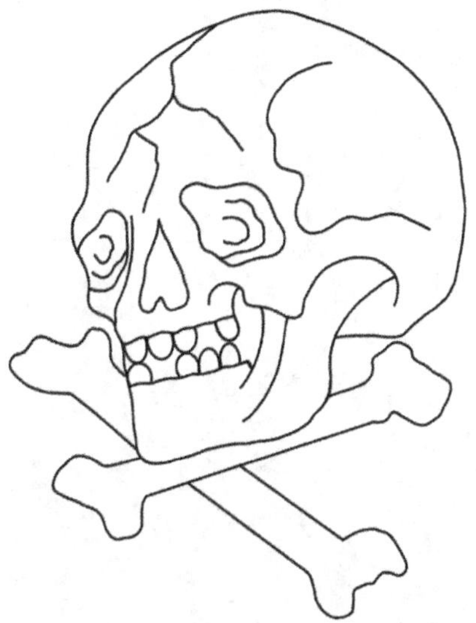

WINGED SKULL

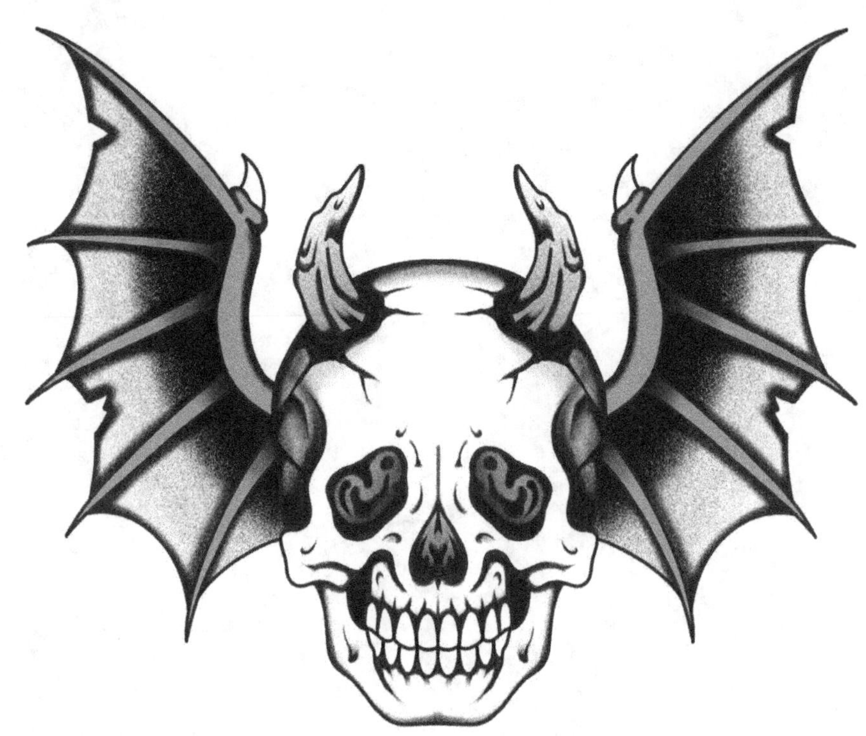

A symbol of freedom and rebellion, the
winged skull reflects punk's defiance of
limitations and its soaring, independent spirit.

01

02

03

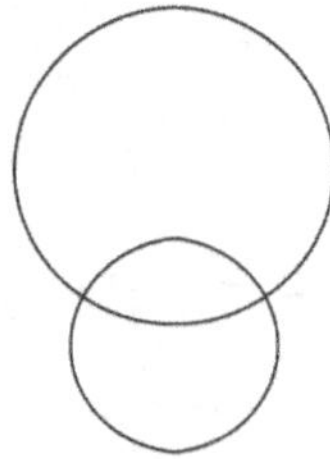

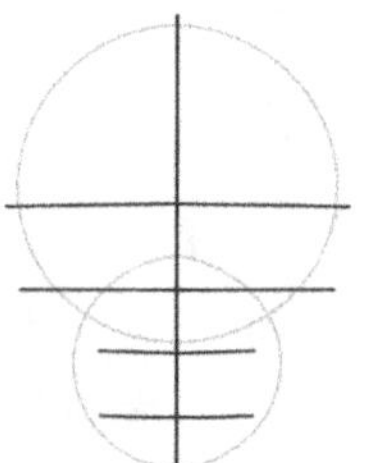

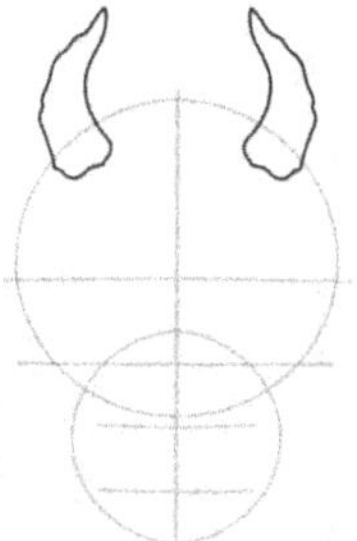

04

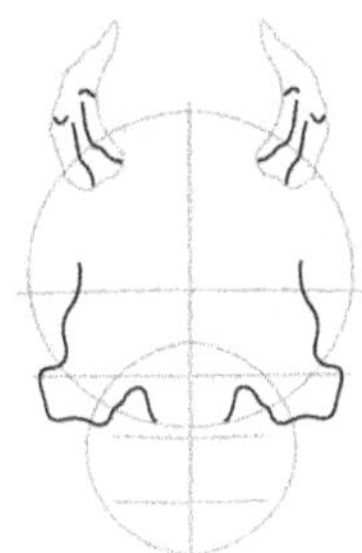

05

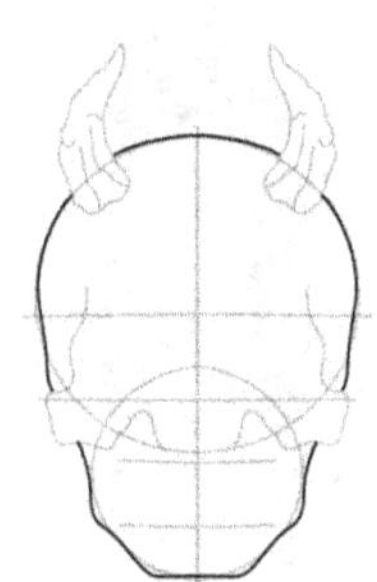

06

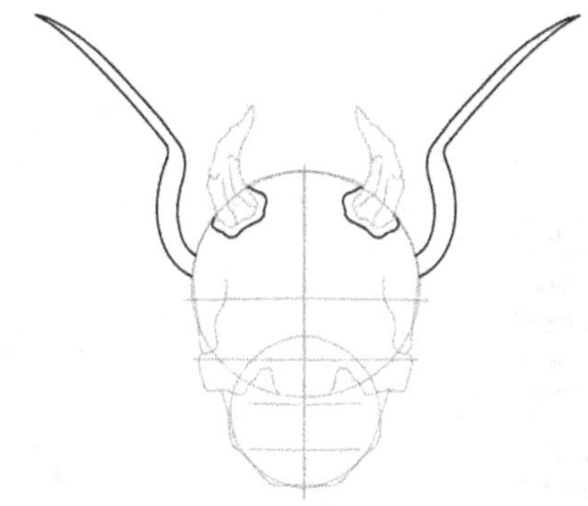

07

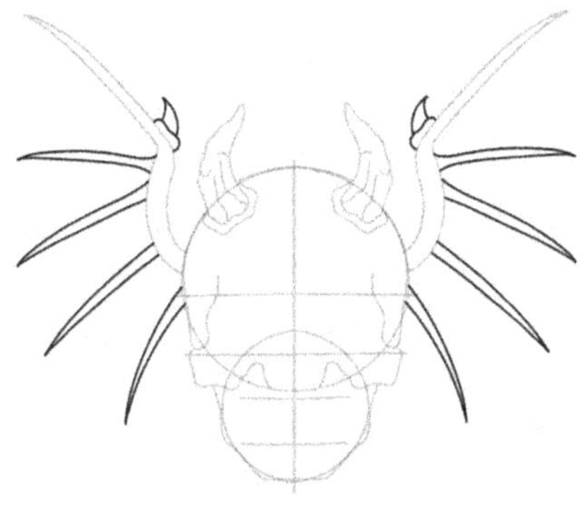

08

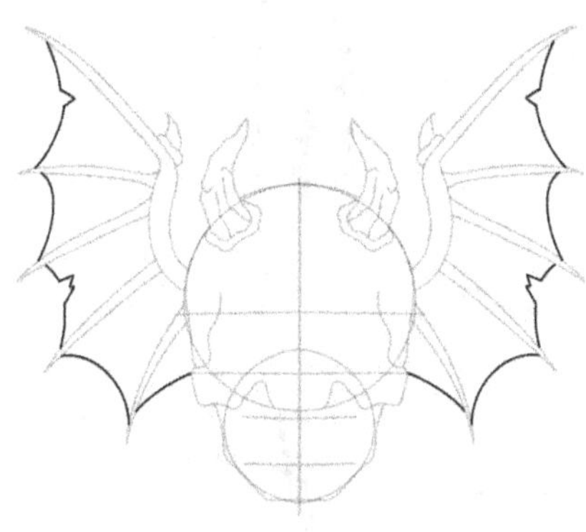

09

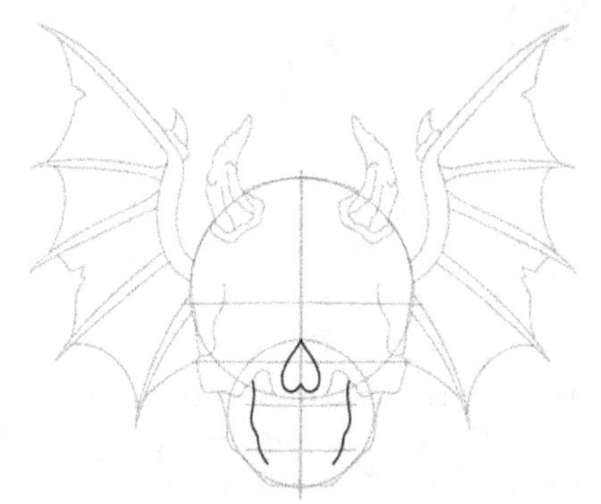

10

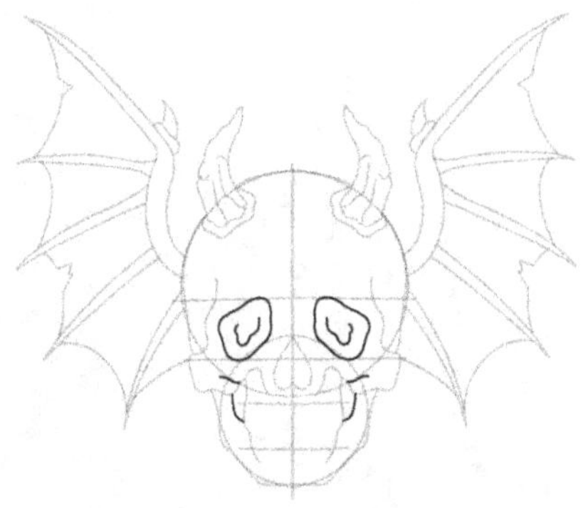

11

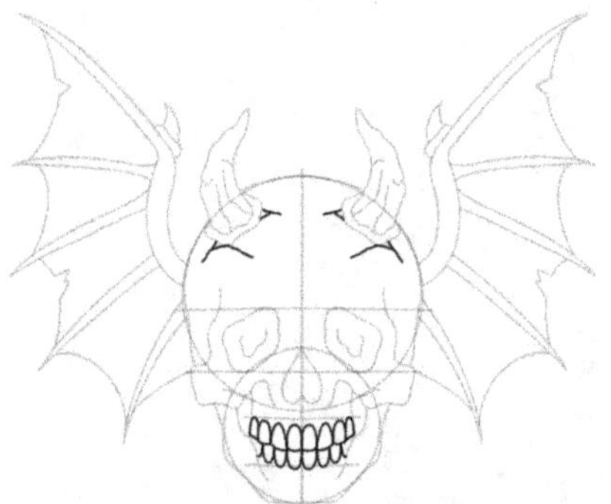

12

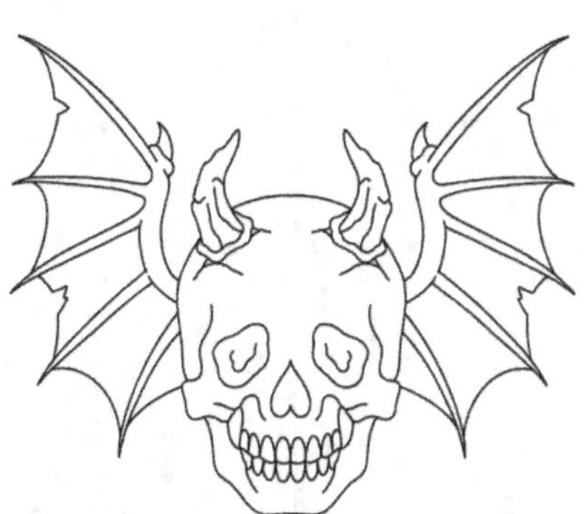

SWITCHBLADE

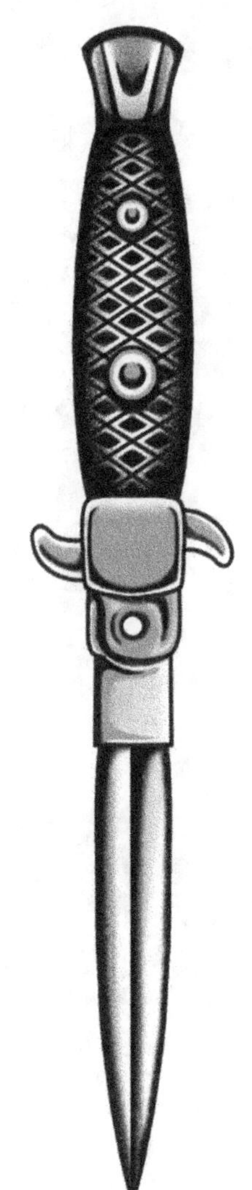

A sharp emblem of danger and rebellion, the switchblade embodies punk's raw edge, self-defence, and refusal to back down.

01　　　　　　　　　　　**02**　　　　　　　　　　　**03**

04

05

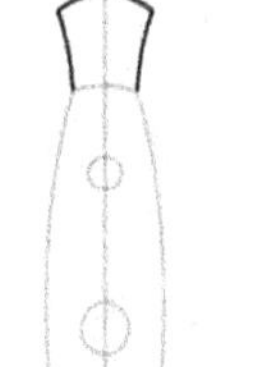

06

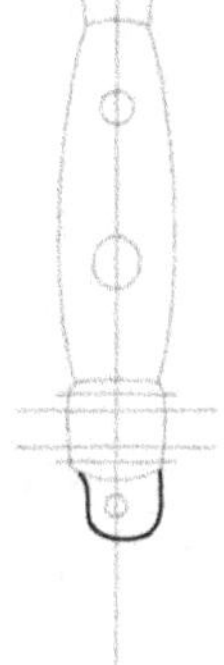

07

08

09

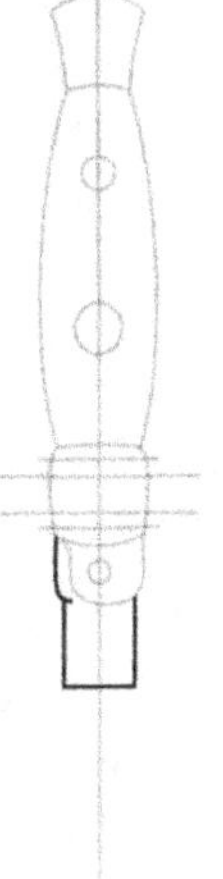

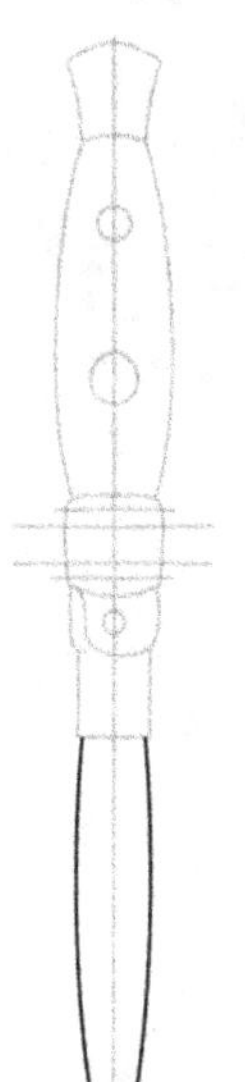

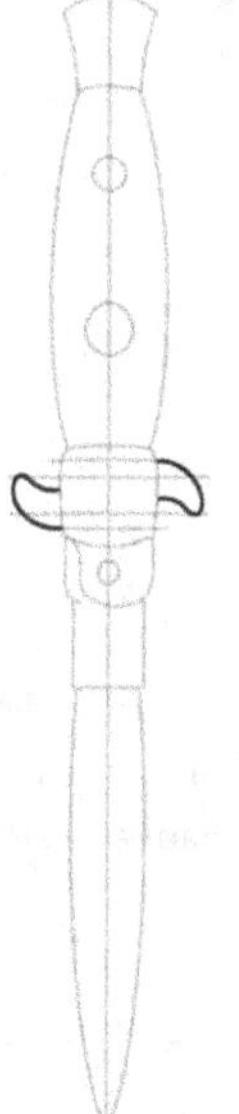

10

11

12

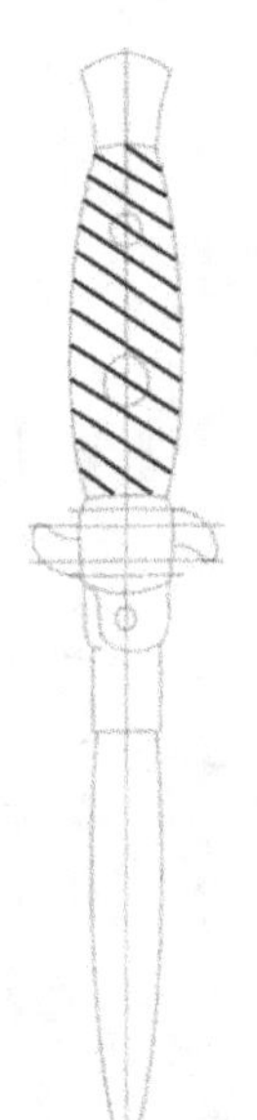

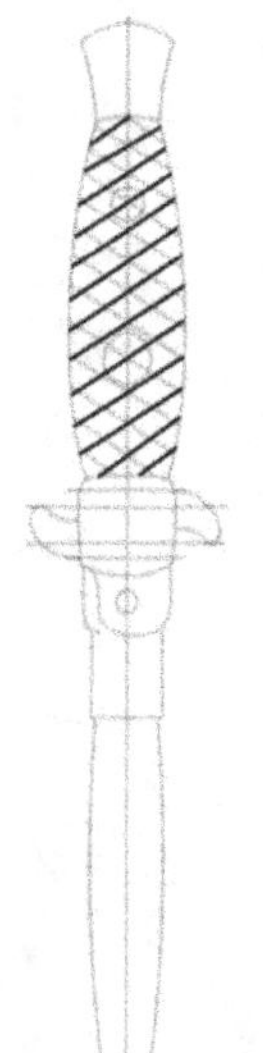

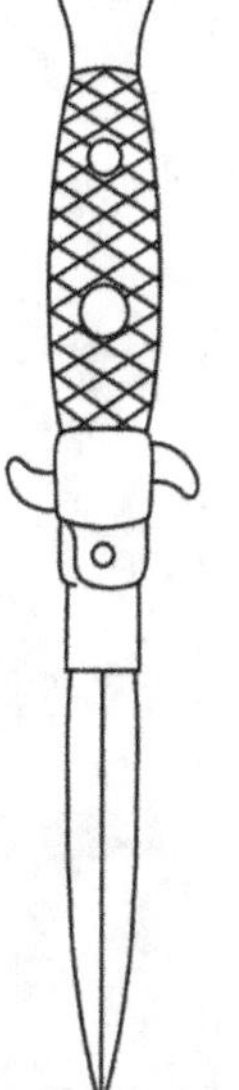

HOW TO DRAW PUNK THINGS

CHECKERBOARD SLIP-ON

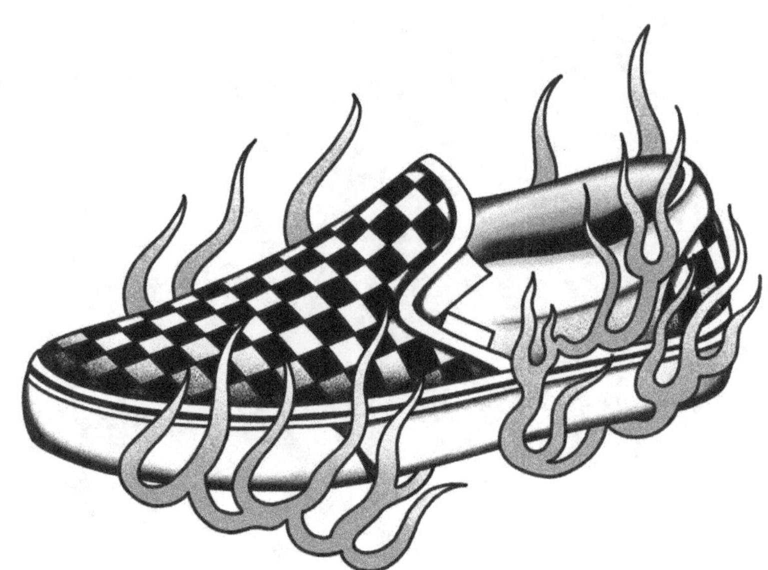

A nod to ska-punk culture, these shoes
symbolise punk's playful irreverence, unity,
and roots in alternative music scenes.

01   02   03

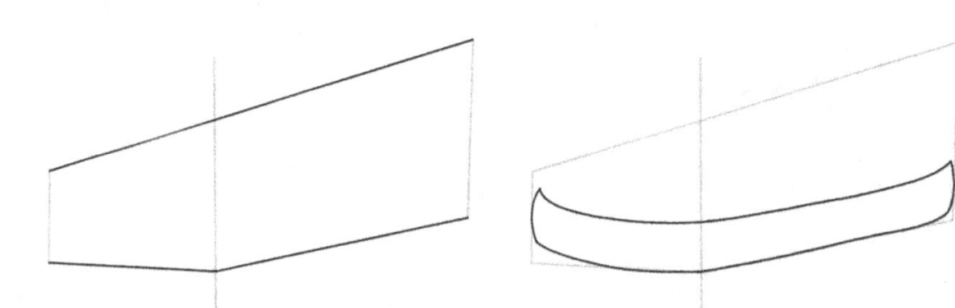

04

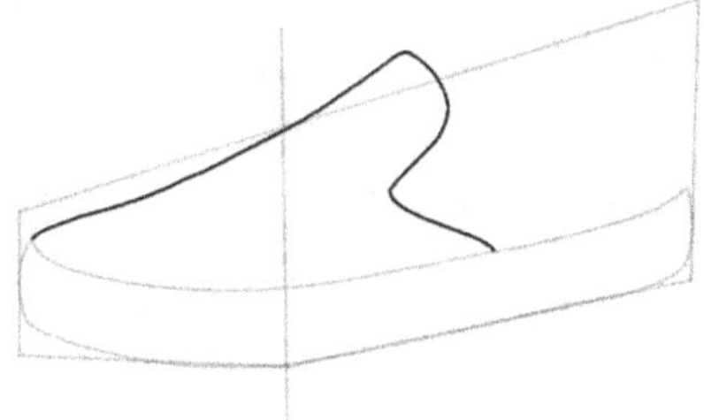

05

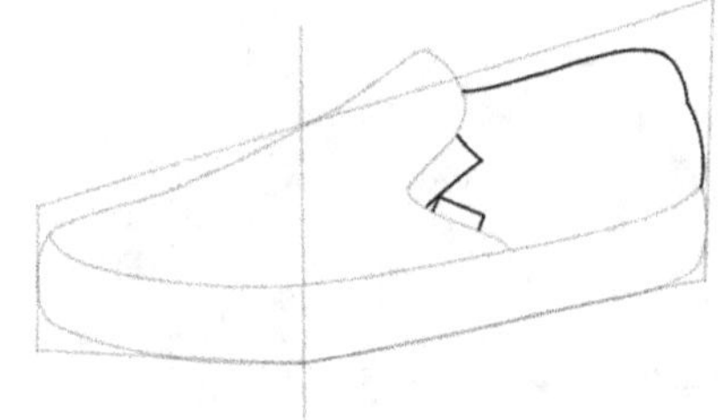

06

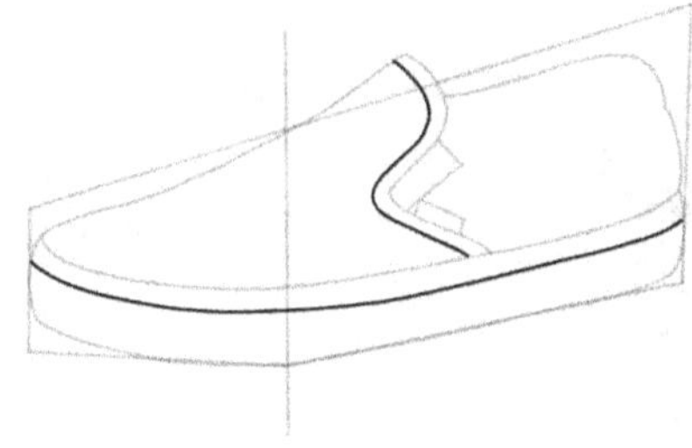

07

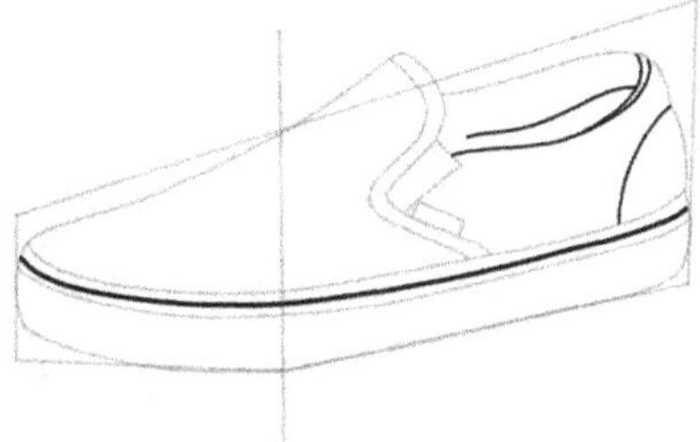

08

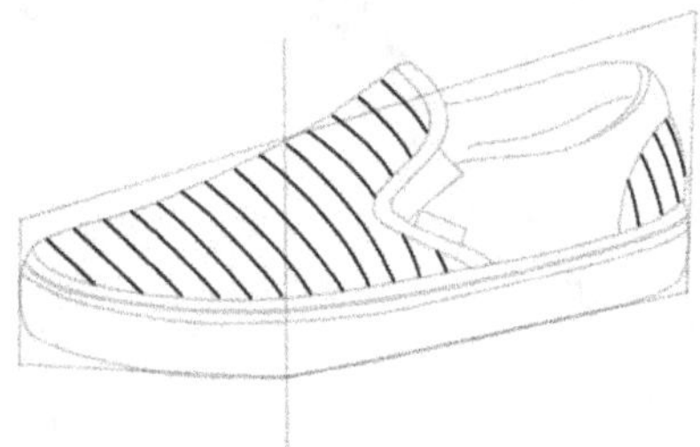

09

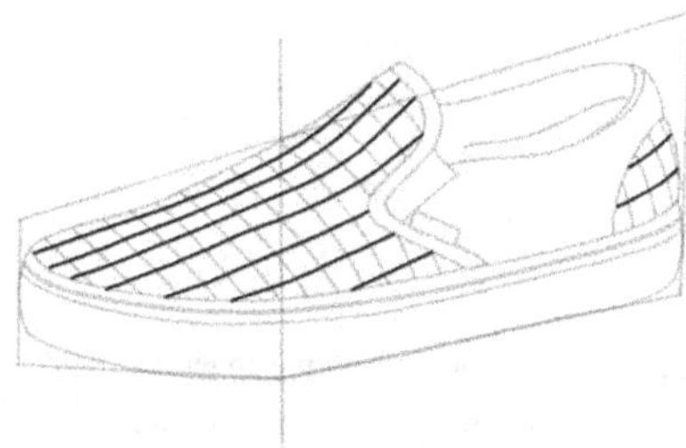

10

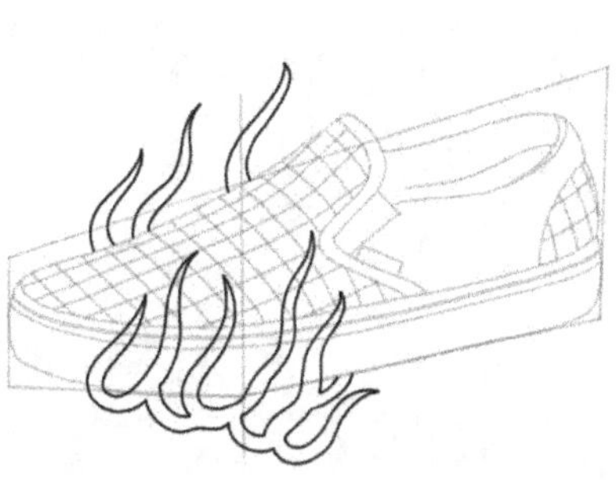

11

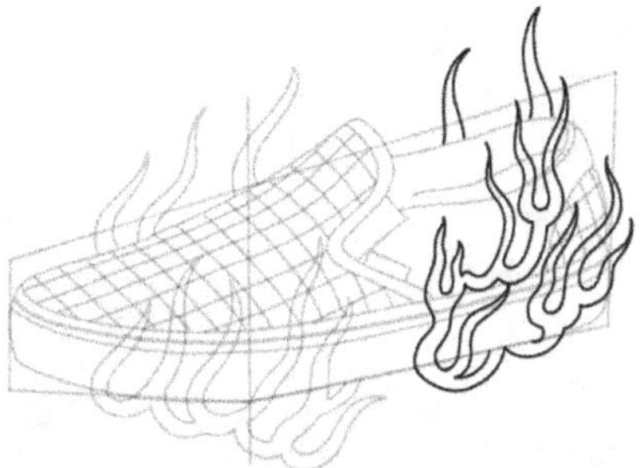

12

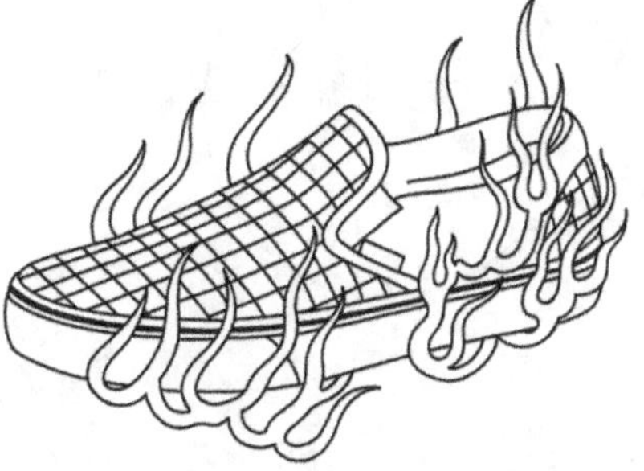

HOW TO DRAW PUNK THINGS

WILTED ROSE

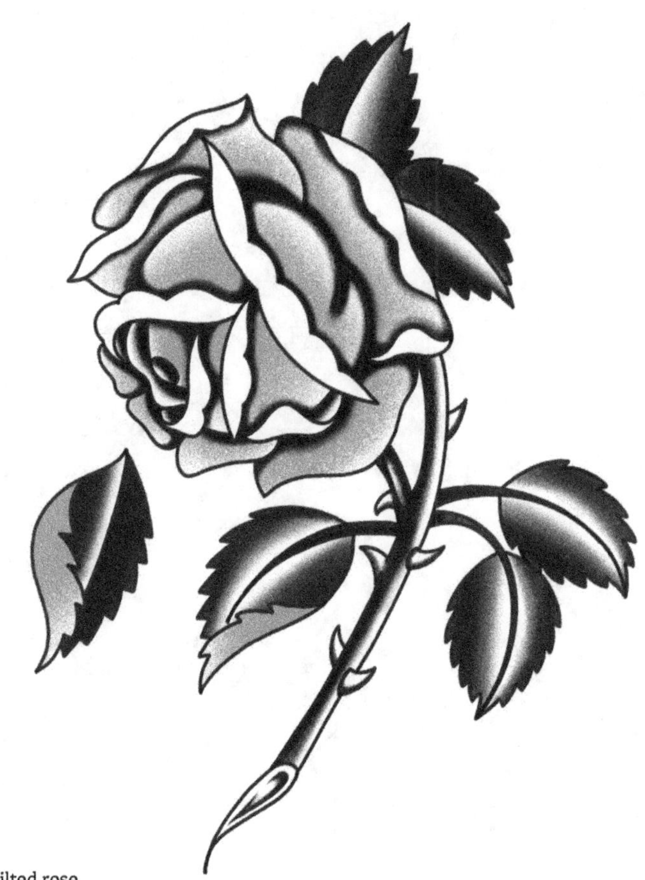

A symbol of beauty in decay, the wilted rose
reflects punk's romanticism of imperfection
and rejection of polished ideals.

01

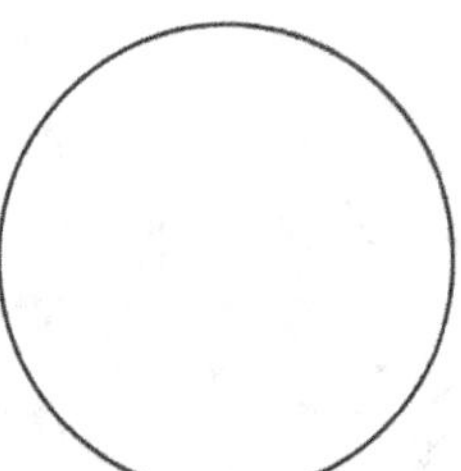

02

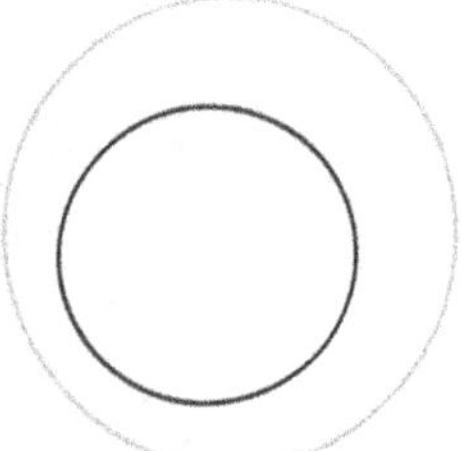

03

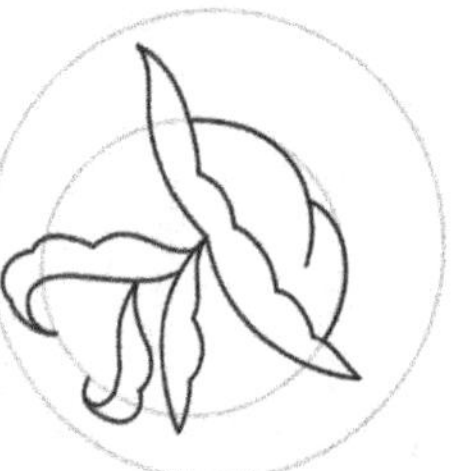

04

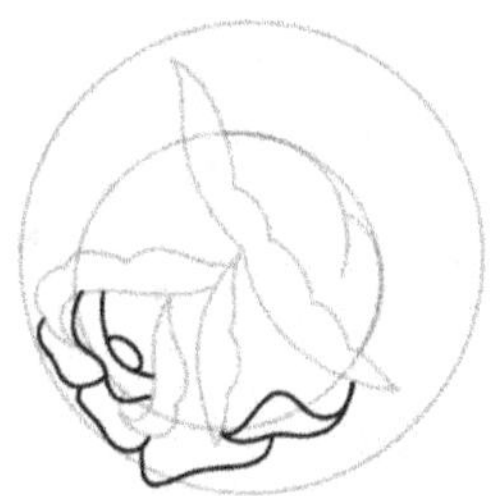

05

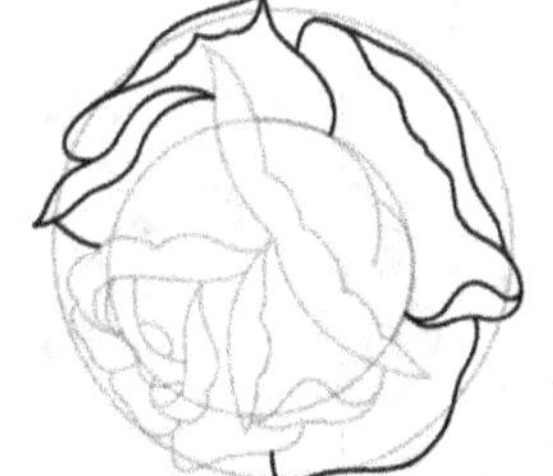

06

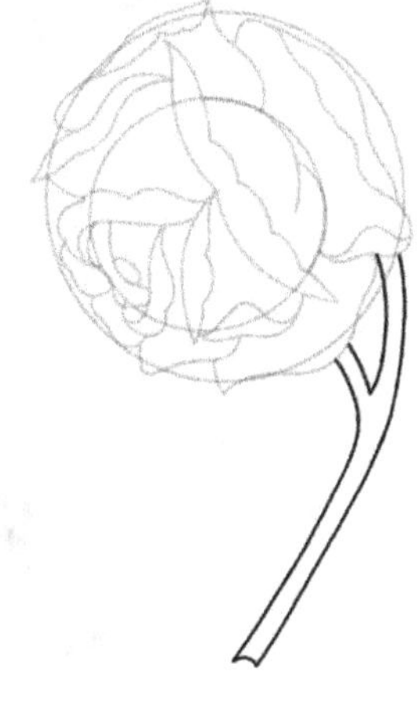

07

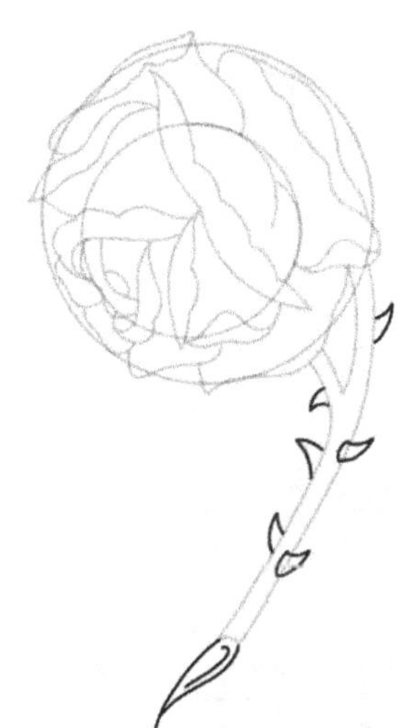

08

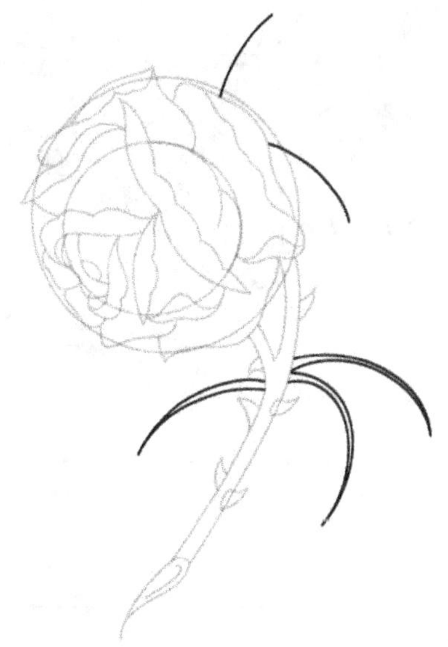

09

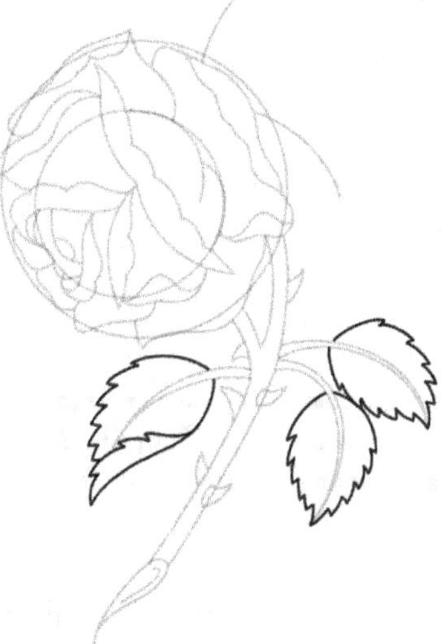

10

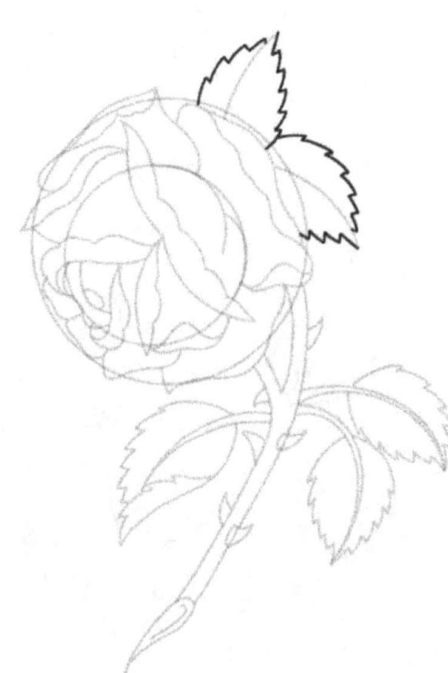

11

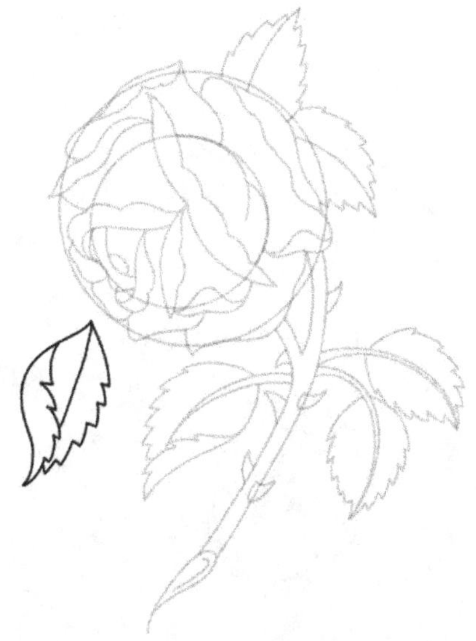

12

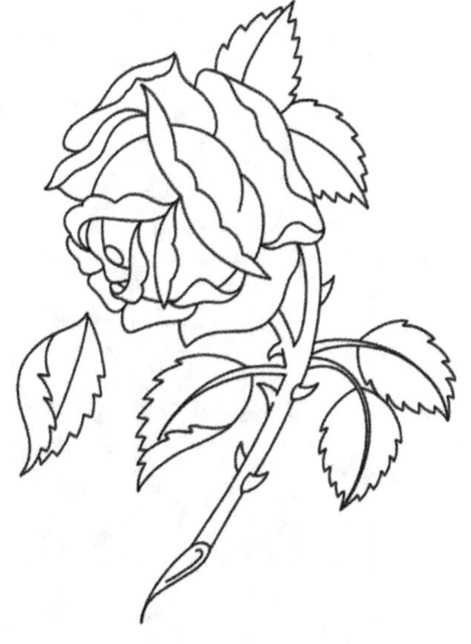

HOW TO DRAW PUNK THINGS

SKULL & SNAKE

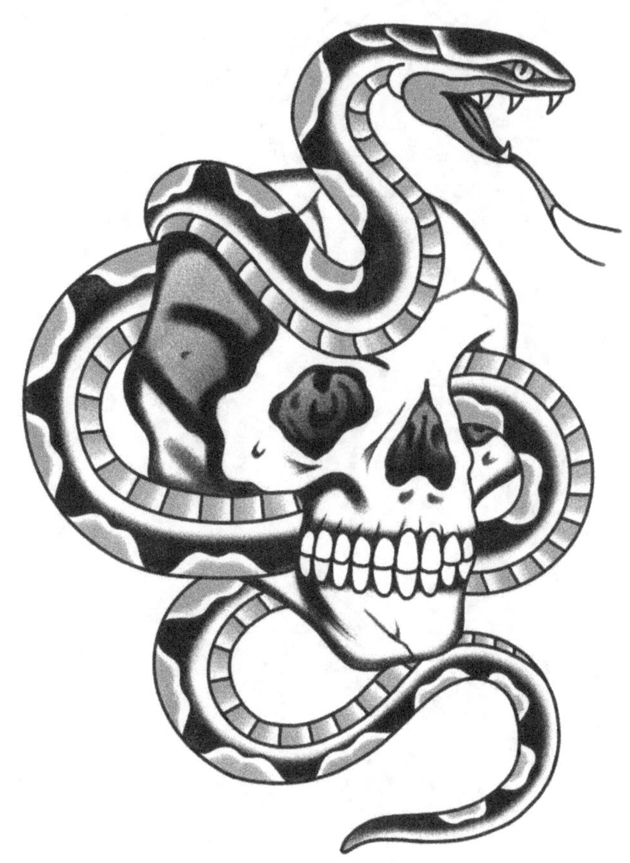

Representing danger and transformation,
the skull and snake embody punk's fierce
resilience and constant reinvention.

01

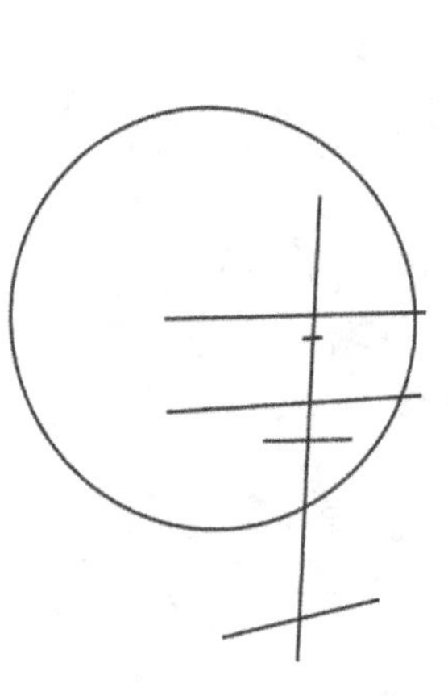

02

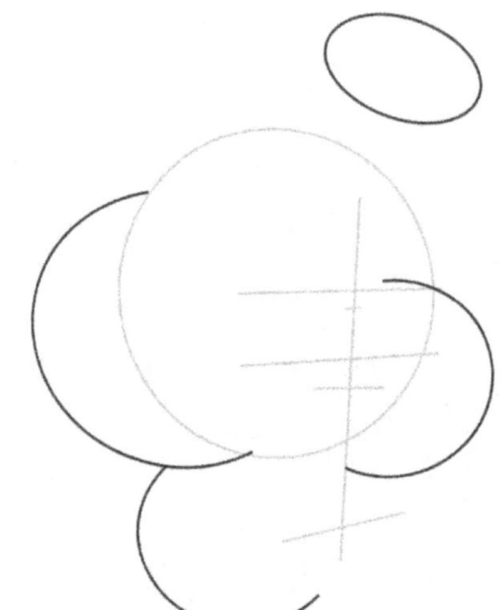

03

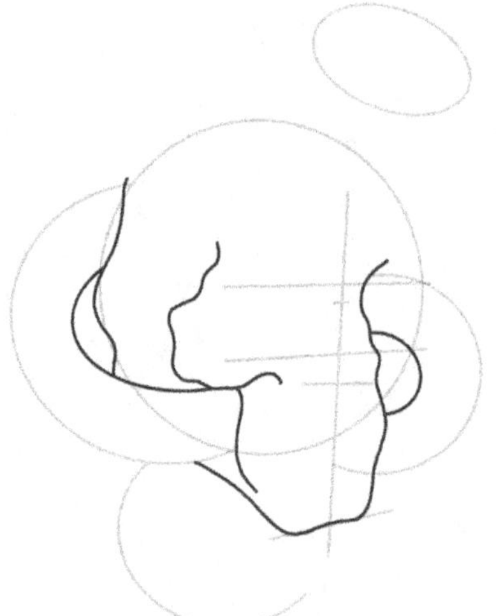

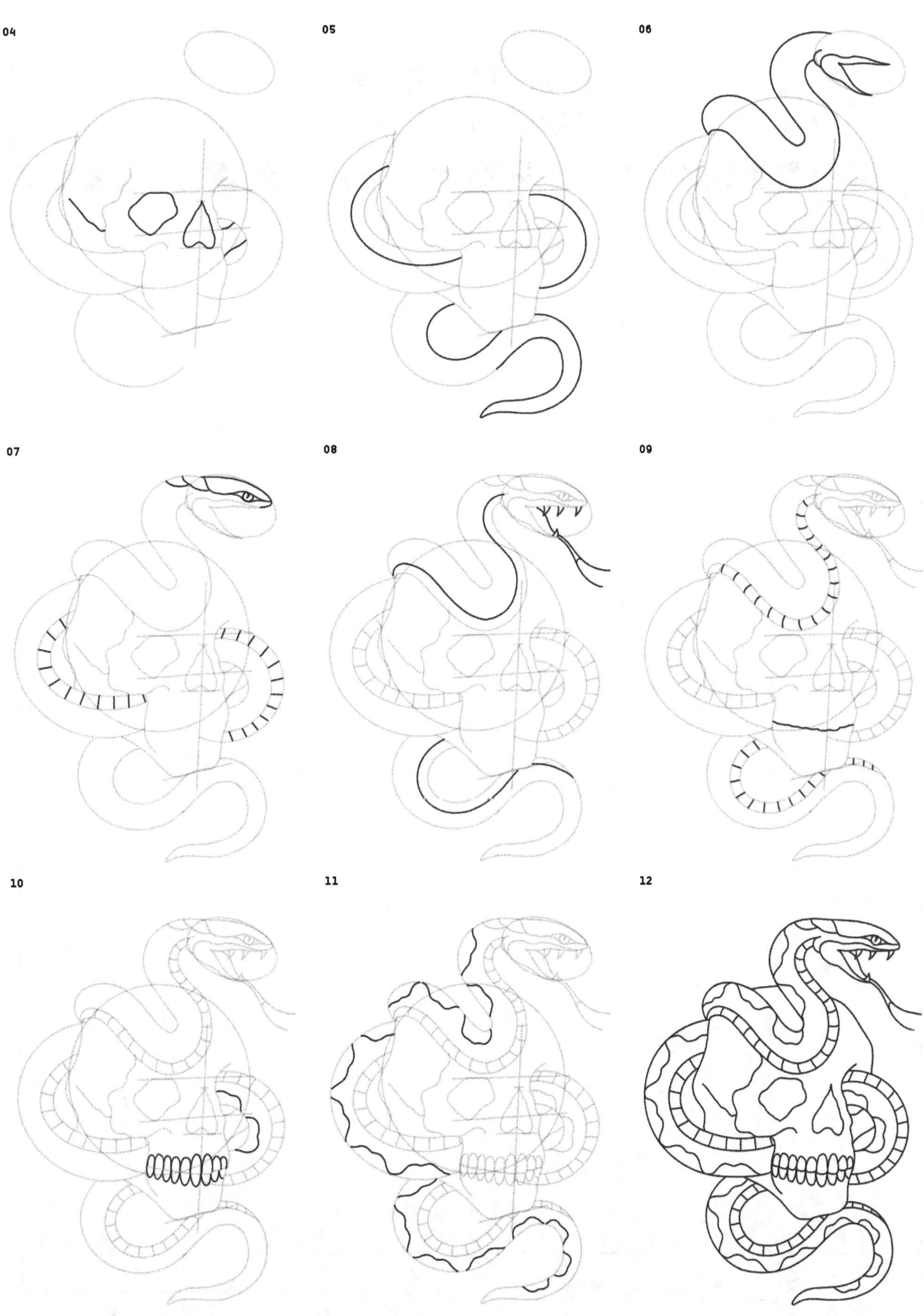

04
05
06
07
08
09
10
11
12
HOW TO DRAW PUNK THINGS

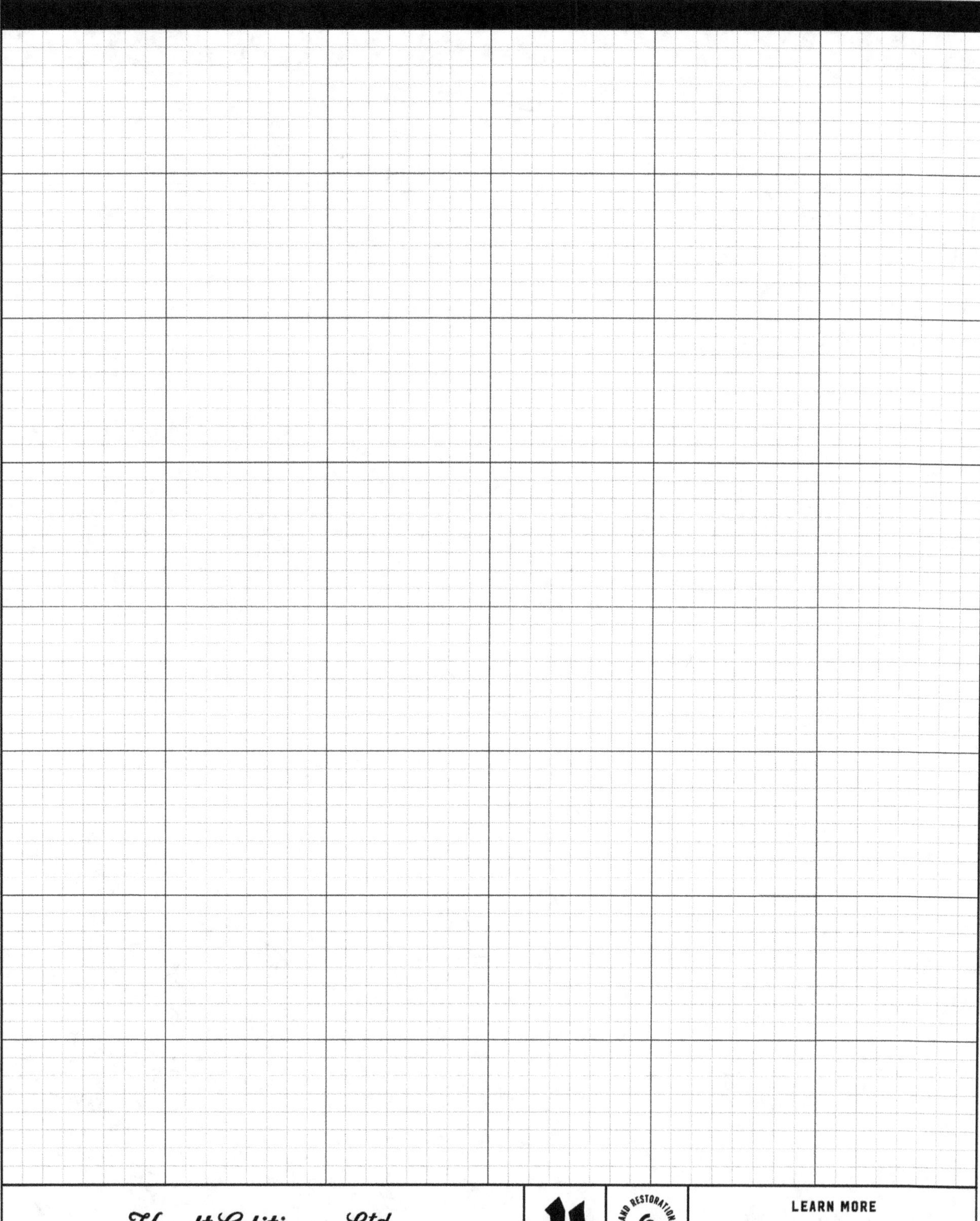

PRACTICE
MAKES
PERFECT
T R D
M R K

HOW TO DRAW
PUNK THINGS

PRACTICE
MAKES
PERFECT
T R D
M R K

Vault Editions Ltd

CURATION AND RESTORATION SERVICES

LEARN MORE
VAULTEDITIONS.COM

PRACTICE
T R D MAKES M R K
PERFECT

HOW TO DRAW
PUNK THINGS

PRACTICE
T R D MAKES M R K
PERFECT

Vault Editions Ltd

LEARN MORE

VAULTEDITIONS.COM

PRACTICE
T R D MAKES M R K
PERFECT

HOW TO DRAW
PUNK THINGS

PRACTICE
T R D MAKES M R K
PERFECT

Vault Editions Ltd

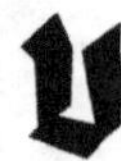
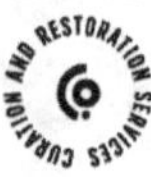

LEARN MORE

VAULTEDITIONS.COM

PRACTICE
MAKES
PERFECT
T R D
M R K

HOW TO DRAW
PUNK THINGS

PRACTICE
MAKES
PERFECT
T R D
M R K

Vault Editions Ltd

LEARN MORE

VAULTEDITIONS.COM

CURATION AND RESTORATION SERVICES

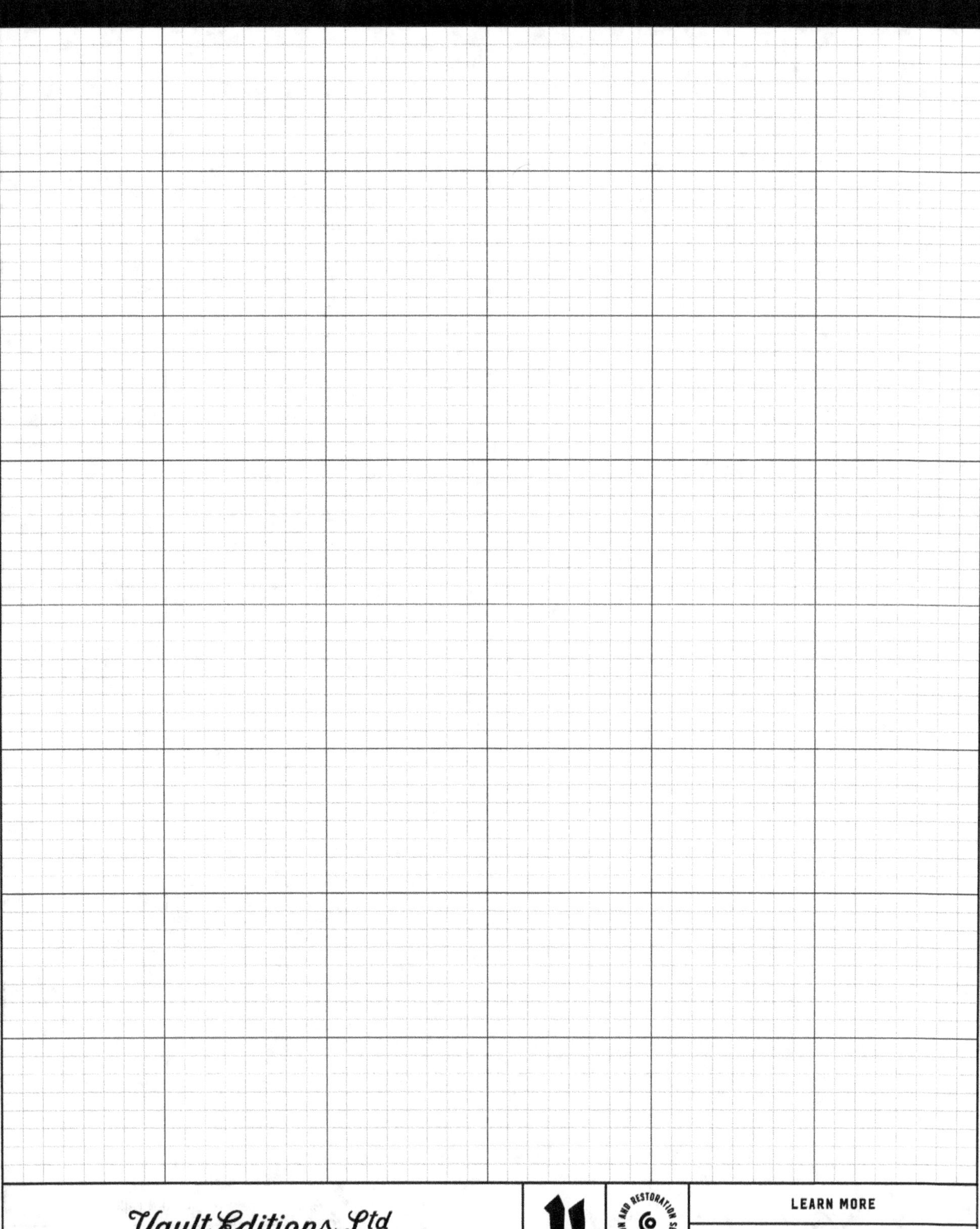
PRACTICE
MAKES
PERFECT
T R D
MRK
HOW TO DRAW
PUNK THINGS
PRACTICE
MAKES
PERFECT
T R D
MRK
Vault Editions Ltd
CORATION AND RESTORATION
SERVICES
LEARN MORE
VAULTEDITIONS.COM

PRACTICE
MAKES
PERFECT
TRD MRK

HOW TO DRAW
PUNK THINGS

PRACTICE
MAKES
PERFECT
TRD MRK

Vault Editions Ltd

CURATION AND RESTORATION SERVICES

LEARN MORE

VAULTEDITIONS.COM

HOW TO DRAW
PUNK THINGS

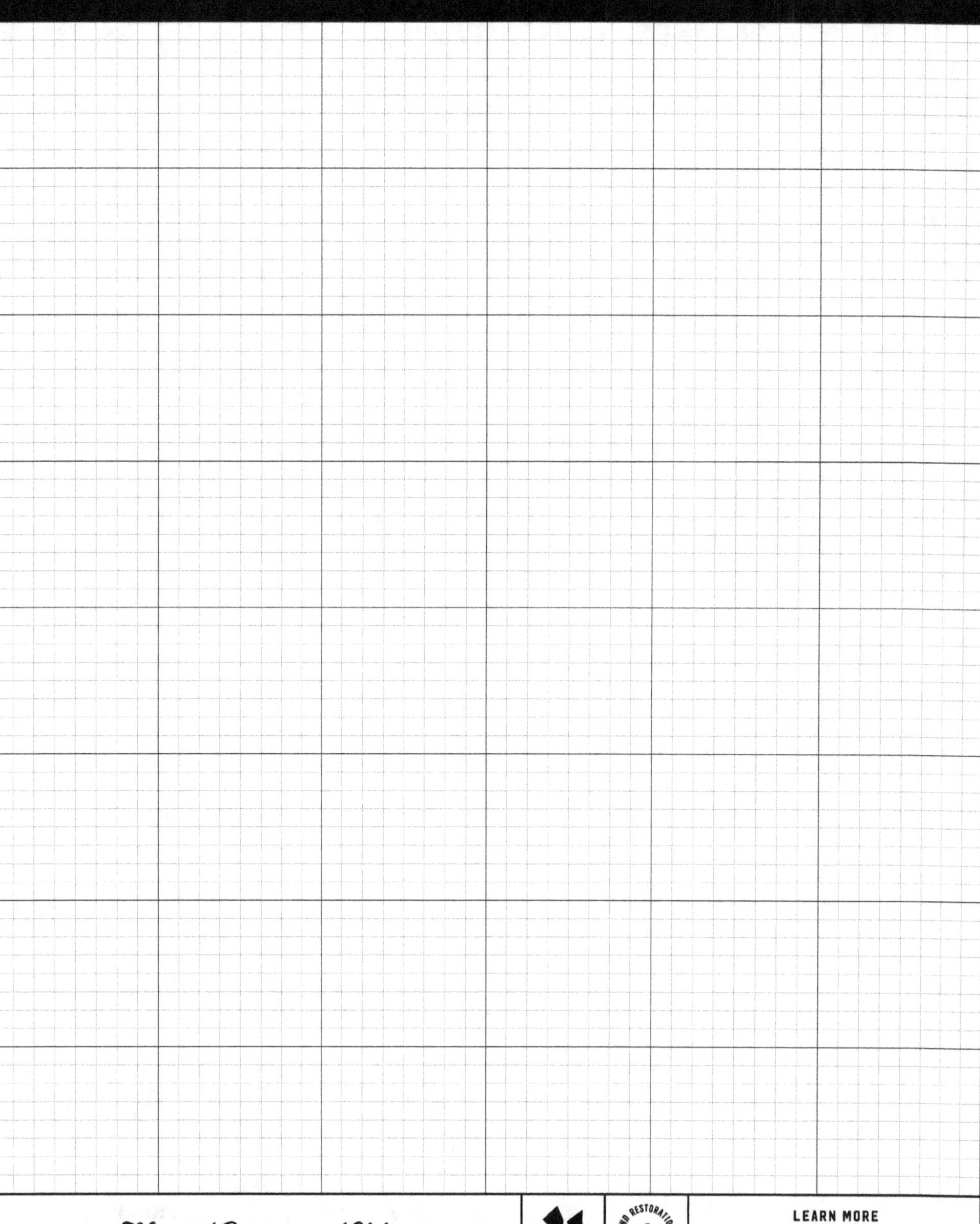

Vault Editions Ltd

LEARN MORE

VAULTEDITIONS.COM

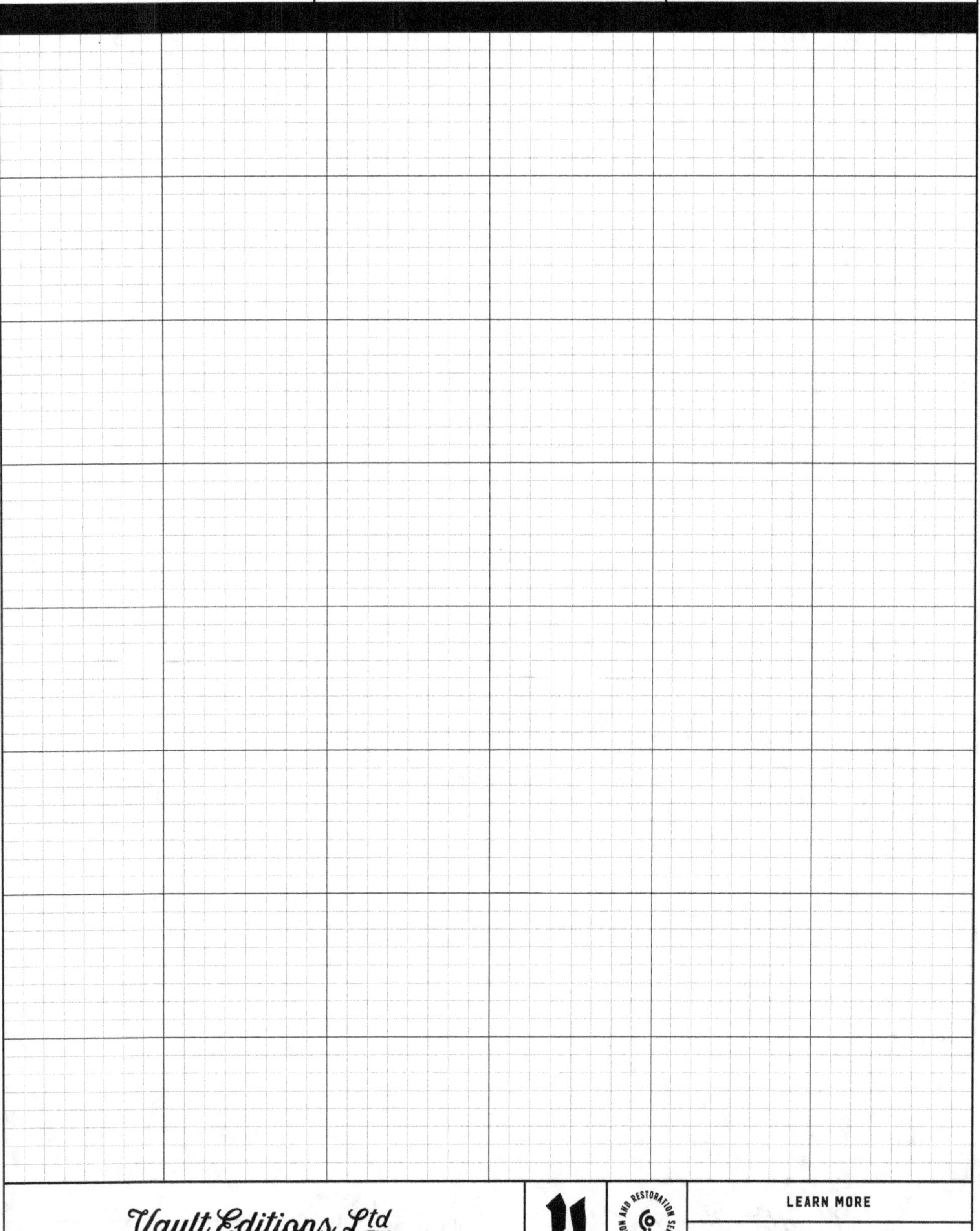
PRACTICE
MAKES
PERFECT
TRD
MRK

HOW TO DRAW
PUNK THINGS

PRACTICE
MAKES
PERFECT
TRD
MRK

Vault Editions Ltd

LEARN MORE
VAULTEDITIONS.COM

PRACTICE
MAKES
PERFECT
T R D
MRK

HOW TO DRAW
PUNK THINGS

PRACTICE
MAKES
PERFECT
T R D
MRK

Vault Editions Ltd

CURATION AND RESTORATION SERVICES

LEARN MORE

VAULTEDITIONS.COM

PRACTICE MAKES PERFECT
T R D   MRK

HOW TO DRAW
PUNK THINGS

PRACTICE MAKES PERFECT
T R D   MRK

Vault Editions Ltd

CURATION AND RESTORATION SERVICES

LEARN MORE

VAULTEDITIONS.COM

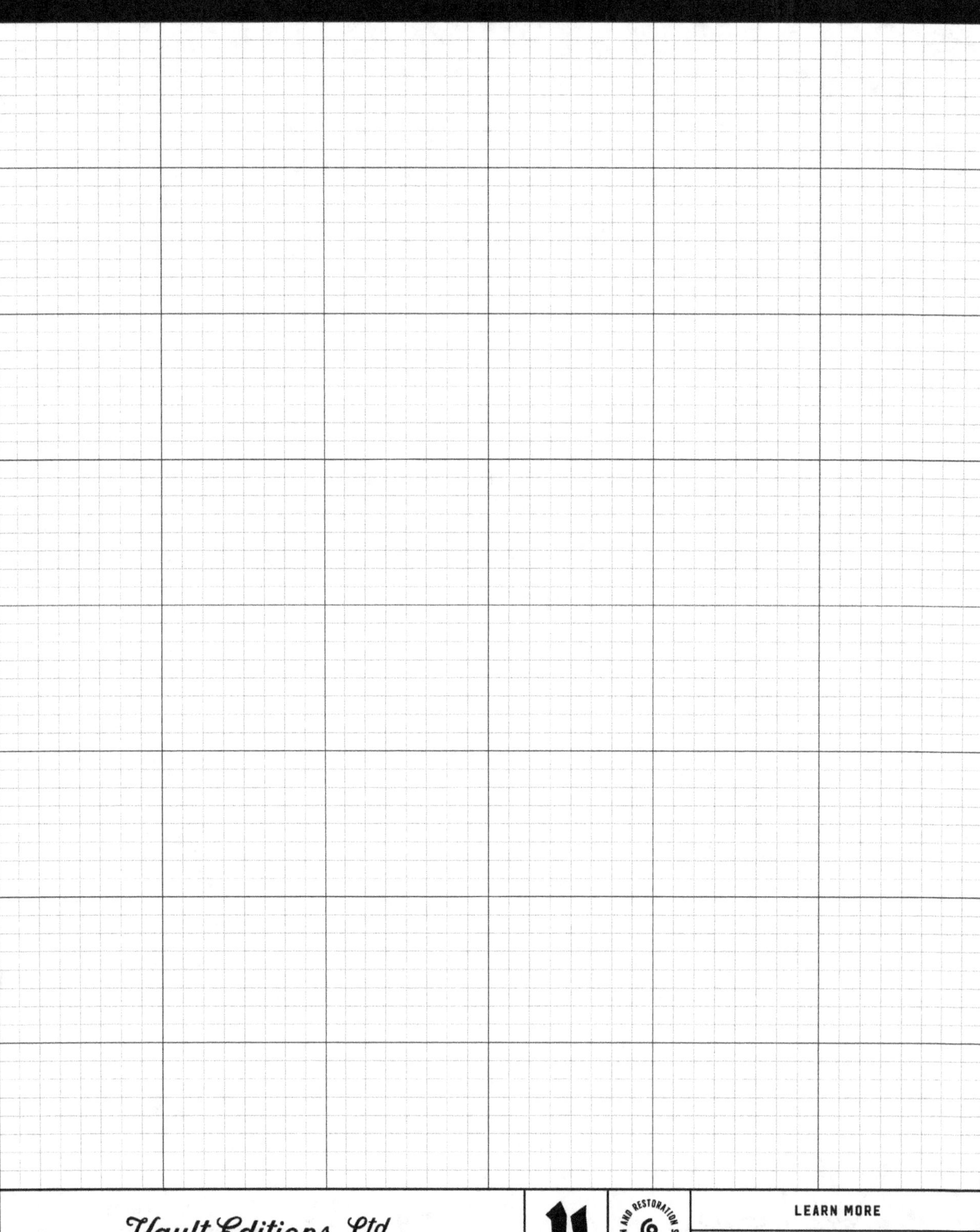
PRACTICE
MAKES
PERFECT
TRD
MRK
HOW TO DRAW
PUNK THINGS
PRACTICE
MAKES
PERFECT
TRD
MRK
Vault Editions Ltd
CURATION AND RESTORATION SERVICES
LEARN MORE
VAULTEDITIONS.COM

PRACTICE MAKES PERFECT
T R D / M R K

HOW TO DRAW
PUNK THINGS

PRACTICE MAKES PERFECT
T R D / M R K

Vault Editions Ltd

CURATION AND RESTORATION SERVICES

LEARN MORE

VAULTEDITIONS.COM

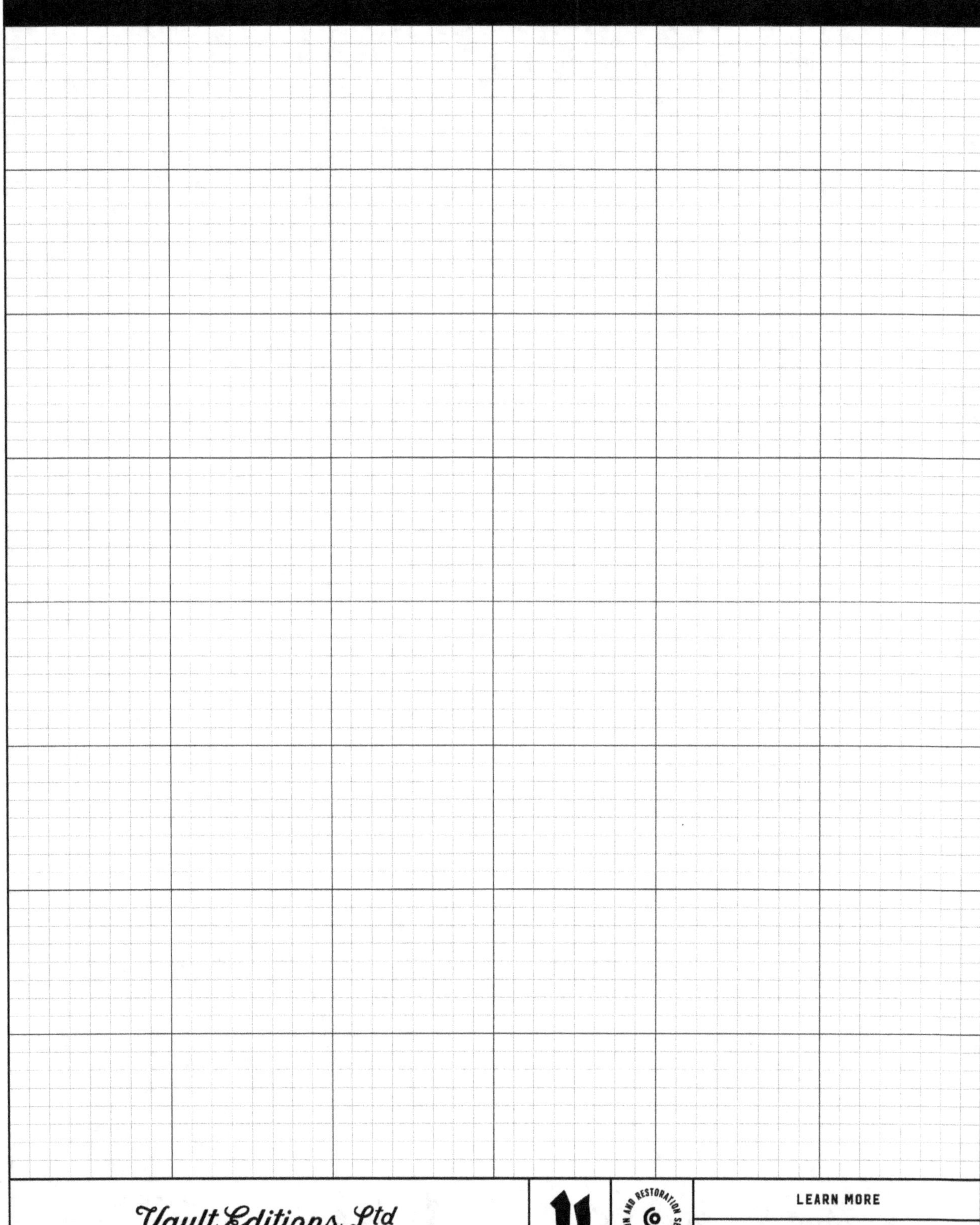
PRACTICE
MAKES
PERFECT
T R D
MRK

HOW TO DRAW
PUNK THINGS

PRACTICE
MAKES
PERFECT
T R D
MRK

Vault Editions Ltd

LEARN MORE
VAULTEDITIONS.COM

HOW TO DRAW
PUNK THINGS

HOW TO DRAW PUNK THINGS

Vault Editions Ltd

CURATION AND RESTORATION SERVICES

LEARN MORE

VAULTEDITIONS.COM

CONCLUSION

As you reach the end of How to Draw Punk Things: A Step-by-Step Guide to Drawing Cool, Punk-Inspired Designs, you've sharpened your drawing skills and tapped into the rebellious energy and creative freedom that define punk culture. Punk is about breaking the rules and expressing yourself without compromise, so take the techniques and confidence you've developed here and keep pushing your creative boundaries. Whether refining these designs, adding your own twist, or creating something entirely new, let your work be bold, authentic, and unapologetically yours.

Thank you for being part of this artistic journey. Use what you've learned to experiment, take risks, and let your art speak with its own authentic voice. Punk isn't about perfection—it's about creativity, self-expression, and staying true to yourself. Keep pushing your creative limits and making art that challenges the ordinary.

ABOUT THE ARTIST

The designs in this book were produced by Aaron Hingston, a highly skilled tattoo artist whose work brings traditional tattoo designs to life by merging classic artistry with modern techniques. Since starting his career in 2009, Aaron has earned a reputation for precise line work and attention to detail. Based in Victoria, Australia, his creations draw from the rich heritage of tattoo traditions while incorporating fresh, contemporary influences, resulting in designs that are both timeless and personal.

Aaron collaborates closely with clients to craft custom tattoos that tell their unique stories. Whether it's a bold new design or an addition to existing work, his creative process ensures each piece is tailored to the individual. To explore Aaron's portfolio or inquire about bookings and commissions, visit his Instagram profile @aaron_hingston.

LEARN MORE

At Vault Editions, our mission is to provide the highest-quality reference materials for artists and designers, offering meticulously curated resources that inspire and empower creativity. If you've found value in this book, we invite you to explore more of our expertly crafted titles at vaulteditions.com, where you'll discover a world of visual inspiration and practical tools designed to elevate your creative work.

REVIEW THIS BOOK

As a family-owned and operated independent publisher, reviews are essential to the success of our business. Please leave an honest review of this book wherever you purchased it.

JOIN OUR COMMUNITY

Are you the creative and curious type? If so, you will love our community on Instagram. Every day, we share bizarre and beautiful artwork ranging from 17th and 18th-century natural history and scientific illustrations to mythical beasts, ornamental designs, anatomical drawings and more; join our community of 300K+ people today by searching @vault_editions on Instagram.

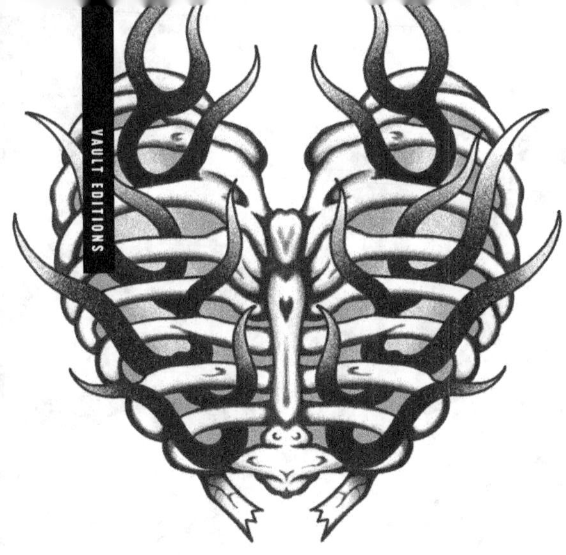

DOWNLOAD YOUR FILES

To enhance your creative journey, *How to Draw Punk Things* comes with a digital PDF version of the book and a specially designed set of Procreate brushes. These resources are tailored to help you refine your skills and streamline your digital creative workflow.

The digital PDF provides easy access to the book's contents on any device, so you can reference the designs anytime, anywhere. It's perfect for artists on the go, allowing you to study and practice whenever inspiration strikes.

The custom Procreate brushes are designed to replicate the look and feel of traditional tattoo flash designs, from bold outlining to shading techniques. These brushes make it easier for digital artists to create authentic-looking designs in a digital medium, offering precision and flexibility as you sketch, refine, and finalise your artwork. Whether you're experimenting with new ideas or perfecting your final designs, these brushes allow you to bring your creations to life with the same iconic style that defines the classic punk aesthetic.

Download yours now and get creating!

STEP ONE

Enter the following web address on a desktop or laptop computer in your web browser.

vaulteditions.com/pages/dpt

STEP TWO

Enter the following password to access the download page:

dpt492745sxda

STEP THREE

Follow the prompts to access your high-resolution files.

CONTACT

For technical support, please email:
info@vaulteditions.com

Copyright © 2024
Vault Editions Ltd

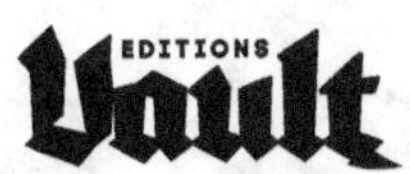

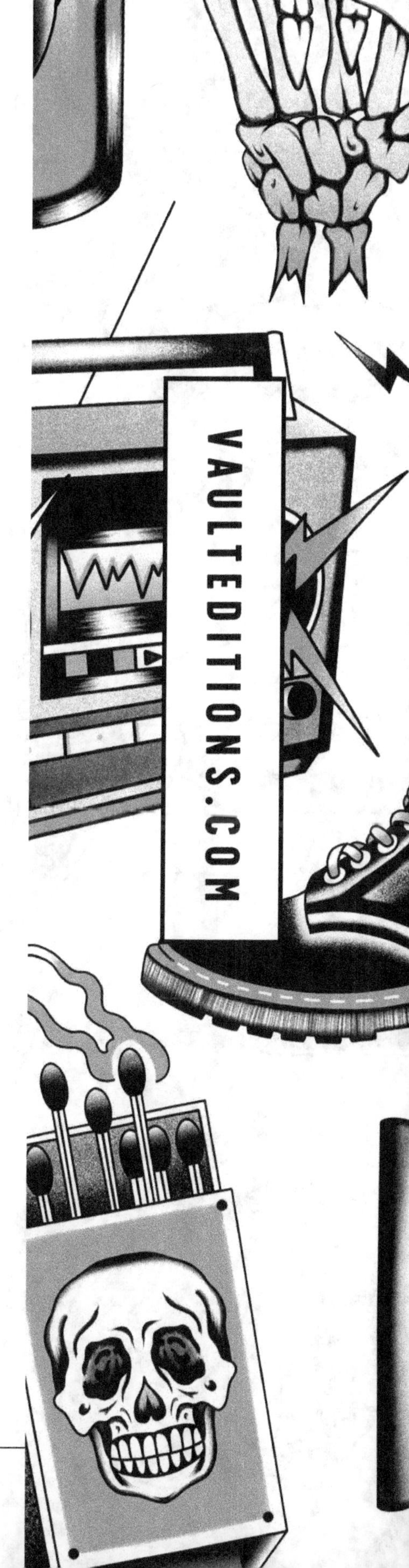

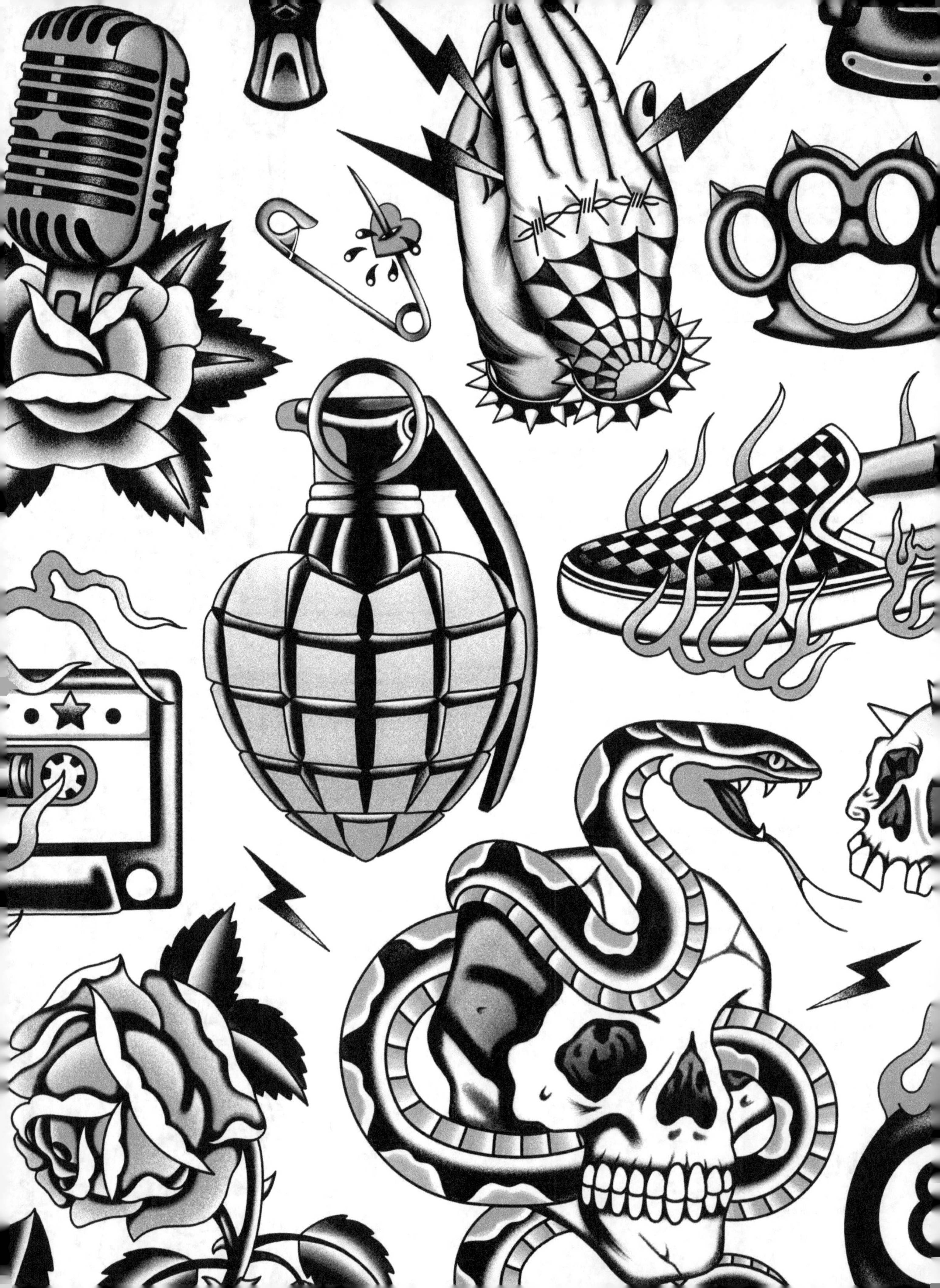

9 781922 966544